ORGANIZING THE EXECUTIVE BRANCH
The Johnson Presidency

An Administrative History of the Johnson Presidency

Emmette S. Redford, Series Editor

ORGANIZING THE EXECUTIVE BRANCH

The Johnson Presidency

EMMETTE S. REDFORD AND
MARLAN BLISSETT

THE UNIVERSITY OF CHICAGO PRESS
Chicago and London

EMMETTE S. REDFORD is Ashbel Smith
Professor of Government and Public Affairs and MARLAN BLISSETT is associate
professor at the Lyndon B. Johnson School
of Public Affairs at the University of Texas,
Austin.

The University of Chicago Press, Chicago 60637
The University of Chicago, Ltd., London

Library of Congress Cataloging in Publication Data

Redford, Emmette Shelburn, 1904–
  Organizing the executive branch.

  (An Administrative history of the Johnson
presidency)
  Includes index.
  1. United States—Executive departments—
Reorganization. 2. United States—Politics and
government—1963–1969. I. Blissett, Marlan.
II. Title. III. Series: Administrative history
of the Johnson presidency.
JK411.R43   353.07'3   81-1142
ISBN 0–226–70675–3   AACR2

CONTENTS

CONTENTS

FOREWORD

This is the first of a projected group of publications that will form the series An Administrative History of the Johnson Presidency. Ten to twelve special studies like this one and an overall volume are planned.

Our objective is to provide a comprehensive view of how a president and those who assisted him managed the White House and the executive branch to achieve the objectives of law and presidential policy. Administration will be studied as part of the responsibility of a president—in this case, President Lyndon B. Johnson.

The view taken of administration is comprehensive. It includes the interrelations between policy, administration, and program development. It encompasses administration in its various aspects: development of the infrastructure, including structuring and staffing the executive branch and budgeting for its operations; implementation of policy; and presidential management of the executive branch.

We aim for an authentic and adequate historical record based primarily on the documentary materials in the Lyndon B. Johnson Library and on interviews with many people who assisted President Johnson. We hope the historical record as presented from a social science perspective will amplify knowledge of administrative processes and of the tasks and problems of the presidency.

The study is being financed primarily by a grant from the National Endowment for the Humanities, with additional aid from the Lyndon Baines Johnson Foundation, the Hoblitzelle Foundation, and the Lyndon B. Johnson School of Public Affairs of the University of Texas at Austin.

The findings and conclusions in publications resulting from this study do not necessarily represent the view of any donor.

EMMETTE S. REDFORD
Project director

PREFACE

This volume presents a history of the actions taken by President Lyndon B. Johnson and his aides to modify the structure of the executive branch of the United States government. It does not encompass policy development or the operation of executive structures, except as they are related to issues of organization that were considered during the presidency.

The history deals with so many pieces of executive structure that it was not feasible to examine all documentary materials in various locations or to interview all the chief actors. It has been built primarily on documents in the Lyndon B. Johnson Library. These often, indeed usually, do not fully reveal the motivations and actions of the president, but they provide the basis for an authentic record of the contributions of the persons who were in a position to influence his decisions.

We present historical accounts of each organizational change, and we believe that these separate accounts are meaningful cumulatively in revealing the processes of organization change, the influences that produce or prevent such change, and the structural problems that are presented to presidents by today's policy complexes.

We are grateful for the assistance given to us. The manuscript was read in nearly completed form by Harvey C. Mansfield, Sr., Harold Seidman, and James L. Sundquist. Parts of it were read by Dean Elspeth Rostow, Jesse Burkhead, Richard Schott, and David Welborn. The chapter on the creation of the Department of Transportation was read by Alan Boyd and Alan Dean. The staff of the Lyndon B. Johnson Library gave efficient and friendly aid. And we were fortunate to have the exceptional research and editorial assistance of Kay Hancock and Robert Blum. All of them saved us from errors and improved the quality of the manuscript. The deficiencies that remain are due either to the time limits that must be imposed on a project of this kind or to our own failings.

EMMETTE S. REDFORD
MARLAN BLISSETT

ONE

INTRODUCTION

The president is at the pinnacle of a structure called the executive branch, which is so vast, so diversified in function, so varied in its tasks, and so important to the well-being of citizens within and outside the country that it is distinct from all other domestic organizations and comparable to few that exist or have existed anywhere in the world. Despite the size and complexity of the executive branch, a president cannot escape considering its effectiveness for the tasks of government and the discharge of his own responsibilities. Nor will he fail to see its importance for implementing his own policies and assisting him in evaluating their effect.

Structure, of course, is only one factor in effectiveness, and it is often questionable whether particular modifications in structure improve performance significantly. Yet, unquestionably, structure is elemental to performance, and a specific structural change can affect not only the extent of achievement but the purposes sought. This book deals with the attention President Johnson and responsible presidential aides gave to organizational change and with the way they viewed—or failed to view—the relation of structure to executive guidance and control.

CONTINUITY AND CHANGE

The president inherits an executive structure that is part of a national historical and political process. It is composed of many separate centers of initiative and power, each preserving in its organization the values of prevailing groups and coalitions. Departments, bureaus, independent agencies, regulatory commissions—in fact, all the structural components of

1

administration—incorporate interests and become major instruments of their survival. Over time, additional interests seek representation and continuity through public organizations. This leads to the creation of new organizations, to adaptations in the structure and policy of established ones, and to marginal adjustments among units with similar, complementary, or conflicting purposes.

In a larger sense, the evolution of the executive branch has increased a president's responsibilities for guidance, policy coordination, and managerial control. Historically, the pattern has been one in which the structures of the executive branch and the presidency were joined to stabilize markets, ensure employment, distribute benefits, provide for the national security, and protect individual rights. The Constitution, reinforced by individual statutes and court decisions, has given the president leverage to utilize structure, but he must still search for pathways through competing departments and programs and must combine resources from different areas of specialization and interest. The legacy of history has given the president no choice but to exert executive direction toward his interpretation of national needs. Future organizational changes become significant as they strengthen or diminish this responsibility.

THE AUTHORITY TO ORGANIZE

Although the Constitution vests the president with "the executive power," it does not state expressly whether the authority to structure the executive branch is part of the executive power or the legislative power. The president may appoint and remove executive officers, but Congress has the power to vest appointment of "inferior officers" in the president alone, in courts of law, or in heads of departments. Further, Congress has the sweeping authority to make laws that are "necessary and proper" for the conduct of government or to carry out any power vested in the government or any part thereof. By implication from this clause of the Constitution, precedent of the First Congress, and the subsequent course of history, the legislative power encompasses the power to create, alter, or abolish departments, agencies, commissions, and bureaus within the executive branch and to determine the powers of each. This power can be, and is, exercised with respect both to legislatively created functions and to those the Constitution delegates to the president. It can be, and has been, used even to establish units of organization within the Executive Office itself, such as the Council of Economic Advisers, the National Security Council, and the Office of Management and Budget, and in the last case to require senatorial confirmation of its director.

This means that the Congress can determine the features of executive branch structure. It can create a structure that is integrated in a small number of departments or dispersed to numerous agencies, bureaus, and commissions, one whose powers are centralized in Washington or decentralized to field officers, one whose processes and subordinate units are defined in detail and tightly coordinated or the reverse. Although one would not expect Congress's decisions to be extreme or unreasonable, a president can be assisted or hindered in his operations by structures he has not designed and cannot modify without congressional authorization.

But Congress cannot destroy the executive branch or remove the president from its pinnacle. It can create structures, define their powers, prescribe their processes, determine the amount of funds available, make rules with respect to employees, and do these things in detail. It can even assign duties that are ministerial in nature and thus subject to official direction by the judicial, rather than the executive power.[1] But the basic unity of the executive branch and the president's position at its head are safeguarded by the constitutional powers the president possesses over diplomacy or defense or other matters, by his constitutional power to select officers, and by the implied power to remove officers with executive duties.[2] Thus, what Congress vests in offices, the president may—possibly subject to some congressional limitation—control through executive officers. An executive structure unresponsive to the president, or executive officers independent of him, would be contrary to the grant of executive power and render impotent his constitutional authority to ensure the faithful execution of the laws.

Yet from an operational point of view the president's ability to guide and control the executive establishment is constantly under challenge. Some structures (such as the so-called independent commissions) restrict presidential intervention and policy direction. An increasing number of federal programs make execution dependent on massive participation by state and local governments. Presidential direction may be further attenuated by institutionalizing group influence, "contracting out" program activities, or requiring prior congressional approval of executive action. Moreover, in cases where more than one program or agency is involved, great strain may be placed on presidential capability for guidance and control.

Although the legislative power dominates in decisions on executive structure, the president exerts great influence, both negatively and positively. His chief influence is through his participation in the legislative process (recommending legislation, vetoing bills, or otherwise indicating his approval or disapproval). Also, Congress has repeatedly renewed grants to the president of restricted conditional power to alter structure through reorganization plans and has often delegated to department heads or bureau chiefs discretion over their internal organizations. The president, finally, as commander-in-chief, has considerable constitutional power to create organizations,[3] and under his duty to "take care that the laws are faithfully executed" has power to impose duties on executive offices.[4]

Perspectives on Organizational Purpose

In practice, the Congress has come to depend on the president, even more than for policy leadership, for decisions on structure for policy execution. Yet the ultimate decisions are made in the contest of political forces characteristic of our pluralistic political system. In this contest actors are influenced by their perspectives on the purposes to be served by organization. Since much of the discussion in this book will show how the president's initiatives and the contests over them reflect these perspectives, it is important that they be set forth. This will provide the foundation for understanding processes of organizational change, the president's leadership in those processes, and how changes affect his position for guidance and control of the executive branch.

The Comprehensive Presidential Management Perspective

The first perspective construes the president's constitutional and political responsibility broadly. It is held not only by presidents but by outside constituencies that evaluate presidential performance. It is thus a perspective of presidents and for presidents. Necessarily, it is presented here largely as the latter, but our analysis will underscore the extent to which the perspective was reflected in the decisions and attitudes of President Johnson and his aides.

From the comprehensive presidential management perspective, administration is viewed as a whole, with responsibility for direction and supervision given to the president himself. Its guiding principle is integrated organization—one that links related tasks at successive levels all the way to the top. Such a structure facilitates leadership, direction, supervision, and evaluation from the responsible chief executive. Although hierarchical by design, the organization is viewed as an instrument of democratic government, since top management is responsible to an elected official and accountable to laws democratically made.

Within the integrated structure, the basic guide for organization is to combine functions according to the purposes served, with increasingly broader units of purpose expanding the scope of organizational control. This does not, however, prevent separate services or controls at any level for planning, personnel, budgeting, legal counsel, public relations, or congressional liaison—activities usually characterized as staff functions. Indeed, a corollary principle is that officials responsible for the administration of government need staff aid, both for technical or special services and for policy and administrative planning. Finally, single officials would be preferred to boards or commissions, since this would provide unified leadership, direction and control, and focused responsibility.

In clear, forceful, eloquent exposition, the comprehensive presidential management perspective was set forth in 1937 in the Report of the President's Committee on Admnistrative Management.[5] After New Deal programs had brought a tremendous expansion in the number of executive agencies and an unprecedented enlargement of the task of presidential direction, President Roosevelt created this committee, composed of Louis Brownlow (chairman), Charles E. Merriam, and Luther Gulick. The choice of the word "management" in the title and its dominance in the report significantly mark the perspective. Even more significant is the emphasis on the president.

Whereas previous studies of the executive branch, whether initiated in Congress or by a president, had emphasized economy through cost reduction and efficiency through eliminating duplication in structure, this one broke new ground in its emphasis on the position of the president. Brownlow stated that "The primary purpose of the study should be to discover and invent ways and means to give the President effective managerial direction and control over all departments and agencies of the Executive Branch of the Federal Government commensurate with his responsibility."[6] More than that:

> Stated in simple terms these canons of efficiency require the establishment of a responsible and effective chief executive as the center of energy, direction, and administrative management; the systematic organization of all activities in the hands of a qualified personnel under the direction of the chief executive; and, to aid him in this, the establishment of appropriate managerial and staff agencies.[7]

With respect to organization, the report had two solutions. One was to give the president help (1) by increased White House staff to assist him in "the great managerial functions of the Government"—these being "personnel management, fiscal and organizational planning, and planning management" (which "comprehended all of the essential elements of business management")—and (2) by managerial agencies, "greatly strengthened and developed as arms of the Chief Executive," again in the three areas of finance (Bureau of the Budget), personnel, and planning (a National Resources Board).

The second solution was to reorganize the executive branch with the primary purpose of reducing "to a manageable compass the number of agencies reporting to the President." The "ends of reorganization" included economy, "elimination of duplication and contradictory policies," "simple and symmetrical organization," but also "one grand purpose, namely, to make democracy work."

Another comprehensive view of the executive branch was offered by the reports of the Hoover commission in 1949. Created by statute, the Commission on Organization of the Executive Branch proposed organizational guidelines that were fully consistent with the comprehensive presidential perspective:

1. Create a more orderly grouping of the functions of the Government into major departments and agencies under the President.
2. Establish a clear line of control from the President to these department and agency heads and from them to their subordinates with correlative responsibility from these to the President, cutting through the barriers which have in many cases made bureaus and agencies partially independent of the Chief Executive.
3. Give the President and each department head strong staff services which should exist only to make executive work more effective, and which the President or department head should be free to organize at his discretion.[8]

Two recommendations of the commission set the pattern for a series of reorganization plans submitted to Congress by President Truman and in most cases accepted: (1) to authorize the president to designate chairmen of regulatory commissions to serve at the president's pleasure and to exercise administrative functions of the commissions and (2) to transfer powers of bureaus to the departmental secretaries, who could redelegate these to such bureaus as they desired.

The comprehensive presidential management perspective—as indicated by both the Brownlow committee and the Hoover commission—is one from which the president can view the problems of organization. It reflects concern for maintaining his power and responsibility. The perspective could interpret the word "management" broadly and in line with presidential responsibility. Management could have a broader purpose than efficiency, more even than effectiveness in execution of law and public policy—more than executive purpose. It could mean management of the executive branch, in addition, to provide aid and support to the president in his function of policy development and political leadership. Organization would be an instrument for placing the president at the pinnacle of an executive structure for policy development as well as administrative functions. Only in this sense would presidential management be a satisfactory general or overall perspective for a president.

The Tactical Presidential Perspective

The presidential management perspective views structure as it affects the creation and maintenance of executive capacity. Still, many organizational decisions are made in a more limited context, where tactical issues predominate. From this perspective, organizational change is associated with attempts to further certain policy or program objectives and to improve the president's political position.

Under these conditions, organization is not considered neutral with respect to policy. Nor is it viewed as having only, or even chiefly, a management objective. It may be thought of as the choices between locating the function of consumer protection in the Department of Agriculture or in the Department of Health, Education, and Welfare, of setting rates or prices in an independent commission or in a department, of placing hospital administration for veterans in a Veterans Administration or a bureau within a department, of administering an antipoverty program in an independent agency, within or outside the executive office, or in a department.

Organizational decisions of this nature are policy-specific and can have substantial implications for the direction of a policy, the rigor of its application, and the program results obtained. The immediate effect will be to create concern within affected components of the executive branch, in Congress, and among parties at interest. Hence such choices are politically sensitive and may be accompanied by efforts to avoid or mediate conflict. Since the ends are limited and specific, the organizational decisions are pragmatic and particularistic.

In concrete instances presidents may act from this perspective and still not forsake the comprehensive perspectives set forth in documents like those of 1937 and 1949. Every president will accept the concept that structure should maintain presidential authority over the executive branch and that this is the dictate of article 2 of the Constitution. A president will seek to protect his position at the pinnacle of the executive structure from Congress and from the separatist influences of bureaus and bureaucrats within the executive branch. Thus his structural perspective can only be semiparticularistic; tactically, however, he may look at organization in a particularistic way.

The Congressional Perspective

The third perspective of organizational development is that of Congress. Its reference points are almost exclusively particularistic. This is an inevitable consequence of Congress's structure and the nature of its work. Its division into committees and subcommittees makes specialized members in particular areas of public policy. Its task of defining policy in statutes leads them to think of the purpose of administration as implementation of the policy of

7

particular statutes. Administrative purpose, for congressmen, may be larger than the demands of self-interested constituents, but it is almost entirely policy-specific and subject-specific. To complete and protect its policies, Congress locates them administratively and safeguards the locations.

The particularistic tendency of Congress is accentuated by the linkages of committees. Inescapably, congressional committees develop a kind of proprietary interest in departments and in commissions or bureaus administering their policies. Both program and appropriation subcommittees seek in various ways to command, instruct, or influence the agencies. Their pressure and oversight are continuous, since program budgets must be approved annually and statutes are frequently amended. Concurrently, the agencies, conscious of the power and interest of committees and members strategically situated within them, cultivate ties and are extremely responsive to committee requests. Whereas presidents and department heads move in and out, the tenure of congressmen on committees, especially those who hold the chairs, is often long. The result can be, and often is, a stronger line of communication, influence, and control from committee to agency than from the president to the agency.

Committee linkages also extend outside government, providing access and influence to groups with special standing, visibility, or expertise. Committee and subcommittee linkage with private interests provides useful input into public policy, but it further fragments decision-making and protects the particularistic relations among executive bureaus, nongovernmental interests, and Congress.

In some cases the concentration of protective influence for certain units of organization is so potent and persistent that an agency becomes untouchable, or touchable only at the fringes. The Corps of Engineers, known to be favorably disposed toward construction expenditures that benefit interests dispersed throughout many congressional districts, is a case in point. Roosevelt found he could not change its location, and, when Eisenhower was said to be contemplating such a change, a critic who wanted to expose the naiveté of the new president quipped, "Why, he even thinks he can move the Corps of Engineers."

The regulatory commissions, too, are usually untouchable. Committees of Congress with jurisdiction over legislation affecting commissions have for more than sixty years called them "arms of Congress" and have supported the tradition that they should be independent of the president's executive supervision and direction. Roosevelt could not disturb their independent locations, and Congress confirmed his defeat with a provision in the next reorganization act exempting the commissions from inclusion in reorganization plans.

Congress may at times choose to protect bureaus from departmental control by vesting power in the bureau rather than in the departmental secretary. Thus Truman's reorganization plan for the Treasury Department was defeated and a second plan was accepted only after the secretary's control over the Comptroller of the Currency was limited, as provided in statute, to giving "general directions."

Although its dispersed and fragmented structure protects and maintains a particularistic perspective, Congress has on occasion, with limitations, accepted comprehensive management objectives. This is patently demonstrated in the successive reorganization acts delegating power to the president. The first such reorganization act (1917) had as its purpose the effective conduct of war. Later acts stressed economy and efficiency objectives, and those of 1932 and 1933 were part of economy acts, so-called. The Reorganization Act of 1949, which gave the president authority to submit reorganization plans, summarized the traditional management perspective in specific statements of purpose: "better execution of the laws," "more effective management of the executive branch," "expeditious administration," promoting economy, reducing the number of agencies through consolidation, eliminating "overlapping or duplication of effort," grouping functions "according to major purposes ... under a single head."

Absent from the statement, however, is any explicit reference to leadership, direction, or control by the president, or to energy and vigor in his administration. In view of the enduring contest for power between the president and Congress, common points of view even on general management objectives will not eliminate the differences in congressional and presidential perspectives about the organization of executive power.

The Bureaucratic Perspective

The structure of executive departments and agencies—like that of Congress—lends itself to specialization, access by affected interests, and protection of existing allocations of functions and resources. These qualities emphasize a particularistic view of change and make the president's efforts to increase central direction and guidance more difficult. From the bureaucratic perspective, organizational problems may demand constant attention, but they are open to incremental adjustments—changes, for example, in line staff functions, headquarters/field responsibilities, intra-agency coordination, and supporting links with other organizations.

The narrow range of the interests and program responsibilities that make up the bureaucratic perspective frequently brings the executive branch into conflict with the president. Departments and agencies prefer an approach to policy that is segmental—segmentally developed, segmentally solidified in structure, and segmentally supported. A president may have different ideas or may want a certain policy enacted without regard for its effect on

9

established programs or the organizational patterns under which they have been developed. An administrator, however, no matter how sensitive to presidential leadership, needs support from Congress and speical clienteles whose desires may run counter to White House initiatives. Thus the presidential use of organizational and program resources is dependent on administrators who frequently have divided loyalties. In analogous fashion, administrators too may be prevented by program clienteles, congressional subcommittees, and professional or trade groups from exercising full control over a bureau within the department or agency.

If the executive branch is viewed as a whole, further opportunities for conflict are opened up by the presence of redundant functions and overlapping responsibilities. Consequently, the organization and management of federal programs, including their implementation at the state and local level, require coordination. Yet coordinating mechanisms—whether interagency or intergovernmental—usually have advisory status only and are at the mercy of agencies with established programs. The particularistic concerns of these agencies and the congressional and nongovernmental interests that support them affect the degree of coordination possible for certain policies and the extent to which executive guidance may be applied.

THE JOHNSON PRESIDENCY

During the presidency of Lyndon B. Johnson an explosion of policy initiatives, added to the usual backlog of problems, forced concern for organization. A war on poverty called for centers of action both within and outside existing structures. New programs in health and education overwhelmed old bureaus with tasks vastly larger than any they had undertaken before. Enforcement of civil rights legislation required new organization within and across departments. New efforts to deal with problems of cities and with transportation were incorporated into movements for new departments. Many of the resulting problems of organization were dealt with as they arose. A new Office of Economic Opportunity, two new departments, reorganizations in education and health and other bureau functions, seventeen reorganization plans, and other initiatives were in most instances immediate responses to the program expansions and changes that were occurring.

Nevertheless, these responses were made under the persistent influence of the comprehensive presidential perspective. Moreover, tactical perspectives on implementation of Great Society programs led, early in the administration, to broad considerations in organization planning, though they were expressed in terms of "policy coordination" rather than "management." Midway in the Johnson presidency this concern led to attention to executive structure generally and to restatement of the comprehensive perspectives on executive guidance and control.

Johnson's concern for organization was influenced by many factors, including his own objectives and his desire to project them in public policy, the necessities of program administration, and the initiatives of his own staff in generating proposals for change. Although his responsibility was not transferable, he was assisted by numerous individuals and institutional aides. We have chosen the word *subpresidency*[9] to denote all those who served the president—continuously or ad hoc, in an institutional capacity or otherwise—in the exercise of his responsibilities. This included, on occasion, individuals in departments or independent agencies who had separate official responsibilities but whose loyalties to the president led them to look at problems from a presidential perspective.

As an activist president, Johnson was constantly in search of new ideas, demanding of others that they give him new proposals and programs, exacting action from them, and counting achievements in number of things done. Yet the cumulative effect of Great Society legislation was to produce far greater problems of executive structure and coordination than had existed at any other time, except perhaps during the Civil War, the Great Depression, and World War II. In retrospect, it appears that the problems of organization created in the sixties were to be permanent, threatening the capacity of the administrative system to fulfill policy objectives.

THE PURPOSES OF THIS STUDY

We attempt to explain major changes in organization within the executive branch that were made, failed, or were only considered during the Johnson presidency. Specifically, we seek to reveal:

1. The extent to which President Johnson personally participated in organization matters or influenced them through the atmosphere he created.

2. The ways he was assisted by a presidential subsystem that we call the *subpresidency*.

3. The processes of initiation and consideration of organizational change and the events and perspectives that influenced results.

4. The way that, in the second half of the Johnson presidency, as a consequence of expanded national policies, attention was focused on structural possibilities for strengthening executive guidance and control.

The focus is on the action of the presidency with respect to creating or changing executive organization. Not included, generally, are departmental or agency operations, or changes in organization made by department, agency, or bureau heads. Although the presence or action of Congress affected structural changes within the executive branch, its responses are noted only to the extent that they reveal the initiatives, methods, and results of presidential action. Finally, although issues of organization for administration of national programs arise because of the coexistence of state and local governments, the focus here is on national executive structure. A companion volume on intergovernmental administration is being written by another author.

TWO

HOUSING AND URBAN DEVELOPMENT
A New Commitment to Urban Problems

The creation of the Department of Housing and Urban Development (HUD) was an event of symbolic moment. Although it did not mark a turning point in federal policy toward the city, President Johnson viewed it as a "new and needed instrument," a "means to respond to new challenges."[1]

Like most cabinet-level additions, HUD was composed of several old agencies with well-established programs and constituencies, together with a broad but imprecise mandate for addressing future problems. The legislation called for a department that would administer existing federal housing programs as well as represent the needs and interests of the nation's metropolitan areas. But other federal departments also exercised urban responsibilities, and the role HUD would play in the organizational framework of the executive branch was not clearly defined.

The law creating the department directed the president to study both housing and urban development functions within the federal government and to advise Congress which ones should be transferred to the new department. Many advocates of the department, both inside and outside government, felt that HUD should become the organizing point for a comprehensive approach to urban problems. But the realization of these hopes would depend on an effective reorganization of the department's constituent units, the outcome of interagency battles, and the mediating role of the subpresidency.

DEVELOPMENTS BEFORE THE JOHNSON PRESIDENCY
Origins of a Probem

The constituent units of HUD had evolved in response to public concerns for slum clearance, housing availability, residential mortgage insurance, and

13

urban renewal. Before the creation of HUD, the individual units—the Federal Housing Administration (FHA), the Public Housing Administration (PHA), the Federal National Mortgage Association (FNMA), the Community Facilities Administration (CFA), and the Urban Renewal Administration (URA)—were loosely organized within the Housing and Home Finance Agency (HHFA). FHA, PHA, and FNMA had been created independently during the 1930s, each authorized by separate legislation and each serving a different clientele. In 1949 Congress approved a presidential reorganization plan establishing HHFA and gave it responsibility for coordinating the major housing programs.[2] Almost twenty years later (1954), CFA and URA were created from existing offices without special legislation. Although HHFA did not have clear lines of authority over constituent units with separate statutory bases, it would nevertheless serve as the lead agency for dealing with physical development programs in urban communities.

The federal government was slow to accept responsibility·for improving urban conditions. The first expression of concern took the form of special studies commissioned by Congress in the early 1890s and later by Theodore Roosevelt. In both instances recommendations were made for improving the nation's slums and constructing inexpensive but sanitary dwellings. In neither instance, however, was a federal program forthcoming. The federal response came as a set of emergency measures to stimulate construction and provide housing relief during periods of national crisis—World War I, the Great Depression, and World War II.[3]

From the beginning, this limited but necessary involvement produced two reactions. On one side federal intervention was alleged to undermine federalism, states rights, and the free enterprise system. On the other, the government was criticized for failing to see housing as but one aspect of an urban economy. Both positions had organizational implications. Either the federal government should step back from its involvement with the cities (reinforcing the integrity of the states) or it should create a national department for dealing with a whole range of urban issues.

This conflict of attitude—which mirrors a deeper conflict within our system—has never been satisfactorily resolved. But, despite what its critics may have imagined, federal urban intervention has been extremely limited. The initial measures were confined to stabilizing the residential housing market—first through the establishment of the Federal Home Loan Bank Board (1932) to provide credit for home lending institutions and then through the creation of the Federal Housing Administration (1934) to insure mortgages for residential buyers. Later, a secondary mortgage market was opened up for FHA-insured loans and placed under FNMA (1938).[4]

Protecting the housing market served two important functions: it helped address the problem of an insufficient housing supply, and it provided stimulus to the economy. It did not, however, improve the living environment of the poor. Not until the creation of the United States Housing Authority (USHA) (1937) was there a federal commitment to slum clearance and public housing. Even then the approach was indirect. The United States Housing Authority subsidized local public agencies to replace slum dwellings with new public housing. Although provision was made for upkeep and rental assistance, the need quickly overran the resources. When World War II broke out, slum clearance was suspended completely, and public housing was reserved for areas in which defense needs were critical.[5]

The early housing programs were the result of economic and political pressures that grew out of the Great Depression. Nevertheless, they revealed something fundamental about federal involvement in urban affairs: the use of incremental approaches to achieve different, perhaps irreconcilable, ends. The viable programs were those in which the federal government either guaranteed or expanded an existing market. The least effective and the least liked among some parts of the population were those organized to provide social welfare. Insuring the home construction industry, for example, was considered an act of policy genius, for it contributed to aggregate economic growth without cost to anyone. But subsidizing public housing had redistributive effects. It took tax resources and allocated them to the urban poor.

The contrast between programs of production and programs of redistribution was made crystal clear in the first attempt to reorganize federal agencies with housing responsibilities. In 1939, through a presidential reorganization plan, Franklin Roosevelt created two distinct operations: a Federal Loan Agency, which included the Federal Home Loan Bank Board and FHA, and a Federal Works Agency (concerned mainly with public housing and employment) composed of USHA and several public works units.[6] The effect of this arrangement, however, was to mobilize two different urban constituencies and make an integrated approach to housing politically impossible.

During World War II (1942) Roosevelt tried to make up for this mistake by regrouping almost all nonfarm housing functions under a National Housing Agency (NHA). But once the war was over a new base of authority was necessary. This was finally provided—after two and a half years of deadlock—when Congress approved an executive reorganization plan transferring the administrative units of NHA to HHFA (1947).[7]

Yet the creation of HHFA did not bring peace and did not redress the equity question; it only perpetuated the status quo. The larger issues of housing policy were reserved for the Housing Act of 1949. Under the legislation, a comprehensive housing policy was envisioned: the federal government would work toward a decent home and suitable living environment for

15

every American family. The programs to realize these objectives called for an increase in housing production (including low-rent public housing), slum clearance, and urban redevelopment (a term for physical improvement projects in blighted neighborhoods).[8]

As anticipated, the availability of federal subsidies helped expand the home construction industry and stimulate private investment in urban buildings. It did not, however, expand the residual benefits to the urban poor. These would continue to remain inadequate.

The greatest beneficiary of the new legislation was HHFA. It was no longer an administrative oddity but became a second-echelon agency with a mandate and a mission. It had been brought into existence to satisfy the demand for housing, but as a result of the Housing Act of 1949 it became an indirect participant in the urban economy. Later, when Congress replaced urban redevelopment with urban renewal—and began subsidizing physical conservation and rehabilitation as well as clearance—the linkage between the agency and the financial community was made even stronger. To emphasize this development, two new units—the Community Facilities Administration (CFA) and the Urban Renewal Administration (URA)—were created in 1954 by order of the administrator.[9]

The involvement of HHFA in the physical revitalization of the citywidened the gap between its economic function (subsidizing housing production and improving central city property values) and its welfare function (public housing). But the problem was further complicated by the internal structure of the agency itself. Only CFA and URA were fully responsible to the administrator. The remaining units—FHA, PHA, FNMA. and FHLBB—were subject only (in accordance with Reorganization Plan no. 3 of 1947) to the administrator's powers of "general supervision and coordination." Even if an attempt were made to bring public housing and urban development closer together, administrative changes would require a presidential reorganization initiative or additional legislation. While prospects for these were not bleak, they would have to be weighed against other alternatives for integrating urban-related functions at the federal level.

Congress and Urban Policy

The dispersed nature of federal urban programs—each having a separate calendar for planning and funding—was a constant irritation to the state and local officials who had to work with the different pieces. Congress was also uneasy, since to deal with the growing list of urban issues required an approach that was considerably broader than any agency's mandate and that probably called for a substantial reallocation of resources.

The congressional response—which began to take shape in the middle 1950s—assumed two distinct forms. One approach was to continue to increase funds for established programs and slowly work out better methods of federal-state-local coordination. The other was to seek a structural solution—that is, a cabinet department that would represent urban interests at the highest levels of government.

The "structuralists," whose first bill was introduced in 1955, wanted a strong, multipurpose department, but one that retained HHFA as its organizational base.[10] Functions other than housing would be transferred from existing agencies to the new department at the president's discretion through reorganization plans. The "incrementalists," on the other hand, sensed that the nation faced not a "monolithic" urban problem but a diverse set of urban conditions that would not be addressed by a single agency. Instead of a new department they proposed a commission on metropolitan problems to study the dynamics of metropolitan expansion, and they recommended measures that could be taken within the existing framework of tripartite (federal-state-local) administration.[11]

Presidential Reaction to Urban Demands

Like Congress, the presidency was divided in its view of how urban policies should be administered. President Eisenhower, who wished to reduce federal intervention in state and local government, rejected the idea of a cabinet department for housing. So did his chief assistant, Sherman Adams, who believed such a department would stimulate demand for increased expenditures.[12] But in 1957 the President's Advisory Committee on Government Organization (PACGO) and the Bureau of the Budget (BOB)—which staffed PACGO—felt that the permanence and national significance of shelter and physical development programs warranted cabinet status.[13] Both supported the creation of a department of housing and community development.

Differing policy perspectives within the subpresidency are not unusual. In fact, many presidents deliberately foster competing points of view to give them a keener sense of the equities and interests that surround a particular issue. The Eisenhower subpresidency had access to a considerable range of thought. But internal memorandums show that the most influential ideas came from a moderate-to-conservative group of political scientists and public administrators—Luther G. Gulick, George Deming, C. McKim Norton, Robert H. Connery, Richard H. Leach, John Bebout, and William Fredericks. What these individuals counseled and what the president found appealing was a White House unit (not a department) for reviewing all federal policies and programs affecting the urban economy.[14]

The Eisenhower approach to urban policy administration emphasized increased staff assistance and improved coordination, but not departmental reorganization. During the presidential campaign of 1960, Richard Nixon also endorsed this point of view, calling for a federal "clearinghouse for

information and advice on such metropolitan problems as . . . growth, renewal, and adjustment."[15] The driving force of urban policy would continue
to be federal subsidies. But the markets affected would extend to entire
metropolitan areas. According to Nixon, this private market strategy would
"propel rather than retard public efforts," giving urban localities an opportunity to "innovate and improvise."[16]

The Democratic party, however, assumed a different posture. Instead of a
staff or advisory mechanism, its platform called for a single department to
handle urban and metropolitan problems—a department with backbone
and a measure of independence. As Democrat Robert Wood argued:

> It is not "representativeness" in the sense of access to the President in a
> "consultative" or "advisory" relationship which the proponents seek
> from Department status. This, too, they could achieve in a staff capac-
> ity and perhaps with easier channels of access and more Presidential
> confidence. It is "representativeness" in the sense of being able to dis-
> agree with the Chief Executive or to influence him in terms other than
> logical argument that the proponents seek.[17]

The Kennedy Administration's Proposal

The proposed department, however, did not rank high on President Kennedy's legislative agenda. Even if it had, the narrow base of presidential
support in Congress would have been a sufficient deterrent. Yet, in view of
the campaign promise, something had to be done. As a presidential adviser,
Richard Neustadat, put it: "The trick [was] to create something bigger and
broader than HHFA with respect to urban development without actually
taking anything away from anyone else, and, at the same time, permitting a
housecleaning at HHFA."[18]

Under Kennedy, attention to the scope and composition of a department
moved in stages. The first stage took place between the general election and
the inauguration, at which time the principal actors were members of a
presidential task force on long-range problems of housing and urban affairs.
Chaired by Joseph P. MacMurray, a former New York State housing administrator and president of Queens Borough Community College, the
group was composed of a university professor (Robert Wood, MIT), a
congressional staff director (John E. Barriere, House Subcommittee on
Housing), and two executives from savings and loan institutions (Harry
Held, Bowery Savings Bank of New York, and Charles Wellman, Federal
Savings and Loan, Glendale, California). In its report, the task force enthusiastically recommended the elevation of HHFA to cabinet status and
urged that the water pollution and waste treatment programs of the Public
Health Service also be included.[9]

The second stage occurred shortly after the inauguration and involved an assessment of the departmental idea by the innermost circle of the Kennedy subpresidency—Theodore C. Sorensen, White House special counsel, and two members of his immediate office—Myer Feldman and Lee C. White. This group reviewed the task force report and a variety of independent appraisals from BOB, HHFA, the Conference of Mayors, and other federal agencies with urban interests or responsibilities.[20]

A number of functions were identified that could be transferred to the proposed department: for example, the Federal Home Loan Bank Board, the Federal Savings and Loan Insurance Corporation, the veterans' housing assistance program, and the water pollution control program.[21] But strategically placed congressional interests—largely from the Government Operations Committees of both houses—were hostile to a department with diverse and wide-ranging urban functions.

Given these constraints, the White House staff and BOB moved with extreme caution. The first tactical consideration was whether to submit a bill or a presidential reorganization plan. Either method could be used to create a department, but a reorganization plan would not contain an expression of national urban policy. In addition, reorganization plans were considered offensive to Senator McClellan, chairman of the Government Operations Committee, who felt they reduced the powers of Congress.[22] A decision was made in favor of a bill.

The second tactical issue was the content of the legislation itself. At the suggestion of Elmer Staats, deputy director of BOB, two bills were drafted—one elevating HHFA and its constituent units to cabinet rank without any internal changes, the other delegating to the secretary the powers exercised by these units.[23]

For the initial drafts Staats turned to B. T. Fitzpatrick, a Washington housing attorney, who worked from contents supplied by BOB staff. Fitzpatrick's drafts were then reviewed by the bureau's legal staff, by Harold Seidman, who was the acting assistant director for the Division of Management and Organization and by the bureau's director, David E. Bell.[24] The review group examined the department from several perspectives:

Would it obscure FHA and PHA?

Would it become a clientele agency for the central cities?

What effect would it have on the coordination of all federal urban activities?

Would it force a change in the federal-state-local system of government?

As it finally emerged, a bill to create a department of urban affairs and housing did not mention a single function beyond those exercised by HHFA, though it did give the secretary full authority over the agency's operations. Even so, congressional opposition proved too strong. The bill was deliberately stalled in the House Rules Committee. President Kennedy then resubmitted the legislation in the form of a reorganization plan,[25] but it too was promptly rejected in Congress.

Congressional critics quickly pointed out that the vote was greatly influenced by Kennedy's desire to elevate Robert Weaver, a black, to the new cabinet post (Weaver had already stirred up controversy as Kennedy's appointee as administrator of HHFA). But a number of other objections were present as well, ranging from opposition to public housing to fear that the proposed department was an unwarranted intrusion into local government. As Weaver recalled, opposition was on two grounds:

> The first was the issue of concentration of federal government and impingement upon local government and so forth, which some people honestly felt and others didn't like it for different reasons. And secondly, the fact that it seemed as though I might become Secretary was another element which was very much involved in the killing of it.[26]

In the budget message of 1963 Kennedy again proposed that Congress establish a department of urban affairs and housing. But Congress was unresponsive, largely owing to Kennedy's inability to demonstrate widespread support for it. An urban consciousness—or more precisely, a general awareness of urban problems—would gradually develop, but only after Kennedy's assassination and the presidential election of 1964.

In 1964 President Johnson proposed legislation for a department of housing and community development, but it was not until after the November election that he pursued its prospects seriously. With a mandate from the electorate and a democratic majority in Congress, Johnson began a search for urban policy initiatives on all fronts—new structures, new programs, more effective processes. Although these elements were clearly distinguishable, Johnson actively searched for combinations that would enlarge the capacity of the Great Society.

The Creation of HUD
The Johnson Approach

To help formulate a comprehensive urban strategy, President Johnson appointed a Task Force on Metropolitan and Urban Problems under the leadership of Robert Wood (1964).[27] At the president's request, the task force was asked to develop a fresh, imaginative approach to urban issues rather than to focus on policies that would be politically acceptable. The result, unlike previous legislative and executive reviews, was a consideration of pathways that diverged sharply from the traditional emphasis on housing.

According to the task force, not only did existing federal programs show an imbalance between physical development and human needs within the city, but they revealed "imbalances between parts of the country, communities of different types, and parts of the population."[28] A more comprehensive urban policy was necessary in which future resources could be allocated to the social, physical, and economic environments of the city. The intent was not to realign federal subsidies, but to increase support and provide better policy coordination for urban social services, the construction of community facilities, and an expansion of federally insured mortgages.

Although many new programs and functions were proposed—for example, rent supplements, below-market interest subsidies, new communities, block grants, and demonstration cities—the major organization recommendations were for the creation of an urban affairs council in the Executive Office and a new department of housing and urban development.[29] The urban affairs council would be composed of representatives from federal agencies with significant urban responsibilities and would include a secretariat large enough to carry out policy-planning functions. The new department, however, would be more limited in scope, extending to the housing and assistance programs of HHFA but stopping short of a comprehensive structure for all urban activities.

From the perspectives of the task force, the imbalance between physical development and human services within the city could not be dealt with by a single act of federal reorganization. Rather, "extraordinary organizational and collaborative efforts [were] required by governments at every level."[30] The proposed cabinet department was only a starting point, for regional and economic differences among urban communities would demand political, not organizational, solutions. Thus the prospect of a viable urban policy was less dependent on a particular administrative arrangement than on the "unifying potential of the offices of President, Governors, Mayors and other local chief executives."[31]

Still, reorganization could be used as a part of the president's strategy for unifying urban policies. It was not his most powerful instrument, but it might create a new balance of interests and influence the distribution of federal subsidies. The Task Force on Metropolitan and Urban Problems recognized this possibility but deferred to a companion Task Force on Government Organization the "detailed development" of the new federal department.[32]

Under the direction of Don K. Price, the Task Force on Government Organization recommended the consolidation of a number of programs from existing departments and independent agencies. Without evaluating political feasibility or effect on urban equities, the task force felt a department of housing and community development should include all the operations of HHFA and the Federal Home Loan Bank Board; the home loan functions of the Veterans Administration and the Farmer's Home Administration (Agriculture); and the grant programs for waste treatment facilities (HEW), water supply systems in small communities (Agriculture), and urban highway construction (Bureau of Public Roads, Commerce).[33] These functions were chosen because of their obvious connection to the physical aspects of community development. Other programs—for example, hospital and health facilities, airports, public works and school construction—were rejected because it was difficult to separate their community and noncommunity development functions or because they were intimately related to the program objectives of the host agency.[34]

The functions that would finally be incorporated into the new department were not left to chance. Both task forces had been assigned an executive secretary from BOB and, at times, a White House staff member to serve as presidential liaison. Through these channels, the practical effects of reorganization were under constant subpresidential review and assessment. As presidential assistant Bill Moyers put it:

> We anticipated the reactions of different constituencies that would be served or alienated by the recommendations . . . and made them part of the process in developing the programs. I think that was the most essential, crucial decision that was ever made.[35]

One constituency that had no intention of being alienated from urban policy recommendations was HHFA. Through Morton Schussheim, HHFA's assistant administrator for program policy and one of the staff members of the Task Force on Urban and Metropolitan Problems, Weaver was kept constantly up to date. "I worked very closely with him [Schussheim] and I had a very, very large role in the '64 task force through this."[36]

Almost all the program recommendations of the task force met with Weaver's approval, but he was strongly opposed to the creation of a council of urban affairs. The task force had paid little attention to Schussheim's arguments against the council, but, once the final report had been sent to the president (30 November 1964), Weaver appealed to a higher level of subpresidential decision-making. In a memo to Bill Moyers in early December, Weaver set down his objections:

> [The] proposal to create an Urban Affairs Council could kill the proposed Department. Private organizations and many in the Congress have recommended a similar Office in the White House as an alternative to a Department . . . . However, the recommendation for the Council (or any similar Office) could lead to impairing Administration legislative strategy, and conceivably the authorization of the Council and the establishment of the Department could both be defeated. . . . Also, by

standing between the Department and the President, the Council or other coordinating office in the Executive Office would tend to defeat one of the principal purposes of the Department, to increase the status of, and level of consideration given to urban matters.[37]

Weaver's view of the new department was clear: it should be concerned primarily with housing and physical assistance efforts, "excluding," he wrote Moyers, "purely social and economic factors involved in the urban programs and the over-all urban policy of the Federal Government."[38] Weaver's memo was perfectly timed to become part of a preliminary assessment of the Wood and Price proposals conducted by Moyers, Richard Goodwin of the White House staff, and BOB during December 1964.[39]

After a review of the benefits, budgetary effects, and political support for the reorganization, a decision was made to recommend cabinet status for HHFA but not to give it additional functions or to change any of the basic laws applicable to its programs.[40] President Johnson went along with the recommendation, and BOB prepared draft legislation giving the secretary power to alter the internal structure of the agency. The question of a larger urban role for the department was left open.

A second evaluation of the proposed department took place after the agencies had been asked to comment on the draft legislation. Nine agencies indicated complete approval, while the remainder raised questions regarding jurisdiction, the number of supergrade positions, intergovernmental assistance, and the effect of the new department of pending litigation.[41] In all but the last instance BOB recommended against new language, indicating that the intent of the bill was sufficiently clear or that to try for greater precision would only call attention to an urban-rural split.[42] Additional wording to prevent the abatement of legal actions, however, was acceptable to both the bureau and HHFA.

What was not immediately apparent at this stage of evaluation was the difference in policy expectations between the White House and HHFA. President Johnson wanted a broad-based urban policy with new programs and organizational instruments. HHFA's goals were more modest. It wanted cabinet status, parity with other departments, protection of its traditional programs, and internal integration. What HHFA did not want was political trouble: jurisdictional wars with other agencies, conflict with congressional oversight committees, a running battle with state and local governments over urban priorities.

The only issue that produced an instant response from HHFA dealt with the pay levels for the administrators of its constituent units. Indeed, this reaction was perhaps the most sensitive point raised during the review and comment process. As BOB described it:

The major issue appears to be the pay level of the commissioners of the constituent units. Under the 1964 executive pay legislation they are at Level IV. In the present draft, these positions were put at Level V. It appears that the question of downgrading is still open, however.[43]

Although seemingly trivial, the choice of pay levels did have important implications for interagency politics and departmental prestige. Executive level IV was reserved for assistant secretaries whose responsibilities were thought to be greater than those of "administrators", "commissioners", and "directors." From the standpoint of HHFA, a level V appointment not only would diminish the importance of the function performed, it would create difficulties in recruiting and training high-quality executive personnel. The bureau clearly understood this, but as a tactical maneuver it sought to keep the matter open.

Another tactical position taken by the bureau was to separate reorganization proposals from new program measures. Mixing the two created problems in Congress, since program proposals went to different committees than did those concerned with administrative changes. Yet it was not clear that President Johnson saw this separation as advantageous. In his State of the Union message on 4 January 1965, the president indicated an impatience with past approaches to urban problems. "The first step," he asserted, "is to break old patterns—to begin to think, work and plan for the development of entire metropolitan areas.... A Department of Housing and Urban Development will be needed to spearhead this effort in our cities."[44] Three weeks later in his message to Congress on the budget he emphasized again the importance of an urban department "coupled with increased emphasis on comprehensive local planning."[45]

After the budget message it became apparent to the bureau that Johnson's view of urban policy was like his view of the country—"free, restless, growing and full of hope."[46] Something had to be done to clarify the extent to which the new department would affect other agencies with urban programs. Each new presidential message seemed to offer an irresistible opportunity to raise urban policy expectations without a corresponding attempt to look at the organizational consequences.

In his budget message the president had promised a special message on housing and urban development. From the bureau's point of view this represented a critical point: without a careful statement of the responsibilities of the new department, serious interagency conflicts might arise. As Harold Seidman observed in reviewing a draft of the housing message:

> There is one general warning I would make. We can note in HHFA and in other quarters a tendency to regard HHFA and its proposed successor department as an agency the scope of which cuts across all things urban. Actually, the primary mission of HHFA centers about the physi-

cal development of urban areas and the provision of shelter. Its successor agency will be named the Department of Urban Affairs. To the extent that HHFA is encouraged in widening its scope beyond urban development, the groundwork is laid for serious interagency jurisdictional conflict and program overlap. Therefore, the message should be very careful not to imply that the HHFA functional and program responsibilities are broader than physical development.[47]

Seidman also noticed the potential overlap between proposed grants for neighborhood health and recreational centers contained in the message, the community centers set up under the poverty program, the community and mental health centers requested by HEW, and the supplementary educational facilities proposed by the president in his message on educational opportunity. "In sum," he concluded, "although the [president's] message has a strong social welfare tenor, it should not imply that, because HHFA programs have all sorts of implications beyond physical development, HHFA should be vested with responsibility for welfare and other programs merely because they are urban or related in some manner to urban development."[48]

Seidman's advice on organization was obviously at variance with program objectives being developed by the president in consultation with other parts of the subpresidency. As a tactical move, Johnson chose not to moderate his position on neighborhood facilities. Nor did he pay close attention to the bureau's advice on HHFA. The proposed department, he announced in his Message on the Cities, not only would encompass the programs of HHFA, but would "be primarily responsible for Federal participation in metropolitan area thinking and planning."[49] In this role it would cooperate with other federal agencies—in health, education, and employment as well as social services—and work with mayors, governors, and state legislatures.

Congressional Consideration of HUD

When the administration bill was introduced in Congress three weeks later, there was still some confusion over assurances from the subpresidency—especially BOB—that the new department would be exclusively concerned with urban physical development and over the president's suggestion that it would serve as a "focal point for thought and innovation and imagination about the problems of our cities."[50] Senator Joseph Clark (D–Penn.), the first witness for the administration bill (S. 1599), tried to put the matter in perspective. He reminded his colleagues on the Subcommittee on Executive Reorganization that HHFA was already administering programs that went well beyond housing or home finance:

Naturally, questions of new functions and new programs will arise in connection with the new Department. If they do not, it will call for an investigation, because I would expect the new Department to concern itself with some of the really pressing problems in the metropolitan areas which are not receiving attention at present. But such extensions of concern arise every year in connection with HHFA. In the last three years, for example, we have assigned mass transit and open space to HHFA even though they have nothing to do with either housing or home finance.[51]

The second witness, Kermit Gordon, director of BOB, reassured the subcommittee that he was against the transfer of existing functions from other departments and agencies to HUD:

I do not want to leave the impression that we have not studied the desirability of incorporating other functions of the Federal Government into the Department of Housing and Urban Development. We have, and we have studied it very carefully, and our conclusion at this time is that we are not prepared to recommend the incorporation of other functions or programs into this Department.[52]

After the testimony of Clark and Gordon, the confusion over departmental scope seemed to evaporate. But to Senator Abraham Ribicoff (D–Conn.), chairman of the subcommittee, the additional transfer and integration of functions would determine the effectiveness of the new department. He urged both the president and members of the Senate to avoid the same mistakes that had been made in creating the Department of Health, Education, and Welfare (HEW). The bureaucracy contained too many "small kingdoms," resistant to any change or shift of emphasis. "If we are going to create a new department, let us try to find out what really belongs in a department responsible for housing and urban development and try to pull some of these things together." "Let us try to do a real job instead of doing it once over lightly."[53] Ribicoff's remarks, however, were not widely shared by members of the subcommittee, for, as a practical matter, the issues raised by a complete reorganization or urban functions would have required a comprehensive committee reorganization of Congress as well.

The real question in the subcommittee was whether to have a new department (whatever its scope) or a presidential mechanism to ensure better coordination of existing urban functions. Most Republicans and a number of southern Democrats were behind Senator Hugh Scott's (R–Penn.) bill (S. 497) that called for an office of community development in the Executive Office of the President. This Office, with the assistance of a community development council—composed of the secretaries of Labor, Commerce, HEW, Treasury, the administrators of Veterans' Affairs and HHFA—would coordinate federal programs with major urban impact.

Everyone sympathized with the need for improved high-level coordination, but the Republican bill did not have sufficient support to challenge S. 1599. Senator Jacob Javits (R–N.Y.), however, was not content to see the coordination issue buried. Although he had cosponsored the president's bill, he felt that even with a department of housing and urban development, urban functions—particularly those in education, poverty, manpower, and juvenile delinquency—would remain uncoordinated. He proposed, therefore, an office of urban program coordination in HUD to coordinate federal programs having a significant effect on community development.[54]

While this provision was attractive, it was also potentially disruptive, for established agencies would not concede the lead role for coordinating urban problems to a department instead of the president. The proposal to locate this office in HUD and not in the Executive Office of the President could be explained only by party politics. The Republican leadership, after all, had called for a roughly comparable operation in preference to a department.

The idea of a departmental focus for urban program coordination struck the subpresidency—this time the president's legislative liaison group—as both misplaced and premature. First create the department, one of its memoranda urged, then, if additional coordination is desired, the responsibility should be given to the "Vice-President in keeping with the mandate given him by the President to provide liaison with the cities."[55]

Interest Groups

In addition to keeping track of amendments, the subpresidency was also at work monitoring interest group opposition to S. 1599. Both BOB and the informal group of White House aides on legislative liaison provided running accounts of the tactics used to defeat the bill by the Mortgage Bankers Association, the National Association of Real Estate Boards, the National Association of Bankers, the American Farm Bureau Association, and the United States Chamber of Commerce.[56]

The most effective critics of the legislation were the mortgage bankers. Polished, well-organized, and articulate, they rested their case on a single argument: since the FHA would not be preserved as a specific legal entity in the department, they argued, the flow of mortgage funds across the state lines would be seriously disrupted.[57] The passage of S. 1599 not only would jeopardize transactions between credit-surplus and credit-short areas of the country, it would inhibit growth and create uncertainties for private credit operations.[58]

Despite assurances from HHFA that the Federal Housing Administration name would be preserved within the new department, the mortgage bankers and their supporters continued to assert that "private housing and private mortgage credit should not be made secondary to the problems of urban

27

development."[59] Although this argument had been historically effective, the mood of Congress and the country was changing. Organized support for S. 1599 represented a greater cross section of political and professional concern than earlier efforts to create a department. It included the National Association of Housing and Redevelopment Officials, the United States Conference of Mayors, the National League of Cities, the National Housing Conference, the American Institute of Planners, the American Federation of Labor and Congress of Industrial Organizations, the American Institute of Architects, the National Association of Mutual Savings Banks, and the United Presbyterian Church. Two groups—the National Association of Counties and the National Association of Home Builders—that previously had opposed a department were now solidly behind S. 1599.[60]

Finding Room to Compromise

Although interest group efforts to influence the fate of the department were felt in both houses of Congress, the issues were identical: Should FHA be given permanent status? What additional functions (if any) were needed to make the new organization effective? What interagency responsibilities should the department have? What intergovernmental role should the agency play?

The House Committee on Government Operations, which scheduled its hearings five days later than the Senate, resolved the first issue by adopting an amendment designating one of the assistant secretaries to administer, under the direction and supervision of the secretary, programs related to the private mortgage market. The Bureau of the Budget concurred in the action, and the Senate Subcommittee on Executive Reorganization followed with a similar amendment. On the floor of the Senate, however, S. 1599 was further amended, on the motion of Senator John Sparkman (D–Ala.), to provide a federal housing commissioner appointed by the president. Although the commissioner was to have his duties and powers prescribed by the secretary, the language was sufficiently different from that of the House to create at least momentary concern within the bureau, which has traditionally supported full authority in departmental secretaries. "While at first blush this seems pretty awful," one of its staff members wrote:

it means that the Assistant Secretary is staff rather than line. Further, since FHA functions are still vested in the Secretary, . . . there is no statutory obstacle to transfer of functions in or out of FHA within the Department. In sum, then, the main objection to this amendment should be respecting the appointment of the FHA Commissioner by the President. In all other respects, it would appear to strengthen rather than weaken the organizational setup we are advocating.[61]

The House had not introduced further significant changes in the administration bill, either to expand the scope of the department or to describe its interagency and intergovernmental responsibilities. But the Senate wanted greater specificity. In addition to the Javits and Sparkman amendments, several other provisions were incorporated. The most important were two amendments by Senator Robert F. Kennedy (D–N.Y.)—one adding mass transportation to housing and urban development in the description of problems to be solved, the other a provision obligating the president to conduct a study of urban development functions that could be transferred to or from the department. The remaining substantial issue was a proposal by Senator Leverett Saltonstall (R–Mass.), that the secretary be required to hold public hearings on questions of federal assistance when asked to do so by a governor.[62]

With the exception of the Sparkman and Saltonstall amendments, the bureau was content to let the others alone, even though it felt that "in some cases they [were] unnecessary or a reiteration of existing law or statutory policy."[63] The Saltonstall amendment, however, might have created special problems. In a memo to the legislative liaison group, the bureau argued that it not only was an administrative nuisance but was "extremely open to abuse and arbitrary utilization."[64] To "negotiate" these and other differences between the subpresidency and the Senate, presidential assistant Mike Manatos was asked to talk with Senator Ribicoff. As he later reported to Larry O'Brien:

> I . . . talked to Senator Ribicoff about the conference on the Department bill and the Sparkman and Saltonstall amendments. Abe has no problem whatsoever in dropping the Sparkman Amendment. He feels somewhat of a commitment to Saltonstall to attempt to work out something that is acceptable in that area. You will recall that Saltonstall switched to support the bill when his amendment was adopted. However, if we feel that the Saltonstall Amendment ought to be dropped I am certain Abe will do it.[65]

The conference committee met on 26 August 1965 to resolve the differences between the House-passed bill and S. 1599 as amended. The Sparkman amendment was combined with the House provision for an assistant secretary in charge of functions affecting the private mortgage market. The result was the designation of an assistant secretary as federal housing commissioner with responsibility for the Federal Housing Administration. The Saltonstall amendment was dropped entirely, though the secretary was required to consult and cooperate with state governors and agencies—even to the point of holding informal public hearings. The remaining amendments, however, met with conference approval. The only change made was the substitution of the word "director" for Senator Javits's "Office of Urban Program Coordination."

On 9 September 1965 President Johnson signed the act that brought HUD into existence. The occasion, however, was largely symbolic, for not only were there conflicting views as to the nature of the department, but its internal structure was still to be worked out.

The legislation provided for a secretary, an under secretary, four assistant secretaries, an assistant secretary for administration, and a director of urban program coordination.[66] The act vested the powers in the secretary; and beyond the requirement that one of the four assistant secretaries administer FHA, there was enormous organizational latitude. Even the responsibilities of the assistant secretary for administration and the director of urban program coordination were left to the secretary's discretion. As a final gesture of good faith, Congress authorized up to six level V positions should the secretary wish to create or delegate additional functions.

The absence of organizational detail can be attributed to the persistent influence of BOB.[67] Aware of the difficulty of separating urban functions from established programs in other departments, bureau staff under both Kennedy and Johnson worked against attempts to gain approval for a comprehensive department of urban affairs. Instead of identifying programs and prescribing a structure for HUD, the bureau advocated complete authority over the existing functions of HHFA and maximum organizational flexibility for the secretary. As BOB's assistant director for management and organization put it: "Our strategy was to make the Secretary strong, give him the authority to reorganize and restructure, and provide him with leverage against the established clienteles."[68]

THE INTERNAL ORGANIZATION OF HUD

President Johnson was not actively involved in the organizational arrangements of HUD, but he clearly wanted an instrument capable of improving the urban setting by "combining construction with social services and community facilities."[69] From the president's point of view, the structure of HUD presented an opportunity for utilizing federal resources more effectively. Urban programs and functions would have to be reevaluated—perhaps even recombined—but not in a way that antagonized Congress or threatened operating interests. In short, what the president wanted was departmental structure, sensitive to the needs of urban development but equally responsive to subsystem politics.

The legislation itself provided a loose framework for internal organizational proposals. In addition, structural mechanisms were required for interagency coordination, intergovernmental relations, and the encouragement of private home-builders and mortgage lending institutions. In response to the act, three centers of activity developed, each characterized by an organizational point of view and each with a different design for HUD. The comprehensive perspective of the president was represented by BOB and the President's Task Force on Urban Problems, while a different approach took shape around Robert Weaver and HHFA.

Weaver's Response to the New Legislation

It was widely assumed that Weaver would be President Johnson's choice for departmental secretary. He was well-positioned with liberal and ethnic interests; he had worked hard to elevate HHFA to cabinet status; and he was familiar with the major federal housing and physical development programs. Although Johnson took pride in building suspense into his appointments, Weaver could not afford to delay organization planning. He moved quickly to design a department that would fulfill the legislative mandate and overcome the administrative weaknesses of HHFA. As Weaver described the situation:

> After the department was established by act of Congress... I had assumed that it might be possible that I would become the Secretary. I immediately began to set up machinery for organizing a new department in the event that I would be. I got the most experienced people we had here in administration, and I then began to indicate to them the structure and the objectives and so forth that I would want to have— that I would suggest would be done.[70]

The most pressing issue was the assertion of secretarial control over the constituent units of HHFA. Hence, structure was seen as an instrument to unify program objectives and departmental operations. "I had a unique problem," Weaver confessed," which I suppose any—well, HEW had it and Alan Boyd has had it in Transportation—and that is that we had five little fiefdoms over here, and each one was pretty damned autonomous and had not only its own autonomy, but had something of its own lobby in the Congress and its own congressional support. Well, the first thing that was obvious to me was that if we were going to have a department, it didn't mean a tinker's damn if you didn't pull this thing together."[71]

Weaver's approach to unification was to group programs and functions so that the organizational context would force resolution of related problems.[72] Programs that had grown up independently but that dealt with similar activities would be structurally drawn together. Although questions of personality and politics could not be avoided completely,[73] Weaver's reorganization design showed remarkable consistency and clarity of purpose. He believed that structure should be an instrument of program objectives.[74] Consequently, his plans for HUD were developed largely to serve existing program elements. Still, the design was not easy to complete, for many of the programs in HHFA had overlapping purposes.

Congress had provided direction by giving separate organizational status to "programs relating to the private mortgage market." But among the unassigned programs were those that dealt with public housing, metropolitan development, open space, urban renewal, urban beautification, neighborhood facilities, and the urbanizing countryside. Here, organizational distinctions could be made only by "drawing artificial dividing lines."[75] Weaver recognized that his decisions might be arbitrary, but he nevertheless developed a rationale:

> I decided that I would take the other [unassigned] programs and just mix them up, and I had to have a rationale to do this. So I hit on the rationale which was those programs which had to do primarily with the inner city would be put under one assistant secretary; those that had to do with the metropolitan area would be put under another assistant secretary—one assistant secretary primarily for urban renewal and public housing, and the other one for metropolitan development.[76]

With existing programs assigned to three assistant secretaries—mortgage credit and federal housing commissioner, renewal and housing assistance, and metropolitan development—Weaver turned to the remaining positions mandated by the departmental act—an undesignated assistant secretary and an assistant secretary for administration. The undesignated slot was transformed into an assistant secretary for demonstrations and intergovernmental relations, who had authority over demonstration programs (such as Model Cities) and over the new functions in intergovernmental assistance and cooperation. The assistant secretary for administration was given the job of consolidating a number of support functions (e.g., personnel, budgeting, automatic data processing, accounting, auditing, procurement) and developing departmentwide standards for their implementation.[77]

Weaver had moved skillfully to design a structure that would bring together related activities and improve program effectiveness. To further break down the existing pattern of HHFA and unify the policy responsibilities of the department, he planned to confer both line and staff functions on the assistant secretaries. "I decided ... that they were going to be staff insofar as they [were] the top advisory group and they got together on policies and so forth; but line in the sense that they [were] responsible for the administration of particular programs which [fell] under their jurisdiction."[78]

Although the arrangement was administratively unorthodox, Weaver was not alone in favoring a mixture of line and staff roles in the upper echelons of the department. Congress had led the way by making the assistant secretary for mortgage credit and federal housing commissioner a line officer in charge of FHA and, at the same time, the secretary's principal adviser on programs related to the private mortgage market—a staff role. Congress did not provide a rationale for its decision, but Weaver felt a combination of line and staff duties would prevent assistant secretaries from neglecting problems affecting the entire department and promote coordinated planning and action between two or more constituent units.

An additional reason for supporting line/staff roles was the prospect that assistant secretaries might be given an opportunity to have more than a passing influence on departmental operations. As Dwight Ink, assistant secretary for administration, put it:

> Assistant Secretaries for the most part had been (and many still are) little more than political figureheads. They do not possess the staff resources to have an in-depth or sustained impact on operations, and their tenure tends to be so short that they leave before they know what is really happening in the organization for which they have some ill-defined responsibility. We equipped each HUD assistant secretary with budget, personnel, and planning capabilities which provided greater capacity to lead and manage, as well as an institutional memory to help bridge the transition from one assistant secretary to the next.[79]

The final means for ensuring the effectiveness of the department lay in the relations between headquarters and the field. Under HHFA, there were four largely separate field operations—one for the Office of the Administrator, another for FHA, one for PHA, and a regional arrangement for FNMA. The Office of the Administrator, with responsibility for urban renewal and community facilities, had seven regional offices, as did PHA. FNMA had five, and the largest of the lot, FHA, possessed seventy-five insurance offices and six offices that dealt with multifamily housing.[80] Historically, the headquarters units of FHA, PHA, and FNMA had exercised control over the applications process as well as the formulation of policy, the development of standards, the unification of procedures, and the evaluation of field office performance.[81] But with the exception of programs under the Office of the Administrator, the regional directors had only limited authority to represent the central office in the field.[82] Weaver found this situation intolerable and proposed a single system of strong regional administrators with authority to make case-by-case decisions. As Weaver expressed it:

> we wanted to have strong regional offices and we wanted to decentralize up to the point where you could decentralize without losing control. By that I mean, for example, we let the regional office process

33

an urban renewal project. But when the urban renewal project is announced it has to come through here so that the congressional liaison can announce it. We can't have ten different people all courting around for congressional reactions, because then when I need to get some support for something, they didn't get it from me.[83]

Since HHFA did not have a tradition of strong regional administration, Weaver relied on both his own experiences and those of his subordinates in designing the field structure of HUD. Of particular significance in working out the details of decentralization was the role of Dwight Ink.[84] Before coming to HUD, Ink had spent considerable time with the Atomic Energy Commission (AEC) and was familiar with its complex pattern of delegating operating authority to the field while centralizing policy decisions at headquarters. Weaver's proposal for integrating and strengthening the regional office of HUD benefited greatly from the AEC model.[85]

As it finally emerged, Weaver's approach to decentralization would employ structure to place regional decisions within the context of related problems affecting a single community.[86] To do this required four major changes in field administration:[87]

1. Each of the seven regional administrators would report directly to the secretary as a line manager in charge of various programs.

2. Each would be given power to represent and speak for the department on all matters within the region.

3. A new position would be created under each regional administrator for making sure that program assumptions and policies were consistent with each other in a given community.

4. Finally, regional operations for public housing and multifamily FHA programs would be united under the regional administrator.

Weaver's deep commitment to the field reflected his concern for improving the outreach of the department. From the start he felt that decentralization was crucial to effective program implementation.

The President's Task Force on Urban Problems

Several changes had taken place in the subpresidency as Weaver worked on his organizational design for HUD. Joseph Califano had assumed the urban policy responsibilities of special counsel Lee White, in an attempt to coordinate White House domestic operations. Kermit Gordon was leaving the Bureau of the Budget to become president of the Brookings Institution, and Charles Schultze had been chosen as the bureau's director. Finally, still fascinated by the prospect of new ideas and programs, President Johnson had ordered another round of task force studies.[88]

Robert Wood—whose 1964 task force had produced a highly sophisticated analysis of urban problems—was invited to the White House in late September 1965 to discuss possible participants in a new urban task force.[89] During the meeting, Califano mentioned names of men with high public visibility—Walter Reuther (vice-president, AFL–CIO), Whitney Young (executive director, Urban League), and Edgar Kaiser (president, Kaiser Industries). With the exception of Wood, the only academic name brought up was Charles Haar, a law professor from Harvard. It was Wood's assessment that the "task force was quite different in terms of the ... decline in the number of so-called 'eggheads.' ... Much greater personalities and reputations came in. It was obviously moving from a Presidential and Executive Office institutional mechanism ... to an immediate concern ... [with] ... location in the White House and the White House staff itself."[90]

As the task force began to take shape, both its membership and its access to the White House suggested that a massive push in the cities was under serious presidential consideration. Wood was asked to chair the group whose members would include—in addition to Reuther, Haar, Young, and Kaiser—Senator Abraham Ribicoff (D–Conn.), Ben Heineman (president, Chicago and North Western Railway), and William Rafsky (executive vice-president, Old Philadelphia Development Corporation). Kermit Gordon also agreed to participate, to the delight of Schultze, who wanted to keep Reuther from "bending the budget completely out of balance."[91]

Since Califano's duties included all domestic policy issues, the day-to-day contact with the task force was taken over by Harry McPherson. John Clinton of the White House also assisted on special projects, as did the aides of individual members. Institutional staff was provided by BOB, whose primary interest was in keeping program transfers and organizational changes to manageable proportions.

The specific proposals for departmental organization were developed by a subcommittee of the task force composed of Heineman, Haar, and Rafsky. Each shared the perspective that "the form of organization must be creatively fashioned to be hospitable to inter-governmental cooperation and to local and private action helpful in solving problems of housing, urban development and mass transportation."[92] But the overriding concern was for an internal structure that "would give the best possible administration to specific programs" and have the resilience "to flex and grow" should new programs be created or old ones transferred or modified.[93]

The subcommittee's strategy was twofold: (1) use organizational structure to bridge the gap between the physical and social environments of metropolitan areas; and (2) organize HUD so it could assist the president in coordinating federal activities in urban and suburban communities. The major provision for "humanizing" urban affairs was the proposed transfer

35

of all community action programs to HUD from the Office of Economic Opportunity (OEO).[94] The subcommittee and all members of the task force except Kermit Gordon and Whitney Young felt that the new department "would tend to make them more successful and meaningful and to give them essential continuity."[95] On the second front, the task force believed that with rearrangement of function and the creation of new structures HUD could play a central role in the executive coordination of urban policy.

The first step in this direction was to give the secretary a unified staff capable of searching out friction points over the entire range of urban activity. Thus the four assistant secretaries would all be staff—one for financial assistance (who would also be the FHA commissioner), one for physical facilities, one for intergovernmental cooperation, and an assistant secretary for Community Action programs. Field operations would also be unified by setting up strong regional administrators, reporting directly to the secretary and under secretary but surrounded by a regional staff for budgeting, public information, and administration. Finally, a council on interdepartmental coordination would be established to provide an integrated focus for the physical, organizational, fiscal, and social programs of metropolitian areas. Chaired by the secretary of HUD, its members would include the secretaries of Defense, Interior, Commerce, Labor, and HEW, as well as the heads of the Federal Aviation Administration, the General Services Administration, and the Federal Home Loan Bank Board.[96]

BOB: The Search for Middle Ground

BOB was well represented on the task force. Its former director, Kermit Gordon, was a task force member, and Bureau personnel served as Wood's institutional staff. Still, seasoned professionals in the Bureau like Harold Seidman were skeptical of task force deliberations, often viewing their work as "off-the-cuff musing of 'experts' . . . not calculated to produce meaningful results."[97] On the proposed reorganization of HUD, the bureau found itself somewhere between the task force recommendations, which would use assistant secretaries as staff, and Weaver's proposals, which would give them line *and* staff responsibilities.

Since the major objectives for the internal organization of HUD were centralized control and unified operations, BOB was critical of Weaver's combination of line and staff responsibilities in the assistant secretaries. As Seidman wrote Schultze:

the proposed organization does not give the Secretary the staff resources which will provide him with adequate review and advice on key objectives of the Department—provision of housing and planned development of urban areas . . . [the] assistant secretaries seem to be placed in the line of command with heavy administrative responsibilities which might tend to limit their ability to provide "across-the-board" advice to the Secretary.[98]

But equally disturbing was the division between central city programs (under an assistant secretary for urban renewal and housing assistance) and suburban programs (under an assistant secretary for metropolitan development). From BOB's perspective this arrangement would split up major programs such as open space and urban beautification and "have a dampening effect on efforts to develop a sense of metropolitan unity and intergovernmental cooperation."[99]

Although Weaver and BOB were in agreement on the need for strong regional administrators, Weaver's method of delegating responsibilities was thought to create a number of administrative problems. Again, it was Seidman who responded:

> We understand that the Secretary proposes to make delegations to each assistant secretary who would, in turn, make re-delegations to the Regional Administrators. This means, in effect, that the regional administrator would be serving four masters on functional matters while acting administratively as the Secretary's man in the region. This presents real problems in terms of the pattern of delegations to the field (the degree to which each assistant secretary is willing to delegate may vary widely), the resolution of disputes between the field and Washington, and the recruitment of able regional administrators.[100]

BOB's organizational strategy was to reduce areas of controversy (by not overly rearranging or adding functions). It recommended that HUD divide its assistant secretaries equally between line and staff. Line responsibilities would go to an assistant secretary for metropolitan development, who would administer programs in urban renewal, community facilities, and urban transportation, and to a federal housing commissioner who would be in charge of FHA, FNMA, PHA, rent control supplements, and college housing. Thus, urban housing programs would be grouped together, as would those dealing with urban physical development.[101]

Having designated line functions for programs in "urban hardware," BOB reserved the department's staff functions for such "software" activities as research, planning, and technical assistance. In keeping with this division, there would be an assistant secretary for policy development and program evaluation and one for planning and technical assistance.[102]

The disagreements between Weaver and BOB over line/staff responsibilities and field organization were not bitter and should not conceal basic areas of agreement.[103] Both wanted HUD to deal with housing and physical development; both wanted a unified department with strong regional administrators; and both wanted improved interagency coordination.

Moving toward Solution

The choice of organizational proposals for HUD, however, rested with the White House, as did the appointment of a departmental secretary. The two decisions were not unrelated, and as the time approached for the legislation to take effect (sixty days after presidential approval), Weaver's position began to erode. Several key staff members in HHFA left their posts, and official Washington was filled with rumors that Weaver had been passed over. Weaver, too, was anxious: "you get an image of lack of impetus and the press just preys on this and they decide the President has no confidence in you."[104]

Then there was the department to think about. Without a secretary, its relation to other agencies and to Congress could be compromised. From Weaver's point of view a decision had to be forced, and what better way to do it than offer his resignation?

> I . . . went to the White House where both Lee White and Joe Califano were—Joe beginning to phase into some of the responsibilities that Lee had and other responsibilities—and indicated that I felt that since the time was coming that I was going to resign because I did not want to be in the unfortunate position of being sort of a hanger-on on the one hand. And secondly, I did not think that anybody who would be the Acting Secretary would be able to get the sort of cooperation that one needed, and the department would not really get going.[105]

Although Weaver was dissuaded from stepping down, he let it be known that his "feelings toward President Johnson were less than warm."[106] He went back to the department but found morale there lower than it had ever been. The whole base of his authority was slipping away, and even with the exertion of personal leadership there was a noticeable slump in administrative operations.

The situation did not improve until President Johnson announced Weaver's appointment on 19 January 1966. At that point Weaver's position was legitimized, and the decision on departmental structure was made. Weaver's line/staff concept was adopted, as was his plan for field organization.

THE ROLE OF THE NEW DEPARTMENT

The role of the department was affected by other developments. HUD, by President Johnson' decision, would not acquire the urban constituencies of the Community Action Program (CAP). As a result of the efforts of Weaver and BOB, it would deal primarily with housing and the physical aspects of urban growth—not with a full range of urban issues. The effect of these decisions meant that HUD would not become a superagency for urban growth or urban economic development.

The subpresidency had recognized all along that it was impractical to place everything urban in a single department, but it tried to "institutionalize" HUD's awareness of cross-cutting problems—problems that either overlapped with other agencies or lay at the margin of departmental responsibilities—in two ways: first, through assigning exclusive staff functions to assistant secretaries for program and policy evaluation; second, by strengthening the leadership of the secretary in interagency and intergovernmental relations.

Weaver's designation of both line and staff functions to the assistant secretaries would provide some measure of assistance. But he needed additional authority to ensure maximum consultation and cooperation in coordinating federal urban programs. The task force recommendation for a council on interdepartmental coordination—which Weaver endorsed—was one approach, but it lacked authoritative support. BOB's solution was to recommend that the secretary be given, by executive order, the power to convene officials in agencies whose programs affected urban areas. This not only would create a forum for the discussion of common problems, it would have formal presidential backing in achieving consistent policies, practices, and procedures. President Johnson was impressed with the idea of coordinating around specific problems, and on 11 August 1966 he signed an executive order giving the "convener function" to the secretary.[107]

The proliferation of separate urban programs, however—each with a different objective and base of support—would continue to frustrate both the president and the Bureau of the Budget. New approaches seemed essential for coordinating Great Society programs. The convener order was one method accessible to the secretary of HUD;[108] OEO's Community Action agencies were another, drawing together federal, state, and other assistance at the local level. Still, more effective mechanisms were thought necessary to consolidate funds and programs, to stimulate local initiative, and to help finance new and additional projects.

Model Cities

The difficulty of coordinating federal programs within urban areas had led the Task Force on Urban Problems to propose a new experimental method for integrating federal resources. Large-scale experiments or demonstrations in selected cities, it was argued, could mobilize money, administrative skill, existing knowledge, and clientele support in an all-out attack on conditions in disadvantaged communities. The object was to develop and apply methods for comprehensive, coordinated planning in projects that would serve as "models" for the rest of the nation. Such efforts, the task force reported, "would show that cities are capable of mobilizing local resources and integrating them with federal assistance to attack urban problems on the huge scale required to create a totally new living environment."[109]

This "total" experiment in the mobilization of urban resources became the centerpiece of the Demonstration Cities and Metropolitan Development Act of 1966. It differed from CAP established by the War on Poverty in that the local organizational unit—the City Demonstration Agency (CDA)—had to be part of city government or have legal status as a local public agency. More than any other program, Model Cities became a test of HUD's decentralized structure and its capacity to coordinate categorical aid programs at the federal level.

Local Administration

In implementing Model Cities, HUD worked toward a balance between neighborhood participants and city officials. Each city was free to develop a mechanism that served the needs of both disadvantaged clienteles and the leadership of local government. The organizational pattern favored by HUD, and followed in most cities, included a policy-making group composed of the director and staff of the CDA, a neighborhood resident organization, and representatives of the city.[110] Many variations of this model were approved, some that provided for neighborhood representation within the planning committees of the CDA, a larger number that gave the resident organization a professional staff and a separate planning function.[111] In all cases, final approval for neighborhood plans was reserved for the city's governing body.[112]

The role of neighborhood residents, however, was never clearly specified. Some HUD officials leaned toward advisory status only, while others supported active participation in all decisions affecting the model neighborhood. In the end, failure to identify the nature of citizen input may have delayed HUD's efforts to have funds from other agencies channeled directly to city hall.[113]

Questions of resident influence were left unresolved, but the Model Cities Administration made a bona fide effort to negotiate a clean and effective review and approval procedure for each locality. The plan was to have the mayor, the Community Demonstration Agency, and local residents (whether in an advisory or a decision-making capacity) exercise review authority over all federal programs in the model neighborhood.[114] But, given locally diverse methods of implementing federal programs and the unfamiliarity in Washington with interrelated neighborhood problems, the proposal was slow to gain acceptance. Even within HUD itself it took almost two years for the assistant secretary for renewal and housing assistance to require regional administrators to give special handling to renewal projects in model neighborhoods.[115] Once this decision was made, however, the regional administrators were obligated to ensure that the director of the City Demonstration Agency and the local renewal director coordinated their review of renewal applications.[116] This step, which was essential to effective local administration, would probably not have occurred had it not been for the staff role of the assistant secretaries.[117] It became apparent that if HUD could not achieve internal consolidation of resources, its appeal for interagency cooperation would be lost.

Regional Administration

The regional offices mirrored the program configurations of headquarters. Each had a mixture of established programs (such as FHA), those a slight step beyond (such as rent supplements), and one—Model Cities—that ranked second only to the Community Action Program in originality.

Under Weaver's decentralized structure, the regional offices were placed in charge of operations and technical assistance for all demonstration cities. A "swing team" of specialists in the Central Office was formed to assist beleaguered generalists (called "leadmen") in the field. The leadmen served as federal coordinators for individual cities and provided support to program specialists in HUD and other federal agencies within the region.[118] The final point of decision for day-to-day operations was reserved for the regional administrator, who had line responsibility for the implementation of all HUD programs.

Weaver recognized the difficulty of coordinating programs within a decentralized structure. He knew that each step beyond the affected community meant that those making decisions were less well equipped to assess local needs and deal with the realities of city government. At the suggestion of Dwight Ink, Weaver decided that the most effective approach was to staff the new regional offices through the career process. This might not produce an immediate solution, but over time the regions would develop greater technical expertise and greater familiarity with local problems. But the attempt to professionalize the regions was not without its political costs. Not only were the commissioner of FHA and the assistant secretary for administration accused by some members of Congress of being disloyal to the president's political allies, but, according to Ink:

> Bob Weaver found himself under heavy personal criticism from within the Democratic Party when he insisted on appointing a regional administrator in Chicago who was not a protege of Mayor Daley. Weaver took the position that either there would be appointed an

individual nominated by Mayor Daley, in which case the individual would be responsible to Mayor Daley and not the President. Weaver felt that if the latter were the case, it was time also to appoint a new secretary of HUD. After a long struggle, Weaver eventually won, and the HUD bureaucracy gained new respect for its leadership.[119]

Although the regional offices increased in proficiency, neither they nor headquarters were able to develop an effective system of federal-state cooperation. This was especially so for Model Cities. Model Cities coordinators in HUD were viewed as "outsiders" by state officials who administered categorical grants from HEW and Labor. The statutory obligations of state agencies, their loyalties to political and professional groups, and federal requirements for separate grant approvals forced attention away from the cities. But in fairness to the states, HUD was slow to recognize their role.[120] Indeed, the initial guidelines for Model Cities did not even acknowledge their existence.[121] Later in the program, regional administrators did solicit state participation, requesting technical assistance from them for City Demonstration Agencies. But the state response was not encouraging.[122]

Centralization and Coordination of Policy

Conflicts or misadventures in the field that raised questions of policy were dealt with in the Central Office. Here, in addition to informal meetings between the secretary and the assistant secretaries, a Budget Review Committee composed of the under secretary and his deputy, the assistant secretaries, the president of the Federal National Mortgage Credit Association, the director of the Office of Urban Technology and Research, and the department's general counsel served as policy review staff for the secretary. The committee's responsibilities were to evaluate budget and program plans, internal forecasts, and estimates and to recommend positions to be taken with BOB and the president.[123] To facilitate special review arrangements for Model Cities, HUD also negotiated an agreement creating an Inter-Agency Coordinating Committee (1967). Its membership included high-level staff from HUD, HEW, Labor, and the Office of Economic Opportunity. But no commitment was made by any of the members to priority funding for the model neighborhoods.[124]

The final attempt to ensure centralized direction and coordination of policy reached into the subpresidency itself. At the request of Weaver, Joseph Califano and BOB director Charles Zwick agreed to urge other agencies to accept HUD's review proposals.[125] But despite a flurry of memos and telephone calls from the White House, most departments found it difficult to develop a flexible approach to existing categorical aid programs. Varying statutory and administrative requirements—including restrictions on agency sponsorship, project strategy, program content, and eligible beneficiaries—worked against the promise of resource mobilization and institutional change. In a statement made two years after Model Cities began, Weaver spoke directly to the issue.

> we have not gotten over and we have not solved . . . the problem of how we get the funds from the other departments which are involved . . . a department like HEW has got its funds in rather categorical areas which have identified clients, professional groups, and often lobbies. . . . They don't have enough left over to do what needs to be done for the model cities. In addition to that, where they do have money that can be used, it's not free money; or, as in the Department of Labor, the grants go to the States and not the cities.[126]

Categorical funding, however, was not all that complicated the administration of Model Cities. Local groups competed for program dominance against one another and sometimes against neighborhood residents themselves. Cleavages of interest and outlook—between the model neighborhood and the city, between the city and the HUD regional offices, and between all three and the state—frustrated efforts to create a unified structure. Eventually it became apparent that, without greater statutory authority, HUD alone could not establish a single entry point for federal funds destined for the 150 demonstration cities.

Conclusion

In perspective, Model Cities was one of several attempts within the Johnson administration to decentralize decision-making. The legislation provided an opportunity to experiment with different methods providing direct representation to client interests in forums of city and federal officials, professional and public interest groups, and, in some cases, state officials who were responsible for administering federal programs. Yet, unlike the Community Action agencies of the War on Poverty, the local unit of Model Cities—the City Demonstration Agency—was tied directly to city government, and both were required to work with the regional offices of HUD.

Under Weaver's direction the HUD Central Office delegated day-to-day decision-making to the regions and assumed the role of overall policy guidance and coordination. This structure made it possible to test the effects on model neighborhoods of decentralized federal operations. It also gave the subpresidency—at the time seeking a system that would give meaning to "creative federalism"—an indication of the problems of program coordination within the network of categorical aid.

To both HUD and the White House, Model Cities contributed one overwhelming piece of evidence: program coordination could not be achieved by either a "top down" or a "bottom up" strategy. Moreover, it provided ample proof that a combined approach had a much greater chance of success within a single department having statutory responsibility for the affected programs. Even here, however—as shown by the attempt to use urban renewal funds in accordance with the objectives of the Model Cities Administration—improved coordination was painfully slow. Had it not been for Weaver's combined line/staff functions in the assistant secretaries, this development might have achieved even less. By giving each assistant secretary staff responsibility for reviewing the performance of the entire department, Weaver created a setting for making programs conform with policy.

As for coordinating the activities of other departments, Model Cities pointed out the obvious. Obstacles to concentrating federal resources were deeply rooted in past legislation and in dispersion of administrative responsibilities for programs in urban development.

If HUD could claim only modest achievements for Model Cities, its larger vision—that of a department coordinating federal activities in housing and urban development—likewise fell short. Externally, HUD was in an even weaker position on other programs than it was with Model Cities. Model Cities, at least, had enough public visibility to provoke periodic intervention by the subpresidency. In contrast, the range of federal programs touching housing and urban development was extremely diverse and involved almost every department. There was no convenient focus for presidential guidance.

Internally, HUD was limited in scope, reflecting in its structure the economic interests and social values of programs in physical development. In urban renewal and housing, HUD had preserved a balance (or imbalance) between the inner city and the suburbs, between the private mortgage market and public housing, between the economically advantaged and the urban poor. In metropolitan development, it had kept a concern for social services from interfering with the construction of highways, water and sewage plants, and other public works.

But if HUD failed to combine physical construction and social services, it represented—at least symbolically—a new commitment to urban problems. At the very least, its cabinet status provided an opportunity to lay claim to future resources and priorities. Although its structure preserved the policy achievements of the past, there was still the flexibility—as Model Cities proved—to incorporate major new programs. Thus, while structural change was not a means for immediate policy change, it held open future possibilities.

The creation of HUD also revealed important aspects of the presidential management of system. It clearly showed how the particularistic goals of professionals, legislators, interest groups, and bureaucrats are mediated by the subpresidency. Whether in the form of the Bureau of the Budget, presidential task forces, White House aides, or interagency committees, the subpresidency intermittently became a center searching for organizational solutions—at all levels of government—that would improve presidential guidance without offending Congress.

THREE

THE DEPARTMENT OF TRANSPORTATION
Integration of Old Functions

The idea for a department of transportation, which goes back as far as the nineteenth century, gained support among the staff of the Bureau of the Budget (BOB) after World War II.[1] The idea gained public notice in 1948 when a task force report on transportation, prepared by the Brookings Institution for the Commission on Organization of the Executive Branch (Hoover commission), proposed a department of transportation that would include the main transportation functions other than economic regulation. The commission, chaired by a former secretary of commerce, recommended instead a transportation service in the Commerce Department.[2] In 1957, when a White House study was being conducted on organization for protection of safety on airways, staff of the BOB pushed vigorously for a recommendation for a department of transportation;[3] but when President Eisenhower was forced to take a position in 1958 on Senator Mike Monroney's bill for creation of an independent aviation agency, consideration of a department of transportation was temporarily derailed.[4] Nevertheless, President Eisenhower, on the basis of proposals by the Advisory Committee on Governmental Organization, recommended such a department in his final budget message.[5]

REVIVAL OF THE IDEA

Two unpublished task force reports helped revive the idea in the presidential offices in November 1964. The Hilton report, *National Transportation Policy*, contained numerous recommendations on all transportation forms and subjects and included, without accompanying analysis, a proposal for a transportation department.[6] The Price Task Force on Government Reorganization presented the rationale for such a department and recommended the units that should be included in it.[7]

The rationale resulted from the delegation to the task force and from the views of the personnel assigned to it. The task force was instructed to study the structure of the executive branch without regard to the political aspects of organization; only the president would deal with potential political problems. The chairman, Don K. Price of Harvard University, had been a member of President Eisenhower's Committee on Government Organization when that body proposed a transportation department. The task force was dominantly academic in composition, and the staff work for it was done by BOB. The rationale was that of classical administrative theory, developed in academic writings and applied through BOB plans. Reorganization of the executive branch was necessary, the report stated, to ensure effective, economical administration and responsiveness to presidential leadership. Transportation presented an organizational problem because numerous agencies shared responsibility for administering policies for the various modes of transportation. The Department of Commerce, to which several of the agencies were assigned after the Hoover commission report, had played a "relatively ineffective role." The report stated that its recommendation for a single department to handle functions that were not economic and regulatory was "based on the premise that such an organization will facilitate the integration" of transportation programs. Such "unified control . . . will enhance comprehensive overall planning of the Federal investment in the various forms of transportation." The department could consider "whether the national interest would be better served by spending more on one form of transportation and less on another." A department could also provide a way for the president to formulate "national transportation policies" on which he could base recommendations to regulatory commissions. It could also "give policy direction on civil navigation projects to the Corps of Engineers."

The White House did not follow up on the recommendations of the Price task force, and only top Executive Office officials were cognizant of the contents of the report.[8] Though its immediate political impact appeared insignificant, it contained the logic that dominated proposals for a transportation department during the next two years: integration, coordination, presidential authority, planned transportation policies, effective administration, and balanced consideration of the government's transportation investments.

Both task force reports contained other recommendations on government structure in addition to that for a single department for primarily administrative transportation functions. The Price report recommended a single

"Transportation Regulatory Commission," with a "strong chairman" who would exercise responsibility for administrative management. The strong chairman would presumably be designated by the president, and in addition the president could "use his position of leadership to supply policy guidance, consistent with law, to the commissions, bringing to their attention urgent public needs, relevant facts, and policy considerations."[9] The Hilton report recommended "an interagency committee to formulate executive branch positions for presentation to the regulatory agencies in important rate cases and in important cases involving operating rights." It also proposed "a Federal Transportation Investment Review Board, to coordinate the Federal transport investment budget and long-run transport investment planning."[10]

THE EXISTING STRUCTURE FOR PUBLIC TRANSPORTATION FUNCTIONS

Although the two task forces had, following instructions, eschewed consideration of potential political conflicts over their proposals, they had touched sensitive political issues: integration of established institutions, balance of investment policies, and strengthening presidential authority. To the transportation interests affected, these issues were not separable even though they were often separated in discussions. The positions set forth in the reports were themselves political positions, favorable or unfavorable to existing interests within and outside government.

It was natural, indeed inevitable, that those concerned with planning either government structure or transportation policy would give attention to the nonintegrated organization for transportation functions. Fragmentation, disliked both by organization theorists and by those interested in transportation planning and related policies, was in matters of transportation perhaps as great as, or greater than, in any other area of national activity. Three commissions shared responsibility for the economic regulation of transportation: the Civil Aeronautics Board (CAB) had responsibility for commercial aviation; the Maritime Commission for oceanic transport; and the Interstate Commerce Commission (ICC) for railroads, motor carriers by land, domestic water carriers, and oil pipelines. In addition, while so distinctly separated in function as to be of no concern to transportation reorganizers, gas pipelines were subject to regulation by the Federal Power Commission. Similarly, safety protection was dispersed: to an independent Federal Aviation Agency (FAA) and CAB for aviation, to the Coast Guard (in the Treasury Department) for the merchant marine, and to the ICC for types of transportation subject to its jurisdiction. Other functions, in general promotional, also fell under the jurisdictions of a number of agencies. As a result of a reorganization order in 1950, the Maritime Administration,

Bureau of Public Roads, Saint Lawrence Seaway Development Corporation, and the Great Lakes Pilotage Administration were in the Department of Commerce, functioning under the immediate general direction and supervision of the under secretary of commerce for transportation. Legislation in 1958 separated FAA from the Department of Commerce. Promotion of water transportation was affected by river and navigational decisions of the United States Army Corps of Engineers. Other noneconomic and nonsafety functions were in ICC (chiefly over car service) and the Coast Guard; the Alaska Railroad was in the Department of Interior, and the Panama Canal Company was under the supervision of the secretary of the army. The urban transportation assistance program was in the Housing and Home Finance Agency (which became HUD in 1965).

A principal result of this disintegrated structure was dispersion of power to influence the government's investment policies supporting transportation by subsidy or by government construction and operation of facilities. Organization according to mode of transportation created separate modal influences for subsidy, construction, or other promotional activities. Policies and budget plans affecting the size of public investments in transportation were developed in FAA and CAB for aviation, the Bureau of Public Road for highways, HUD for mass transportation, the Corps of Engineers for river navigation, and the Martime Administration and Coast Guard for shipping.

Each of these administering agencies operates in association with powerful external interests. Opportunities for investment and employment and for regional and local development are strongly affected by the size of public expenditures for transportation. In 1964 the national government expended $3.645 billion from the highway trust fund, $835 million for civil aviation safety and subsidy, $660 million (Department of Commerce and Coast Guard) for support of ocean shipping, and an undetermined amount for river navigation as part of over $1.5 billion for water resource development. Potent interests for each mode of transportation were organized to promote these expenditures. In turn, certain committees of Congress were attentive to the lobbies for the separate modes of transportation and to the operations of the administering agencies. Thus, each mode of transportation had a government subsystem of interacting influences supporting it: administrative agencies, private interests, and strategic congressional committees and committee chairmen.[11]

The structure of continuing interests in separate modes of transportation, reinforced by the strength of jurisdictional interests in Congress and concerns for autonomy in the agencies, gave support to the existing organizational arrangements. Proposals for unified transportation policy, balanced investment policies, integration of structure, and strengthened presidential power threatened the independence of the separate modes of transportation.

Reorganization was inherently political: it endangered existing flows of money and supporting power structures.

SUPPORT ARISES FROM BELOW

A department of transportation could be constructed by consolidating functions of the independent FAA, transportation-related bureaus in the Department of Commerce, and certain other bureaus. Normally, an independent agency, such as FAA, or department, such as Commerce, will oppose consideration of a reorganization that destroys its independence or jurisdiction. The course of events leading toward a transportation department was distinctive, if not unique, in that the initiative came from within FAA and support came from Commerce.

The history of aviation safety made the initiative from FAA exceptional. Aviation safety functions had been centered in the Department of Commerce until 1958. Senator Mike Monroney (D–Okla.), chairman of the Subcommittee on Aviation of the Senate Committee on Interstate and Foreign Commerce, had become convinced that a much larger effort toward airline safety was needed, and he had been pressing for the creation of an independent agency. Two serious air accidents had provided the opportunity for him to get legislation to place primary safety functions in an independent agency. The industry and the airline pilots supported this change, accepting the argument that safety would be protected best by an agency responsible directly to the president.[12]

Nevertheless, as N. E. Halaby, administrator of FAA, prepared to leave his post, he sent a letter to the president proposing a department of transportation. Halaby's position was the result of earlier events in his agency. An internal task force, created by Halaby early in 1964 and chaired by Robert T. Norman, concluded that, though aviation had been well cared for, "the honeymoon is over" and that "a Department of Transportation would best protect the long run interest of aviation."[13] Those views had the support of the activist assistant administrator for administration in FAA—Alan Dean, who had come to his position in FAA from BOB in 1959. In September 1964 Halaby asked Dean to prepare a statement for Halaby's use in a scheduled meeting with Don Price, then chairman of the Task Force on Government Reorganization. Dean's memorandum set forth positively the argument that "it is better even from a parochial aviation point of view for the FAA to be the dominant element of a powerful cabinet department than to enjoy the apparent blessings of independent agency status while being excluded from the President's cabinet and inner councils "[14]

Halaby's letter to the president on 30 June 1965 did not speak of aviation needs.[15] It took the broad position that organizational arrangements were needed "to develop consistent, integrated transportation policies and a balanced national transportation system." It argued that a department of commerce and transportation was not the answer, because, first, this was "politically unattainable"—the Department of Commerce had not handled its aviation functions satisfactorily—and, second, giving general attention to business and giving special attention to transportation were incompatible. He proposed that the president ask Secretary Connor of the Department of Commerce, Alan Boyd, undersecretary for transportation, and Charles Schultze, director of BOB, to draft a reorganization proposal and that, in the meantime, the president should create an interagency national transportation council.

Halaby's letter could not, of course, assure the president of support from the aviation community in Congress and outside the government. It could indicate agency support if Halaby's successor concurred. Halaby's letter referred to the leadership of Connor and Boyd in Commerce as providing a present opportunity for support from that department.

Connor wrote to the president concerning transportation on 18 August. He presented forcefully the defects in organization for transportation, but he did not argue at this time for a transportation department or any other form or organization. He proposed the creation for the present of an interagency national transportation council "to accomplish policy coordination" and attached a draft of an executive order for this purpose.[16]

Two days later Schultze sent a memo on transportation organization to Joseph A. Califano, Jr., special assistant to the president. Referring to Halaby's letter and to the two task force recommendations for a department of transportation, he agreed that this "represents the best long-run solution."[17] He added that this "may not be expedient at this time," and hence the president might want to consider transitional steps. He had "serious reservations" about a National Transportation Council, which would reach compromises "geared to the most acceptable common denominator." Schultze included a recommendation that thrust to the heart of the issues in transportation policy and organization and reflected BOB's concern for effective budgetary processes for transportation. He wrote that steps should be taken to create a transportation investment review board; and that, before this, investment criteria should be developed, with BOB taking the lead.

Thus, in the summer of 1965 FAA had expressed support for a department of transportation; a statement of needs pointing in that direction indicated the possibility of support from Commerce; and BOB had again asserted its position in favor of such a department and had shown major concern with integrated planning of investment policy and criteria.

INITIATIVE FROM THE PRESIDENT

Califano reports that while they were swimming in the pool at "the ranch," shortly after he joined the Johnson staff in mid-1965, Johnson said, "There are three areas of urgent concern for the 1966 legislative program. The transportation system of this country is a mess. I want to do something about it." The president told Califano to "give me something big in each of these three areas"[18] (transportation, "to totally rebuild the ghettos," "an open housing bill"). Thus transportation was added by presidential initiative to the legislative agenda.

The president had already conferred with Connor and Boyd and instructed them to develop a bold and imaginative program for transportation.[19] On 6 August Bill Moyers held a meeting with Connor, Boyd, Secretary Weaver of HUD, and others to discuss the 1966 legislative program in the area of transportation.[20] Thereafter Califano assumed responsibility for transportation matters, beginning with appointment on 12 August of a task force chaired by Boyd. It was an inside task force with top officials or their representatives from the Commerce and Treasury departments, Housing and Home Finance Agency, Council of Economic Advisors (CEA), Office of Science and Technology (OST), and BOB. Califano asked for a "rigorous and imaginative program" and a paper on each of ten numbered topics. The topics covered a wide span of transportation policy issues and included an assignment "to develop alternative plans to improve the efficiency of Government transportation functions."[21] On 27 August he requested supplementary studies relating transportation needs to social goals, with cost and time requirements for attaining each goal.[22]

CONCURRENCE ON A DEPARTMENT OF TRANSPORTATION

The events of the next few months determined the basic elements of the president's transportation package for 1966. The president was interested in transportation policies. He had announced in his State of the Union Message in January that he would recommend "heavier reliance on competition in transportation and a new policy for our merchant marine."[23] Califano's list of subjects for study in his two directives to the Boyd task force also showed the administration's concern with transportation policies. Moreover, the president had demanded something big and imaginative. From this position we are able to see the movement from policy to structural considerations, produced in part by an early agreement on the need for a comprehensive department of transportation and further by the complexities of transportation policy.

The responsibility for transportation studies rested with Boyd. He had come to his position as undersecretary on 1 June from CAB, where he had served since 1959 and had been chairman since 1961. As undersecretary he had immediately become engulfed in the government's efforts to deal with a maritime strike. Now, after six weeks in office, he had the task of developing studies and recommendations for transportation reforms.[24]

Studies were quickly produced and were followed by other studies. Boyd's own staff coordinated the effort and BOB provided help on organization studies. On 2 September Boyd transmitted nine reports to Califano. To make the additional studies requested in Califano's supplementary assignment of 27 August he expanded his task force to include the administrators of FAA, the Maritime Administration, and the Bureau of Public Roads, and the chairmen of CAB, ICC, and the Federal Maritime Commission.[25] He convened a first meeting of his expanded group on 10 September , but there was at this stage no deliberation about the choices of policy to be proposed to the president. Indeed, in a memo of 7 September Boyd reported to the members of the original task force that because of the short deadline (imposed by Califano) for reports, the task force had had no opportunity to meet and review the final papers. Boyd also gave instructions for the copies of these reports to be picked up from the task force, thus indicating that at this stage secrecy was considered of greater importance than deliberation in the task force.[26]

Boyd's first reports on 2 September included a recommendation for a department of transportation.[27] When Boyd came to the task of preparing transportation recommendations with some ideas about changes in regulatory policies and procedures, he quickly learned about the reports from Halaby (a friend with whom he was in communication) and the earlier task forces recommending a department. He has reported:

> I was a bit leery about the thing because I didn't know Jack Connor very well, and I didn't know how he would react to it. Anyway, I went back and talked to Jack, and he said, "Fine, go ahead. I think it makes a lot of sense to try to create a Department of Transportation."[28]

Boyd has given his views on the need for such a department. Before coming to the Department of Commerce he had concluded that something had to be changed in the government's handling of transportation matters; within the department, he found the position of under secretary frustrating. Agencies would send up requests for approvals with short deadlines, and the under secretary was forced to act without adequate staff aid. The result was that "all the office of Under Secretary really got into was paper shuffling."

After discovering how feeble the position of under secretary of commerce for transportation was, he quickly concluded that a department was a good idea. He saw two needs: "One, to provide a base from which it would be possible to get the resources to look at the whole system of transportation ... means for articulating to the Congress the need for research and economic studies of the whole system. And second to bring these various operating agencies together so that they would not be completely captive of their constituencies."[29]

Certain persons in the Executive Office had strong convictions that a legislative program on transportation should undertake more than organizational change. One of these was Arthur Okun, a member of the CEA. After the meeting of the Boyd task force on 10 September he wrote to Gardner Ackley, chairman of CEA, that "except for the one bold proposal for a Cabinet Department of Transportation," the task force reflected "the philosophy of a small, politically feasible program." He feared the president was not going to get a bold and imaginative program. A similar conclusion was stated in a memo to the director of BOB. Both memos stated that action was needed promptly to get information to Califano: the president, one said, "is going to be disappointed, unless something is done to break the traffic jam." For Boyd himself the difficulties of developing bold recommendations were further increased by the addition to the task force—at the direction of the president, Boyd said—of the chairman of the regulatory commissions and the heads of additional agencies.[30]

At certain points in the decision process disparate ideas are pulled together and a determination sets the course for further consideration. Such a point was reached on 22 September. Califano had received from Ackley a copy of the Okun memo, and he was promptly ready to have the objectives clarified. He reported to the president that he had "just been over the first cut of the proposals and ideas" on transportation. Echoing the words of Okun's memo, he added, "The proposals are not imaginative enough and will not give you the opportunity to select a variety of alternatives." He referred to agreement between Okun and Schultze that there were major things to be done. He stated that unless the president had objections, he would ask Connor and Boyd to "consider and prepare papers" on four ideas:

1. A Department of Transportation (or some reorganization of the executive transportation functions).
2. Reorganization of the regulatory transportation functions.
3. Program of deregulation to make transportation rates more competitive and rational.
4. A major highway safety program.

The president's reaction was a check on the approval blank of the memo and the addition of "Hooray!"[31]

A memo from Califano to the president on 12 October summarizing plans from fourteen task forces and other sources for the 1966 legislative program repeated the four ideas for transportation legislation.[32] Highway safety was to be retained in the package for presidential recommendations and was being considered on a separate track from the other three. At a meeting of the task force on 15 September Califano asked Boyd for papers on the two ideas for organizational reform: a department of transportation and reorganization of transportation regulatory functions. Boyd's two papers were sent to Califano on 22 October. In a covering memorandum he stated "that there is ample study and consensus to enable a decision to be made on the general merits of the Department of Transportation." As for reform of regulatory administration, the paper noted that BOB concurred with the staff and chairman of the task force that while a long-run desirable objective was a single transport regulatory agency, existing differences in the substance of regulatory statutes for different modes of transportation and in the procedures accompanying them would not make feasible the operation of such a commission. Instead, "An interim policy of Presidential appointment of the ICC chairman [then selected by members of the commission] plus the transfer of safety and subsidy functions of regulatory agencies is suggested."[33]

Boyd stated his belief that reform "should proceed in four phases": (1) concentration of transportation functions other than economic regulation in a transportation department; (2) interim reforms of ICC to include presidential appointment of the chairman; (3) reform of the philosophy of regulation to simplify regulation and emphasize competition and economic performance; and (4) concentration of regulatory authority in a single regulatory agency.

Boyd did not submit the remaining seven task force reports on the substance of transportation policy until 3 December. The reports suggested a range of modifications in policies but outlined no program for the fundamental changes that would constitute a new philosophy and a system capable of administration in a single regulatory agency.

In the meantime BOB elaborated its position to Califano.[34] It endorsed a department of transportation. It agreed with the task force report that a single regulatory agency was not feasible under existing laws and concepts, but it embraced the idea of presidential appointment of ICC's chairman. The Bureau position on two administrative reforms concurred with the first two phases of Boyd's proposal and was to become, along with a highway safety program, the president's legislative program on transportation.

As consensus for a department of transportation was developing at the upper levels of the executive branch, an outside threat arose. On 9 November Schultze reported to Califano's staff that eight bills had been introduced in Congress to make the Maritime Administration an independent agency.[35] Maritime interests were unhappy with the level of public expenditures for ship construction and were disappointed and agitated by information they had gained on the recommendations of a Maritime Task Force report. Bills for an independent maritime agency could derail a transportation department in the same way Monroney's bill for an independent aviation agency had in 1958.

Knowledge concerning the deliberations on changes in transportation organization and policy were confined, until December, to the top echelons of the executive branch and to Boyd's and BOB's staff. In mid-December Califano and Lee White of the White House staff held exploratory discussions with selected persons from the railroad, trucking, inland waterways, and airline industries. A presidentially designated chairman for ICC was acceptable to most; on a department of transportation there was diversity of opinion but considerable support, albeit with clear signals that each mode of transportation would be concerned with its own interests and position; a spokesman for one industry indicated that it would resist changes in policy leading to increased competition. All in all, however, the meeting with the chosen few failed to signal the issues that would precipitate congressional objection to a department of transportation.[36]

Califano reported to the president that these meetings were being held and asked whether he should inform Senator Warren G. Magnuson (D–Wash.), chairman of the Senate Committee on Interstate and Foreign Commerce, "on what we are doing." The president approved and suggested talking also to congressmen Oren Harris (D–Ark.) and Harley O. Staggers (D–W.Va.), chairman and ranking majority member, respectively, of the House Committee on Interstate and Foreign Commerce.[37] Conversation with Magnuson and Staggers brought assurances of support for a department of transportation and a presidentially appointed chairman for ICC. Staggers thought suggested changes in transportation policy were "worth striving for" but predicted bitter opposition; Magnuson thought they should not be submitted and "won't get anywhere if they are."[38]

Yet problems of maintaining support for a department of transportation, for which unity among strategically located officials had seemed apparent months before, now appeared. Connor reasserted his support.[39] But General William F. McKee, successor to Halaby as administrator of FAA, prepared a statement in which he suggested several alternatives to such a department.[40] Moreover, the under secretary of the treasury, supported initially by Henry Fowler, secretary of the department, objected to transfer of the Coast Guard. Clearly, loyalty to the president would be the basis for ultimate support from Fowler and McKee. In the case of the Coast Guard, Califano could report to the president that McNamara preferred incorporating it into the Navy, but realizing that this was unrealistic, supported moving it into the proposed transportation department, and also that Califano, Schultze, White, Connor, Boyd, and Ackley recommended moving it "as a single unit" into the proposed department.[41] The Maritime Administration, however, had no problem with the idea of a transportation department. Nicholas Johnson, its chief and a member of the Boyd task force, supported such a department in a statement distributed to employees of the administration.[42] Also, the chairman of ICC was supportive of changes related to it.

By mid-December the Johnson presidency's position for a department of transportation seems to have firmed, contingent only on reactions from the outside. With regard to a presidentially designated ICC chairman, the president explicitly approved a recommendation by Califano and White on 1 February 1966.[43] When Califano reported to the president on 28 January on a variety of matters on which decision would be needed—components to go into the proposed department, the differences over the Coast Guard, transfers of safety and subsidy function from the CAB, and the problem of the division between HUD and the new department of duties related to mass transit—the president wrote to Califano, "I don't know enough—Can't you reconcile differences before I act."[44] When Califano set forth alternative suggestions on transportation policy—propose the entire package of reforms, send up the easier and less controversial ones, hold all proposals until next year—the president approved the last.[45]

The bold and imaginative program had become, for the moment, two structural reforms—a department of transportation and a presidentially designated chairman of ICC. The first of these was included in the recommendations of the president in his State of the Union message on 12 January and in the president's message to Congress on transportation on 2 March.

To understand the development of executive policy in this instance it is necessary to inquire, What brought about the decision to propose two structural reforms? First, an opportune moment had arrived for two concerns of professional organization planners in BOB to be included in a presidential program. Those ideas represented professional inputs into policy planning, unsupported by any interest group influence from outside the government. A department of transportation was a response to BOB's interest in structural integration and presidential power. A presidentially appointed chairman for ICC was in accord with BOB's policy positions since the report of the first Hoover commission. The objective was to strengthen management in commissions and give the president access to them—an objective already attained for all regulatory commissions except ICC. Avoiding the usual opposition of executive entities to moves toward integration was possible because N. E. Halaby, outgoing administrator of FAA, had recommended that his agency be included in a comprehensive cabinet department. Halaby's position was based on the arguments of his assistant administrator, Alan Dean, who had previously worked in BOB. Finally, Connor, the secretary of commerce, responding to the positive influence of Alan Boyd, his undersecretary for transportation, concurred in the plan for a department of transportation, even though it would strip his department of functions. Development of bureaucratic opposition was averted by secrecy during the planning stage and was overcome, after the decision was firm, by loyalty to the president.

The planning was entirely internal. Characterizing it were task force studies under aggressive and prestigious leadership, cooperation between the task force leadership and Executive Office staff, and the skill of the responsible White House staff member in focusing and choosing issues and submitting positions on those issues for timely approval by the president. The internal process was supplemented by rather limited consultation with affected interests and a few strategically located members of Congress.

The choices for the transportation package can be explained in terms of the distinction between allocative and structural policies.[46] Allocative policies are those that confer benefits upon individuals and groups, while structural policies establish structures or rules to guide future allocations. The effect of the latter may be to avoid or defer allocative decisions. Structural decisions may be constructive in that they facilitate desired policy moves in the future, or they may be face-saving or propagandistic when allocative decisions become impossible or require an excessive expenditure of political capital. Allocative policies in transportation show a high degree of rigidity because of the built-in protections in law, bureaus, and congressional committees for strong interests; hence successive administrations have been frustrated in their desire to effect changes. The Johnson administration's task force foundered on the recalcitrant issues, and in turn the administration found support lacking for the limited policy changes that did emerge. It regarded the structural reforms as meaningful enough to justify a tough contest in Congress.

THE PLANS FOR THE DEPARTMENT

How bold was the plan for the Department of Transportation? Bold, indeed, in three organizational ideas of central significance: (1) to include in the department all the major transportation functions except economic regulation; (2) to give strength to the secretary in the direction and administration of the department; and (3) to locate in the department the power to influence future allocative decisions.

Decisions on these matters were made in a new ad hoc group responsible for elaborating plans for a department. When Secretary Connor affirmed his support for a department of transportation to Califano on 22 December, he added that, following "regular procedure," he had assigned to the general counsel of the Department of Commerce the task of drafting legislation for a department. For BOB, however, regular procedure in reorganization matters implied coordination by the Bureau. Moreover, a BOB staff member, sensing that the general counsel's office in Commerce might not be enthusiastic about the creation of a transportation department, contacted McKee, who in turn arranged a conference with Califano and Schultze. It was agreed that Schultze should appoint a task force.[47] It was chaired by Charles J. Zwick, assistant director of the bureau, and included, from the bureau's professional staff, Harold Seidman, assistant director for management and organization, and Arthur Kallen, senior management analyst. Other members represented the Department of Commerce, FAA, the Coast Guard, CAB, the Corps of Engineers, and ICC. Alan Dean of FAA and Cecil Mackey, who had worked with Boyd's task force and who was director of the Office of Transportation Policy Development, joined the group. The Zwick task force met frequently and submitted its conclusions to a review group that included among others Connor, Schultze, Boyd, and Califano.

Components of a Department of Transportation

In preparing a first draft of legislation, the general counsel of Commerce could rely on lists of transfers proposed by the Boyd task force and BOB staff memoranda to Califano. Further deliberations by the Zwick Task Force enabled Califano to submit to the president a list of units to be included in a new department; with a few modifications the president incorporated those suggestions in his transportation message. From the Department of Commerce, the new Department of Transportation (DOT) would receive the Bureau of Public Roads and the Highway Safety program, the Maritime Administration, and the policy and research functions of the under secretary of commerce for transportation. Also to be transferred were the Coast Guard from the Treasury Department, the Alaska Railroad from the Interior Department, the safety and car service functions of ICC, "the safety functions and policy control over the subsidy functions of the CAB," and "nuts and bolts" research in mass transit from HUD. FAA and the Saint Lawrence Seaway Development Corporation, independent executive agencies, were also to be included.[48] With these components the department would have about fifty thousand employees and control the expenditure of approximately $5 billion yearly.

Differences arose over the inclusion of some of these agencies, and Johnson instructed Califano to resolve them. When Secretary Fowler received a commitment that the Coast Guard would remain intact in the new department, he withdrew his objections to its transfer in a letter of 11 February.[49] Charles S. Murphy, chairman of CAB, although mildly opposed, accepted the transfer of CAB's safety functions, but he strongly objected to the transfer of its subsidy functions. Califano's idea for resolving this was to find legislative language that would authorize DOT to give policy guidance on subsidies to CAB while leaving the application of policy to CAB on a case-to-case basis. The compromise at that time granted DOT less authority: the president's message said that the secretary of transportation "will develop principles and criteria which the Board will take into consideration in its proceedings," and the draft bill included these words. Legislative language to this effect, in Murphy's opinion, did not add authority DOT would not have without delegation and left CAB with complete independence in judgment.[50]

The "nuts and bolts" on mass transit could not be agreed on in conferences between HUD and DOT advocates. Consequently, the president proposed that the two secretaries recommend to him within a year after creation of DOT the means for cooperation between the two departments.

There were other issues to be resolved as a result of department and agency comments. DOT's authority with respect to Corps of Engineers projects will be discussed separately as an issue on investment standards. When objections arose, especially in the aviation community, to vesting all safety functions in the secretary, this question became a major addition to the deliberations. The president decided to recommend a national transportation safety board "independent of the operating units of the Department." The administration draft of a bill provided that a board composed of five members appointed by the president with approval of the Senate would determine the cause of accidents and review, on appeal, license or certificate decisions adverse to a licensee or an applicant for a license.

A Strong Secretary

Since the report of the first Hoover commission, the Executive Office position, reflected in reorganization orders and BOB papers, has been that functions, powers, and duties should be assigned to the secretaries of departments rather than to directors of bureaus or administrations within departments. The secretary would thereby have power to structure his department, assign or reassign tasks, and maintain legal control over the exercise of powers. The framers of the DOT bill began with these assumptions. Objections came immediately from the Coast Guard and FAA. In a memo to Califano on 25 January, Joseph Barr, under secretary of the treasury, stating the case against the transfer of the Coast Guard, argued for the need to retain the Coast Guard as an entity, citing among other things the expectation that the Coast Guard would be transferred to the Navy in case of military conflict. Schultze argued for the transfer in a reply to Barr, assuring him that the Coast Guard would remain an entity within DOT.[51] The president's transportation message said, "The Coast Guard will be transferred as a unit from the Treasury Department."

Assurances to Barr were quickly followed by a plea from McKee to Schultze for preservation of the integrity of FAA.[52] He suggested in his comments on the draft of the president's message that the words "as unit" or "as a separate entity" be used. A master draft of the message shows that Zwick approved "as a unit," but the president's assurance in his message was "transferral in its entirety. . . . It will continue to carry out these functions in the new department." The administration bill, however, provided that the functions, powers, and duties would be transferred to the secretary and did not contain the assurance.

Secretarial control of performance might still exist even if there were a guarantee of organizational identity for component units. To support such control, the plans for the department sought organizational strength at the secretarial level. A subcommittee of the Zwick task force, chaired by Alan Dean, was assigned the task of considering organizational and management problems in the department. It accepted the draft bill's proposal for an under secretary, four assistant secretaries, a general counsel, and an assistant secretary for administration. Rejecting a proposal that modal administrators in the line hold the title of assistant secretary, the subcommittee proposed a line/staff structure in which program-oriented administrations and corporations would report to the secretary, but "all other officials (such as the Assistant Secretaries) will be regarded as staff to the Secretary and will assist him in the general leadership of the Department and its external relationships."[53]

This provision for visible high-level staffing at the secretarial level was a significant feature of the reorganization plan. It could, even with the survival of modal operating structures within the department, correct the deficiency Boyd found in his position as under secretary of commerce for transportation and provided the capability for research, planning, and policy development for transportation at the secretarial level.

Planning for a strong department included attention to the number of supergrades and compensation levels. Solution to these and other personnel problems were worked out by the Zwick task force in consultation with, and with the agreement of, John Macy, chairman of the Civil Service Commission.[54] Moreover, the administration bill would vest in the secretary, rather than in the president, the power to appoint assistant secretaries and modal directors.

Investment Criteria

With the exception of railroad transportation, the several modes of transportation—air, road, water—were subsidized directly or indirectly by the government. The expenditures were large and were supportive of highly organized economic interests. Those interests were protective of the agencies, bureaus, and commissions operating for their respective modes of transportation, and the agencies and bureaus were supportive of the modes of transportation subject to their jurisdictions.

Advocates of a department of transportation hoped that a functional departmental staff at the secretarial level could provide for a view of total transportation needs and an evaluation of the comparative claims of each mode for public assistance. As we noted above, in the early discussion of a transportation package, Schultze recommended the creation of a transportation investment review board and the development of investment criteria. When the idea of a transportation department firmed, the discussion of a board disappeared and the development of investment criteria became a function proposed for the new department.

The drafting of legislation on investment standards applicable to the Corps of Engineers was obviously a delicate task and one that could arouse controversy. The Corps is a construction agency, and transportation is only one of the considerations in decisions on its projects. Its independence is highly valued by interests that benefit from its projects and by congressmen seeking benefits for their constituencies. In 1966 dissatisfaction arose over criteria, reputedly developed by BOB, for calculating water transportation costs and benefits on projected corps projects; those criteria had been adopted in 1964 and were less likely to result in approvals than earlier criteria.[55] Moreover, there was a new structure—the Water Resources Council, founded in 1965—that was to establish, after consultation with other entities and with the approval of the president, "principles, standards and procedures" for federal participation in preparation of regional or river basin plans and for the formulation and evaluation of water projects.

Alfred S. Hitt, general counsel of the Department of the Army, helped prepare the language of the president's message. At one time he reported that he was asking for two changes: (1) to make sure that DOT would not be setting engineering standards in Corps projects; (2) to assure that the standards would govern all agencies, not just the Corps. He wrote that he had the unqualified support of the Corps for the investment standards provision as written. Nevertheless, one staff aide reported at about the same time that it was obvious from congressional consultations that the Corps was laying the groundwork for possible opposition to a secretarial voice in navigation projects.[56]

Those preparing the president's message and a draft bill were cognizant of the variety and strength of interests that would be affected by centralized authority to establish investment standards applicable to the Corps and other transportation authorities. Nevertheless, the message asked for comprehensive delegation: "With the approval of the President, the Secretary of Transportation should also issue standards and criteria for the economic evaluation of Federal transportation investments generally." (In the case of multipurpose water projects, consultation with the Water Resources Council would be required.) Section 7 of the draft bill included such a provision, with exceptions for national defense enterprises and some other activities. In addition, section 7 provided that every survey, plan, or report formulated by a federal agency with respect to which standards or criteria had been promulgated should be prepared in accordance with those criteria and upon the basis of information from the secretary, coordinated with the secretary, and transmitted to the president for approval "in accord with law and procedures established by him." Those were bold proposals indeed, for they would centralize influence within the executive branch on decisions over which the Congress had long cherished its independence and the influence it shared with the executive branch.

Legislative Consideration

As the date for the transportation message approached and as the draft bill was perfected, the White House staff had further consultations with Senator Magnuson and his staff, Congressman Staggers, and others in strategic congressional positions. They reported that Magnuson strongly supported DOT and wished to introduce the bill and speak for it.[57] Connor recommended appointment of a prestigious private committee to support the creation of the department. Johnson approved but believed that the list of members should be enlarged.[58]

When the delivery date for the transportation message approached, Califano reported on the steps already taken or to be taken on the delivery date.[59] These included: briefing about 35 members of Congress the evening before the message; on the day of the message, briefing separately about 100 government officials and the press, with in-depth briefing of about 10, and about 150 persons from industry. Present in all of these interviews were Connor, Boyd, Schultze, and Califano. From the White House staff, Larry O'Brien met with the Speaker, and Mike Manatos met with the majority leader of the Senate. Press clips and congressional statements were prepared. The president showed keen interest in these plans and made suggestions.

Consultations by White House staff with a considerable number of members of Congress, including members of the Government Operations committees—which would have jurisdiction for considering and reporting on the bills—indicated wide support for the proposal for a department of transportation. Manatos, following congressional contacts, reported to Califano, "I would say this is a very popular undertaking."[60] Yet danger signals had been given: Senator Monroney had expressed serious reservations about transferring the FAA and the safety functions of the CAB into the Department of Transportation; Senator McClellan (D–Ark.) wanted to know whether the department would take anything from the Corps of Engineers;[61] bills for a separate maritime agency were in Congress; and some agencies to be transferred were expressing concern about whether their identities and independence would remain intact. As Zwick, from his BOB perspective, had indicated at an early date, it "will be *controversial*," with opposition from transportation interests—especially aviation—some members of Congress, and agencies.[62]

Conflict between Executive and Congressional Purposes

The president's special message to Congress transmitting "A proposal for a cabinet-level Department of Transportation Consolidating Various Existing Transportation Agencies" went to Congress on 2 March.[63] The administration bill was introduced as S. 3010 by Senator Magnuson and as H. 13200 by Congressman Chet Holifield (D–Calif.) who became House manager for the bill. The bill went to the Government Operations Committee in each house, with Senator John L. McClellan (D–Ark.) and Congressman William L. Dawson as chairmen.

The president's proposal came to Congress with strong ideological consensus in the executive branch. The objectives were those stated in the report of the Price task force: integration, comprehensive planning of policy, centralized control of investments, and presidential leadership. The usual politics of agency objection had been avoided. The administration had a proposal in favor of a department of transportation by the outgoing head of an independent agency (FAA) that would be integrated into the new department, acceptance by the secretary of a department (Commerce) that would lose large functions, acceptance by another department secretary (Treasury) whose under secretary had opposed transfer of one of its oldest units, unqualified support by the head of an agency to be transferred (Maritime Administration), and cooperation from the officials of agencies whose independence from outside direction was traditional (CAB, ICC, Corps of Engineers).

In Congress, despite widespread agreement on the idea of a department of transportation, acceptance was contingent on the reservation that reorganization should not fully achieve the objectives set forth in the Price report and accepted as Executive Office doctrine. Three concerns dominated congressional deliberations, and all were reflected in a statement by the bill's Senate sponsor, Senator Magnuson, at the beginning of Senate committee hearings.

First, Congress and the transportation interests were more concerned with policy outcomes to be anticipated from a new department than with structural reform. Sentor Henry M. Jackson (D–Wash.) said on the first day of Senate hearings: "we are not dealing with a mere pulling together of agencies" but "we are getting into the area of substantive changes in transportation."[64] The industry and labor representatives were fearful that changes would threaten benefits to their modes of transportation. Members of Congress were concerned that organizational change not threaten policies enacted earlier. Senator McClellan, brashly asserting his concern for river projects in Arkansas, said, "I want to be thoroughly briefed and advised in this area before I make any commitment on this bill or this part of it."[65] Senator Magnuson had warned that policy changes for transportation would get nowhere; now, in the middle of hearings, the *Wall Street Journal* could predict that although the organization bill was shielded from "outright objection," the modal interests had "ganged up" and "the current ways of doing things are likely to stay the same."[66]

Second, just as persons in the executive branch were concerned with presidential leadership, those in Congress were interested in preserving the legislature's prerogatives. Section 7 especially threatened the ways of doing things in the triangle of Corps, Congress, and private interests. In his initial statement Senator Magnuson said the section "needed clarification"; "it should not infringe on the prerogatives of Congress."[67]

Third, opposed to the executive branch interests in creating a strong departmental secretary and capability for planning and evaluation of modal needs for investment were the interests of the modal groups in maintaining structural arrangements to protect and foster their interests.

The Major Issues

While other issues were raised in Congress, four were of central significance: modal protection, safety, section 7, and maritime inclusion.

Modal Protections

In Senator Magnuson's opening statement he wondered why, for operational continuity, the maritime, public roads, and aviation organizations should not be transferred as legal entities in the same fashion as the Coast Guard. He was concerned that the president intended to appoint assistant secretaries "for policy purposes rather than by modal assignments." And he recommended that the maritime administrator and the head of FAA be continued as presidential appointees with the advice and consent of the Senate, and that the committee consider the same procedure for the head of the Bureau of Public Roads.[68]

From the beginning of congressional hearings, sponsors for the several modes of transportation shared this concern for modal independence and status. General McKee, caught between his position as the president's appointee and his knowledge of the antagonism to the bill in the aviation community, favored transfer of powers to the secretary, adding that the "operational integrity" of FAA would be maintained by redelegation from the secretary—though "it is not written quite as clearly as I think I expressed it."[69] Pushed by questions, he concluded that senatorial confirmation would not be harmful, and that he favored a higher classification for the FAA head than was provided in the bill. The views of those segments of the aviation community that did not oppose the bill in its entirety were reflected in statements by the president of the Air Transport Association, who wanted FAA to be included "intact,"[70] and by Senator Monroney, who wanted it to be, like the Coast Guard, a "legal entity" with an administrator appointed by the president with consent of the Senate—one who did not report to the secretary "through a barricade or layer of assistant and under secretaries."[71] Similarly, the president of the American Association of Highway Officials desired that the Bureau of Public Roads have "autonomy and authority," subject only to the policy guidance of the secretary. He did not want the power of the director over highway administration to be "diluted by going through intermediate administrative levels."[72] Representatives of the waterways industry wanted an assistant secretary for each mode of transportation.[73] By the end of two weeks of hearings, Senator Jacob Javits (D–N.Y.), while supporting the bill, reflected the views of the modal communities by arguing that the Maritime Administration, Bureau of Public Roads, and FAA should be transferred into the new department as legal entities.[74]

In May, Schultze defined the administration's withdrawal line in a memorandum to Califano. On presidential appointments with senatorial confirmation "we can easily yield"; on defining the modal subordinate units in law "we would prefer that this not occur," but the damage would not be great as long as the powers and functions of those units rested with the secretary.[75]

The results were not to be as favorable as the administration had hoped. The withdrawal line held in the House committee and the House, but in the Senate committee the exercise of safety functions in the modal units was protected. Functions, powers, and duties transferred to the secretary from FAA and ICC were to be exercised by the federal aviation and railroad administrators established by the act, and their decisions regarding safety were to be made administratively final and thus not subject to secretarial review. To protect those delegations, no functions that the act specified were to be carried out by an administrator could be transferred elsewhere in the department except by statute or reorganization plans, and the modal administrators could not themselves redelegate such functions outside their administrations. The House conferees accepted provisions of the Senate bill, and they were included in the act passed. Califano's assessment of these provisions was that the secretary's power was "seriously weakened."[76]

Following the provisions of House and Senate bills, the act also provided that the modal administrators and the commandant of the Coast Guard would report directly to the secretary. The hearings reflected fear in Congress that the strength of the modal administrators would be weakened by interposing assistant secretaries between them and the secretary. This had not been the administration's purpose, for it had desired to use the assistant secretaries as staff aides to create secretarial capability for planning and policy leadership. The act retained the provisions in the administration's proposal for an under secretary, a general counsel, four assistant secretaries, and an additional secretary for administration. Thus the act safeguarded the operating jurisdiction of the modal administrations and also provided the basis for intermodal planning and policy initiative at the secretarial level.

Finally, the act provided that, except for the assistant secretary for administration, these officials—like the heads of the modal administrations, the members of the Safety Board, and the head of a new National Traffic Safety Bureau—were to be appointed by the president with the advice and consent of the Senate.[77]

Safety

Proposed for transfer to DOT were FAA, whose purpose was aviation safety; the Coast Guard, whose functions included marine safety; the safety functions of ICC, principally inspection and enforcement of safety functions for railroads, motor carriers, and pipelines; and the safety functions of CAB, which included appellate functions on various decisions of FAA on air safety certificates, and investigations and determination of the cause of air accidents. Within DOT, but independent from the secretary, would be the National Transportation Safety Board; this board would exercise appellate jurisdiction on airline and marine certificates and determine the cause or probable cause of transportation accidents. Investigation of accidents would not be a function of the board but would remain, as in the past, with the modal organizations or be vested in the new secretarial Office of Accident Investigation.

Although objections to these proposals arose in the various transportation services, the critical issue was in the area of aviation. Only eight years had passed since FAA had been created to meet the aviation community's belief that safety on the airlines would be better protected by an independent (nondepartmental) agency, accompanied by appellate and investigatory powers in a board (CAB) itself independent of the operating agency. It is not surprising, therefore, that highly positioned persons in the aviation community would either oppose the bill or accept it only with reservations.[78] When the president sent his message to the Congress, members of the White House staff knew that Senator Monroney, legislative father of FAA, was uncertain about his position on the DOT bill; one senator even reported that he had obtained Monroney's agreement to oppose it.[79] To gain acceptance for the transfer of FAA, it was necessary to make the arrangements on presidential appointment, organizational integrity, and compensation of the aviation administrator discussed in the preceding subsection. In addition, certain congressmen questioned transferring CAB's safety functions, exercised by a Safety Bureau. In his statement to the Senate committee, Senator Magnuson, although supporting the consolidation of transportation safety functions in a department, was "not persuaded" that transfer of CAB's appellate functions was essential to the purposes of the bill, and he spoke strongly in favor of preserving the board's authority in accident investigation.[80] The sentiment of the aviation community was probably best expressed by Stuart G. Tipton, president of the influential Air Transport Association, who said that "it doesn't really make any sense to disturb" something "that works," as does accident investigation in CAB[81]—a sentiment also shared widely about FAA.

The administration had regarded the functions and independence of the proposed National Transportation Safety Board as sufficient to allay the industry's fears about transfer of CAB's safety functions. It was, however, willing to ensure that the authority from CAB to investigate accidents would be independent of FAA functions in the new department, or even to transfer that authority to the Safety Board. But it regarded the transfer of all of CAB's Bureau of Safety functions to DOT and Safety Board as crucial for the DOT proposal: without it the opposition of some truckers to the transfer of ICC's safety functions would increase, and undermining the consolidation of safety functions would jeopardize the entire DOT venture.[82] Consequently, the administration gave considerable attention to winning Senator Monroney's support for transfer of all CAB aviation safety functions to DOT or the Safety Board.

Monroney reported in Senate floor discussion the amendments he had proposed—and the Senate committee accepted—to remove "harmful effects on aviation safety."[83] Without these he would find it "extremely difficult to support the bill."[84] First of these were amendments delegating FAA functions to the aviation administrator and prohibiting transfer of those functions without a statute or reorganization order; those amendments, as noted above, were incorporated into the act. The second amendment provided for transfer of all of CAB's safety functions to the Safety Board.

Some legislators favored the administrator's proposal for separating accident investigation from the Safety Board's functions, either through delegation to modal administrators or by creation of a separate accident investigation bureau. The first alternative would have kept intact the Coast Guard and ICC safety functions, but not the activities of CAB's Bureau of Safety. The bill passed by the House would have created within DOT a separate office of accident investigation. But the conference committee accepted the Senate provisions, incorporating Senator Monroney's amendments.[85] Thus Monroney received assurance that the solution of 1958 would endure: both FAA and CAB safety functions would remain intact and in separate organizations. Accompanying this solution was the extension of similar powers to the Safety Board to investigate accidents occurring on other modes of transportation.

Section 7

The sensitivity of Congress to the possible effects of section 7, which would have delegated to the secretary of DOT powers with respect to standards and criteria for transportation investments, was apparent from the outset of committee hearings. The Senate sponsor suggested that the section should be clarified, and the House sponsor requested an explanatory memorandum. Some legislators expressed concern over the effect on highway expenditures, but the real tempest arose in the ranks of water resource interests and was represented most forcefully in Congress by Senator McClellan.[86] A memorandum filed by Schultze and statements from officials of the Corps of Engineers attempted to minimize the changes that would result. Standards and criteria could not change existing law, for example, on the scope of the interstate highway system; on inland navigation investments the criteria would be presented only as executive branch proposals to be submitted to Congress, would need to be consonant with the nontransportation standards of the Water Resources Council, and would give the secretary no veto power over Corps projects.[87]

Nevertheless, Senator Monroney expressed the prevailing sentiment in the water resource community: section 7 was "too broad and vague." "Its effect on the future development of inland waterway projects could be particularly harmful"; deletion of the section was "strongly recommended."[88]

Boyd quickly recognized that the administration was helpless on section 7. In a memorandum to Connor on 11 May he concluded that the DOT bill could not be enacted without elimination or drastic amendment of the section. "There has been no support for Section 7 from any segment of the industry and no member of either the Senate or House Committee favors the section." He recommended letters to McClellan and Holifield withdrawing the section.[89] Two days later Schultze suggested to Califano several fallback positions to meet opponents' criticisms.[90] The president also learned of McClellan's threat to try to write pre-1964 criteria into the bill, with the possible result that railroad interests' support of the bill would be lost. Califano and Barefoot Sanders of the White House staff recommended to the president that he reinstate the earlier criteria, and he approved, adding, "Why not do this at once?"[91] The president's willingness to accept the pre-1964 standard administratively, though not in law, was reported to McClellan.[92] McClellan, however, had additional concerns—primarily a hydroelectric standard that could adversely affect power development at a project in Arkansas.[93]

The administration succeeded in securing Congressman Holifields' support for section 7 by accepting an amendment that provided for public announcement and opportunity for presentation of views before standards and criteria were made final for submittal to the president.[94] With this and amendments that greatly weakened the provision, the House committee approved section 7.[95] But when a barrage of other amendments was offered in the House, Congressman Holifield accepted an amendment to strike the section entirely.[96] The Senate diluted the section to virtual insignificance by requiring approval of Congress, instead of the president, before promulgation by the secretary of standards and criteria; exempting water resource and legally authorized grant-in-aid programs; continuing the authority of the Water Resources Council to establish standards and criteria for water resource projects. The secretary of DOT was, however, added to the council. Especially negative, from the perspective of executive reorganizers, was the inclusion of the pre-1964 standard in the law.[97]

The Senate provisions prevailed in conference and were included in the bill that passed.[98] It was in effect status quo legislation minus some preexisting flexibility for the executive branch.

Maritime Inclusion

Maritime interests were very unhappy with the Johnson administration in 1966. Indeed, maritime labor was angry, and its most vocal representative, Paul Hall, was unrestrained in his criticism of the president. The industry desired a construction program for fifty ships, and the administration was supporting only about one-fourth that number. A Maritime Task Force report in 1965 was favorable to the industry in certain respects, but its recommendations were not acceptable to some within the administration; when its contents were leaked, discontent with the administration was aggravated.

Antagonism surfaced in bills in the House proposing an independent maritime commission even before the bill for a department of transportation was sent to Congress. The bills went to the Committee on Merchant Marine and Fisheries, chaired by Congressman Edward A. Garmatz (D–Md.), who had introduced one of the bills and who was also a member of the Government Operations Committee. On 21 June Garmatz obtained from the Marine and Fisheries Committee a resolution that the committee favored the establishment of a separate maritime commission and instructions to seek deletion of maritime matters from the DOT bill. In House deliberation on 30 August on the DOT bill, Garmatz offered an amendment to strike maritime matters from the bill, stating that he and his supporters believed independent status would assure these matters the attention from the "executive" that they deserved.[99]

Another factor in the discussion was the industry's desire for a maritime subsidy board that would have status and independence. Secretary Connor reported to Califano in July that he, Boyd, and Harold Seidman of BOB had concluded that the existing arrangements on subsidy were unsatisfactory. Connor leaned toward creation of a board composed of the maritime administrator and two independent members appointed by the secretary. He thought such a change would offer an acceptable alternative to ship-owners and ship operators who had declared themselves in favor of an independent agency.[100] Califano subsequently sent a draft of such an amendment to the Speaker of the House.[101]

Such an arrangement, however, was an inadequate compromise in that it did not meet the maritime interests' central criticism of the administration: that the amount of money to be approved as a budget item for subsidy was insufficient. Maritime interests were concerned with maritime policy, meaning budgetary policy. Structural discussions floated above the real issue of money, and on that the president was unwilling to make the concessions required for consent.

The leader of the opposition was Paul Hall, president of the Seafarers International Union of North America. The White House was aware of his position in 1965, and his opposition ultimately defeated administration efforts to gain consent by concessions on structure. Negotiations were directed by the president himself, and the record demonstrates how the power of a president can wither in the face of a single strategically located private person. This is the recorded "Chronology of the Negotiations at the White House."

Tuesday, August 23; 6:00–8:00 p.m.—Reynolds [James J. Reynolds, Department of Labor] is in Chicago at the President's direction to work out a settlement with *Hall* and *Curran* [Joseph Curran, Maritime Union]. (The decision to send Reynolds out was made by the President at a meeting Monday night, August 22, with O'Brien and Boyd present). First word is that the unions will forego their demand for a separate, independent Maritime Administration if a Presidentially appointed 3-man Maritime Subsidy Board could be created *within* the Department of Transportation. Califano drafts language to accommodate this and sends copies to *Hoyt Haddock* (Curran's man in Washington) who says he will get final approval of the unions and the industry.

Wednesday, August 24; 12:15–2:30 p.m.—The Tuesday night solution is not acceptable to *Paul Hall.* A six-man negotiating group (Haddock, Al Maskin—a union newsman, *Ralph Casey, Howard Adams,* and *Earl Clark*—shipowners representatives, and *Ray Murdock*—Hall's man) meets at the White House with Califano. This group is a special subcommittee of a larger 20-man committee representing all the maritime interests. The group says the Tuesday night proposal does not go far enough in insuring a preferred position for the Maritime Administration in the new Department. After caucusing, the six members agree to language worked out jointly with Califano for a subsidy board within the Department and for a special statutory delegation of authority on maritime matters to the Maritime Administration within the Department of Transportation. Later that afternoon, the 20-man committee approves the agreement—subject to final approval by Paul Hall and Joe Curran, who are in Chicago.

Wednesday, August 24; 8:00–10:00 p.m.—Murdock and two of his associates meet with Califano at the White House and announce that the afternoon's compromise is unacceptable to Paul Hall because it does not provide for sufficient independence of the Maritime Administration in the Department of Transportation.

Additional language is drafted by Califano and Murdock to meet the objections. Murdock also asks, "What else can be offered to sweeten this?" Califano writes out a 3-point plan in which the President would (1) meet with Meany [George Meany, president, AFL-CIO] or any one Meany designates and hear the Maritime case presented, (2) call the Maritime Advisory Commission report a "thoughtful" document and (3) charge the new Department to come up with a new maritime program as its first order of business. Murdock takes a copy of the 3 points and revised language and says he will check it out with Hall.

While these negotiations proceed at the White House, Meany sends a telegram (around 9:40 p.m.) to every Member of the House (received at 10:47 p.m.) reporting the AFL-CIO Executive Council passed a resolution urging support for an independent, separate Maritime Administration outside the Transportation Department. The President (at 11:45 p.m.) talks to *Meany* about the Maritime problem. Meany does not mention the telegram he has just sent to the House members.

Thursday morning, August 25; 10:00 a.m.—At a meeting in the Speaker's office, we learn for the first time of Meany's telegram. *Reynolds* is advised by *Hall* that there can be no deal short of the Maritime

Administration as a separate independent agency. *Curran* in the meantime calls Califano and tells him he has assented to the language worked out the day before. Upon hearing that *Hall* has taken a hard and uncompromising line despite all the negotiations *Haddock* says he will issue a public statement saying that all of Maritime industry and labor favored reaching agreement with the Administration except for *Hall*. *Haddock* never issues the statement.[102]

Also on 25 August, Secretary Wirtz sent the president this addition to the chronology of events:

Now, within the past 45 minutes, Jim Reynolds and I have been advised by Paul Hall and Lane Kirkland [Meany's assistant] that this entire position of the AFL-CIO will now be *reversed* if a commitment is made that there will be a statement, either public or private, by "someone in the White House" as follows:

"The Administration reaffirms its support of the Maritime Act of 1936 and will direct the new Secretary of Transportation and Maritime Administration to develop a program to implement that Act *within the framework of the Maritime Advisory Committee Report.*"

Larry asks your advice as to whether any attempt should be made at this point to give this kind of statement or an equivalent to Paul Hall. If this is done, we would then try to get George Meany to send another telegram immediately countermanding his telegram of last night.[103]

In a press report Hall charged that the Johnson administration had offered to build twenty-five cargo ships if organized labor would forget about an independent maritime administration. Hall was reported as saying: "We're not about to make such a deal"; "Lyndon B. Johnson's word is not worth 2 cents so far as the maritime end is concerned."[104]

Garmatz was able to present to the House on 30 August an impressive set of telegrams favoring an independent maritime commission—from labor and others in the maritime industry, all dated between 23 and 29 August, and including one from Meany, dated 24 August.[105] Some twenty persons representing organized labor were reportedly lobbying for an independent commission.[106] On the other hand, Holifield told the House the president had told him four days earlier that the Maritime Administration "ought to go in the Department of Transportation." Holifield said, "the President is not going to let a man like Paul Hall blackjack him." [107] Garmatz's amendment to delete the transfer of the Maritime Administration from the DOT bill passed a few minutes later—190 to 63.[108]

Exercising great care to avoid public commitments on policy, the president's men were able to keep the Maritime Administration in the bill in the

Senate with provision for a bipartisan maritime board to exercise subsidy functions, as Connor had proposed. But the Senate yielded in the conference committee. Reorganization had been swamped by policy dissatisfaction, a decision on the structure of the executive branch defeated by essentially irrelevant considerations—ultimately, neither independence nor bureau status could assure affirmative budget decisions.

Final Action of Congress

One White House aid reported to the president:

> the House bill is infinitely better than the Senate bill.... Put another way, the House bill contains four-fifths of the original proposal in excellent shape, and the Senate bill contains four-fifths of the original proposal in bad shape.[109]

Califano regarded the House bill as "excellent" except for the exclusion of the Maritime Administration.[110] The administration group hoped for a conference committee report that accepted most of the House bill but included the Senate provision on the Maritime Administration. Given this, the president could then "negotiate with the lobbyists to get the conference report adopted."[111]

But the opposite occurred. The conference committee accepted the House position on the Maritime Administration, the Senate provisions on delegations to modal administrators on safety, as well as its provision to reinstate pre-1964 water resource development standards. Strategically located senators and lobbyists had won—for aviation, water resources, and maritime interests—what each desired; the president was left with nothing on which to negotiate.

Other important adjustments between the houses or variations from the administration bill deserve notice:

1. The administration proposal included transfer of car service functions of ICC, except for certain matters of economic regulation, to DOT. ICC joined BOB in support of the transfer, but industry generally favored retention by ICC. Those opposing the transfer argued that all car service functions, partly operational and partly economic-regulatory, should be in the same agency. The administration proposal was deleted from the bills in both houses.[112]

2. The conference report accepted a Senate amendment providing that the secretary should carry out the provisions of the National Traffic and Motor Vehicles Safety Act of 1966 through a national traffic safety bureau.

3. The Senate restored a provision that required the secretaries of HUD and Transportation to report to the president and Congress within one year after the effective date of the act "on the logical and effective organization

and location of urban mass transportation functions in the Executive Branch."

4. Senate provisions for transfer of the Saint Lawrence Seaway Development Corporation and the Alaska Railroad to DOT were included in the conference report. The administration and the House had assumed that these transfers would be made by reorganization order. The Senate amendment for the corporation attempted to prevent a downgrading of the organization; the amendment gave the corporation protection similar to that given other transferred units by providing that the administrator report directly to the secretary. The amendment transferring the Alaska Railroad was designed to preserve the existing situation in which the ICC had control over rates.

Both houses accepted the conference report. The act was signed by the president on 15 Oct. 1966. Its trade-offs and the losses for the administration, as in preceding congressional steps, demonstrated that congressional as well as presidential perspectives will influence decisions on executive organization, whenever the reorganization must be accomplished by statute.

THE COONSKIN ON THE WALL

The president, signing the bill in the presence of many invited guests, remarked that it was "another coonskin on the wall."[113] What did the coonskin represent?

First, a reward for great effort: Califano has said that "The Transportation Department bill had been the toughest legislative fight of the 89th Congress, it had taken perhaps 15 percent of my time in 1966 and required almost daily presidential attention."[114]

Next, from the viewpoint of those seeking reorganization, some losses, some retention of the status quo, some gains. Among the losses were the failure to include the Maritime Administration in DOT (it would remain in Commerce) and the statutory prescription of an unwanted inflexible investment standard for public waterways expenditures. Preserving the status quo were arrangements for protecting modal functions and operations, existing policies, and congressional prerogatives. Among the gains was the creation in the office of the secretary of offices through which research and planning, policy development, and budgetary control might be achieved. These offices would make the secretary a new center of power and influence—immeasurably stronger than the under secretary of commerce for transportation—to countervail in part the pressures that would emanate from strong protections in law, administration, Congress, and interest groups for existing modal policies.

No bold new transportation policies, no new public programs, no changes in allocation of resources were achieved or sought through this legislation. DOT represented a structural change that, if followed by aggressive departmental leadership and adequate staffing, could lead to new policies, programs, and allocative decisions in the future. As had occurred in the Department of Defense and in the Department of Health, Education, and Welfare (including its predecessor, the Federal Security Agency), the use and extension of staff resources could increase the capability for secretarial guidance on policy and administration.

What did the coonskin signify for the process of reorganization? That fortuitous circumstances, coordinated staff work, and effective employment of presidential influence on Congress can produce structural change. That the president must have the support of a subpresidency that guides, coordinates, pushes, perfects plans, and adjusts proposals to the positions of others. That the rival perspectives of different actors must be compromised. That structural change is more likely to be achieved if it does not threaten allocations of benefits. Finally, that reorganization is a political process from start to finish—a politics of achieving internal executive consent and support, a politics of winning or losing lobbies, and a politics of gaining congressional consent—to be achieved only if congressional prerogatives, entrenched interests, and the concerns of strategically located members are not threatened.

In more general terms, the coonskin symbolizes how difficult it is to reorganize the executive branch in the absence of a visible crisis or a compelling mandate. The creation of DOT was not accidental or without significance, but its potential for determining the distribution of benefits was of limited value immediately and was dependent on further processes for policy effect.

FOUR

THE OFFICE OF
ECONOMIC OPPORTUNITY
Organizing for New Program
Development

The War on Poverty was a major policy thrust of the Johnson presidency. Innovative and dramatic, and wide in scope, it has captured the attention of numerous writers and has been the subject of extensive historical summary, analysis, and evaluation.[1] While interesting for policy drama and significance, it perhaps looms even larger as experience in administration. For it presented one presidency with difficult choices on organization and raised problems of coordination that are recurrent in the functioning of the executive branch. Although the choices on organization were made at the beginning, they were constantly questioned. Program coordination was the main theme in these choices and one test of their correctness. In a fundamental way, the War on Poverty mirrors the critical aspect of administration of Great Society programs.

CREATION OF THE OFFICE OF ECONOMIC OPPORTUNITY (OEO)

"That's my kind of program.... Move full speed ahead," was President Johnson's reaction, according to Walter Heller, chairman of the Council of Economic Advisers (CEA), when Heller presented the developing anti-poverty program two days after Johnson became president.[2] It was, however, only an idea or vision at that time, just beginning to evolve as a program concept. The program and its administration took form during the Johnson presidency.

The idea had been accepted and lines of thought had originated before Johnson's accession. His presidency followed a period of intellectual ferment and search for policy approaches focused on the social conditions of

77

the poor.[3] Undoubtedly cognizant of some of the ferment, President Kennedy said to Heller in December 1962, "Give me facts and figures on things we still have to do. For example, what about the poverty program in the United States?"[4] The facts and figures were assembled by Robert J. Lampman of the CEA staff, and they showed that the policies of government were not reaching the poor. It was obvious that the tax reduction then being considered would not correct this failure in policy. By the spring of 1963 it was reported that President Kennedy "was reaching the conclusion that tax reduction required a comprehensive structural counterpart, taking the form, not of piecemeal programs, but of a broad war against poverty itself."[5]

This language—"comprehensive structural counterpart"—is retrospective and in all likelihood not Kennedy's articulation. There was indeed seeding for such in the experimental projects of the Ford Foundation and the experience of the President's Committee on Juvenile Delinquency and Youth Crime. The common feature in both efforts was subsidy for *community activity* for attack on the problems of the "other America." But discovery of this as a linchpin for the poverty program was a later contribution of the subpresidency.

The initial components of the antipoverty program were joint products of a complex of actors in the subpresidency. Walter Heller, Kermit Gordon, director of the Bureau of the Budget (BOB), and Theodore Sorensen in the White House were the responsible first-level actors. But in this instance the contribution of the second-level actors, particularly William M. Capron of CEA and William B. Cannon of BOB, was important. In and out of the subpresidency were certain cabinet officials and agency heads. And, finally, a few persons active in the community programs—David Hackett from the Juvenile Delinquency Committee and Paul N. Ylvisaker from the Ford Foundation—gave advice at crucial moments.

On instructions from Sorensen to pull together measures for the president's consideration, Heller on 5 November 1963 sent a memorandum to relevant cabinet officials, with copies to a large group of other officials, asking for program suggestions on the topic: "1964 Legislative Proposals for 'Widening Participation in Prosperity'—An Attack on Poverty."[6] The first of these terms was then prominent in discussions and emphasized the antipoverty effort as complementary to the tax reduction plan. The result was a laundry list of suggestions from departments, each interpreting needs in terms of its own mission and the programs it desired to expand or initiate. These were variously regarded by the central planners as too costly, unimaginative, unrelated to the problem, or defensive of current positions. At least one cabinet official was reported as being reluctant. Cannon was in consultation with the experts on the community activity projects and began to press the idea as a new approach. Jointly with Phillip S. Hughes, also of

BOB, he proposed on 12 December 1963 "a series of State and Local Development Corporations, which would develop a plan, to be approved by the President, to conduct action demonstration and testing programs simultaneously in 10 poverty areas—5 urban, 5 rural—over a 3-year span.... Such development corporations should be the subject of one bill and this should be *the poverty* bill."[7] Capron reported to Heller that, though objecting to the word "corporations," "I am enthusiastic—this may be the way to really make something of this poverty program. Please hold this close until I have had a chance to give you some background."[8] Five days later Cannon elaborated a plan for a "local organization under the aegis of a local government" to submit "an integrated action-demonstration plan for attacking poverty in a defined area," to be carried out with responsibility to a local government coordinating public and private resources.[9]

This and other parts of a program were presented by Heller to Sorensen for a meeting in the latter's office on 20 December with the principals in departments and the Executive Office. The main proposal was a *"Coordinated Community Action Program"* for about ten demonstration areas, relying on local initiative and coordinating existing and new programs. Several packages of new legislation and selected expansions of existing programs were put together. By this time BOB had prepared a budget plan that included $500 million as a special allowance for the poverty program, $130 million in new appropriations already included in agency budget plans, and presidential authority to reallocate $300 million of regular agency funds to the purposes of the poverty program.[10]

The subpresidency had, as Johnson directed, moved "full speed ahead" to provide him with a program by the time Heller met with him at the ranch in late December. It was a small program, complementary to a tax cut, glued together from agency pieces, with one new element—unexpectedly added and experimental for ten areas. From this base, Johnson elevated the vision.

> Gordon and Heller had been thinking in terms of a pilot venture to be carried out in a limited number of "demonstration project" cities. But I urged them to broaden their scope. I was certain that we could not start small and hope to propel a program through the Congress. It had to be big and bold and hit the whole nation with real impact....
>
> The challenge I presented to my advisers was the development of a new concept. I didn't want to paste together a lot of existing approaches. I wanted original, inspiring ideas.
>
> The title War on Poverty was decided on during those days at the Ranch.[11]

In the State of the Union message on 8 January 1964 he declared an "unconditional war on poverty," pursuing poverty "wherever it exists," and setting forth the need for new and expanded legislation on a broad front.[12]

The Organizational Problem

The program objectives, as they had already developed, dictated the need to search at once for an appropriate structure for implementation. This effort took a distinctly different path from what might have been anticipated from the initial emphasis on local initiative and coordination. The subpresidency had put together legislative and budget plans for a variety of national moves, and the president had embraced the idea of a national program attacking poverty nationwide. Existing departments and agencies would have new or expanded programs. A new community action program and funds for new program initiatives would raise issues about whether new agencies or old ones should handle them. Hence the immediate attention was to a national structure for administration. Consideration of local planning and coordination was subsumed or subordinated.

In his budget message to Congress on 21 January the president proposed a "unified and intensified approach" "on which each separate element reinforces the others."[13] How could the government be organized to combine new and old purposes, a "unified approach" and separate administrations? How could horizontal programming be superimposed above the vertical activities of agencies? How could internal dissonance and noncooperation, creating program ineffectiveness and political criticism, be avoided? The search for structural solutions to this problem of leadership and coordination, which must recur in comparable situations, is one of the phenomena that give OEO significance in the history of the executive branch.

The early discussion centered on a cabinet council for poverty with a chairman having "full powers,"[14] but the existence of departmental sensitivities to strong controls led to suggestions that the attorney general be chairman. By early January internal struggles existed, and exhaustive BOB memorandums were circulating. On 6 January 1964 there were two alternatives in front: administration by the Department of Health, Education, and Welfare (HEW) or by a council with a chairman appointed by the president. In either case, contact with the White House would be through a special assistant to the president, though this was quickly questioned as downgrading the authority of the coordinating department or council.[15] Officials within HEW wanted the responsibility,[16] and Department of Labor officials preferred HEW to a new level of operations in the Executive Office. Wilbur Cohen of HEW outlined the appropriate internal organization.[17] At this stage expert opinion in the Division of Organization and Management in BOB supported location in HEW.[18]

Division over the alternatives led to discusson in a meeting of major participants with Sorenson on 23 January. At this meeting Secretary of Labor Willard Wirtz proposed a specific variation of the proposals that had been made for some combination from a council, presidential assistant, and HEW administration of community action:

1. A Human Resources Council made up of the President, the Vice President, and heads of interested agencies. The staff would consist of a Special Assistant for Human Resources Affairs and an Executive Secretary....

2. A Citizens Advisory Committee would meet with the council....

3. A unit in HEW, working with an interdepartmental committee, would administer a program of developing, staffing, and providing administration grants to Community Action Program units.

In a subsequent memorandum to the director of BOB, Harold Seidman, head of the Division of Management and Organization, interpreted this as a proposal for high-level policy decisions in a council chaired by the president, with operating responsibility in HEW.

Seidman also summarized the rejection of this proposal at the meeting on 23 January in favor of a modification of the other alternative that had been proposed:

Under the modification agreed at the White House meeting, as we understand it, overall operating responsibility would be vested in the President. The general appropriation would be made to him for allocation among the agencies. Community action plans would be approved by him, presumably after consultation with the Human Resources Council. The President's functions, except chairing the Council, would be delegated to a Special Assistant on Human Resources Affairs.

Seidman objected strongly to these solutions. In addition to opposing the strange idea of a citizens' council "meeting with" the president's advisory council in the Wirtz proposal and fixing organization structure within the presidency by statute, he pressed the point that this proposal had "serious implications" for the president. He thought an analogy was improper between the National Security Council (NSC), dealing with policy where the president had special constitutional responsibilities, and the proposed human resources council; moreover, problems had arisen in NSC use by the president because of the legal prescription of organization. The president, under the proposal, "would be placed in the untenable position of chairing an advisory committee." Also, leadership would be divided between the president and HEW in a manner that would impair leadership with Congress. Yet Seidman thought that the solution in the conference (placing operating functions in the president) was even worse: the president would lack a strong agency head, a special assistant could not perform the functions outlined and maintain a confidential relationship with the president, and the Congress would suspect that the president might use the program for political purposes.[19]

Schultze now asked Seidman to outline the alternatives for organization. Finally, three precise alternatives for giving strength to the coordinating purpose were defined and weighed:[20]

"1. *An independent agency.*" This would dramatize the War on Poverty, offer prestige to attract a director, and allow recruitment of new, creative personnel not committed to present programs; yet the director's bargaining position would be less than that of a department head, his position would deteriorate as pressures limited the president's attention to the program, and he would lose valuable time in building an organization and support services.

"2. *A new unit in the Executive Office.*" While the advantages and disadvantages of an independent agency would exist, there were particular considerations. Location of the director in the Executive Office would tend to offset the disadvantages in relations with Congress and the departments. On the other hand, this alternative would confuse the character of Executive Office agencies that provide staff services to the president, increase the difficulty of resisting pressure supporting fifteen to twenty other proposals for new units in the Executive Office, and encourage those who preferred an Executive Office position for urban affairs rather than a new department.

3. *HEW with delegation to a newly authorized official to be appointed by the president with Senate concurrence.* This alternative would provide an operating base with established professional and administrative support at headquarters and regional offices; it would provide "the best assurance that new programs will mesh smoothly with existing operations," including those of the states, and that staff support would be available at minimum cost. Yet it would obscure the "government-wide character of the program and make it more difficult for the public to understand the Secretary spoke for the President;" old line agencies could resist new policies. "Finally, all of the participating agencies except HEW and Labor have taken the position that coordination cannot be effective from the departmental level. Therefore, this location might militate against optimum use of the resources of other departments, particularly Agriculture, which have a major role in rural areas."

The President Makes a Decision

These alternatives appear to be the obvious ones for a new program in which need is seen for coordinated action across departmental lines. Their identification, however, though it clarified choice possibilities, came too late for deliberation in the subpresidency or for influence on the president on the first organizational issue to be decided. The president had already made a decision, as decisive as the earlier one at the ranch on program scope. He had decided to place the planning and the administration of the antipoverty program in a strong leader reporting directly to him.

The influences on the president's judgment on the most important issue related to government structure in his presidency are, unfortunately, unclear. He apparently had no document that adequately weighed, or even articulated, the options for organization—the sort that planners regard as essential for wise decision. He may have been unhappy with the tension among his advisers and the tardiness in planning as the January events moved at a snail's pace. He had, it is reported, received advice that he needed someone who would have strength with Congress for enactment of the antipoverty bill, and had been presented with names of persons—including Sargent Shriver—who could provide positive leadership.[21] He was probably influenced by the report of the White House conference on 23 January recommending placing authority in the president personally rather than in HEW.

Whatever the influences, the president asked Sargent Shriver a few days later to head the antipoverty war, and on 1 February 1964 announced the appointment. It is obvious the president wanted quick action, for he pressed Shriver for an answer within the hour, as the press conference approached. Johnson designated Shriver special assistant to the president[22] and told him,

> As my representative, you will direct the activities of all executive departments and agencies involved in the program against poverty. You will also be my representative in presenting to the Congress the Administration's view with respect to necessary legislation.

Subsequently, he would refer to Shriver's role as being to "run" the program and would call Shriver his "chief of staff." When designating Shriver, he asked him to attend cabinet meetings.[23]

Other Decisions on Organization

While this settled the issue between departmental location and direct responsibility to the president, in opposition to HEW and Labor and BOB, it left open the choice among the first two alternatives in Seidman's last memorandum—an independent office or location in the Executive Office. BOB was committed to separating operating from staff functions and was fearful of pressures that might result from a precedent in establishing a large operating function in the Executive Office. It supported the location of the functions in an independent agency.[24] Again, as the discussions on a draft bill moved forward, Johnson overruled the BOB position and chose to put the new agency in the Executive Office. BOB was able to salvage agreement that the antipoverty agency could be transferred by the president after a year, and this concession to its view was included in the subsequent legislative enactment.

This left two other organizational problems to be resolved. One was the programs to be operated through the Executive Office agency, the other was the relationships to be defined for it in its coordinating role. These problems were to be given attention in the next phase of planning, in which Shriver provided a new unity and direction for that portion of the subpresidency working on the antipoverty program. Beginning with a conference the day after his designation and continuing two days later with another that included all the major participants, he moved vigorously and feverishly into a planning effort whose intensity and speed can be understood best by those who have participated in speedy responses of government to new situations of high urgency. He assembled a task force of seventeen members—whose work was quickly apportioned—consulted with more than seventy-five leaders in state and local government and the private sector, and coordinated the efforts with the executive branch.[25] Complementing this program planning was the work of an administrative task force, with representation from BOB and the Civil Service Commission (CSC), to recruit a skeleton staff, plan internal organization, assign space, and in general aid in the establishment of a new agency. Shriver submitted a report to the cabinet on 18 February; but submission of legislation to Congress was delayed as resolution was sought for various issues, on some of which there were conflicting positions among the departments and Shriver's advisers.

The bill that was sent to Congress with a presidential message on 16 March was—by Shriver's choice, in concurrence with previous planning—an omnibus bill. The Economic Opportunity Act,[26] signed by the president on 20 August 1964, followed its pattern with few substantial alterations. That pattern was as shown on page 85.

The act confirmed the president's decision for an office, the Office of Economic Opportunity, within the Executive Office of the President, subject to transfer after one year by reorganization plan. It delegated, subject to some qualifications, all the programs to the director of OEO, including allocation of funds. It thus avoided placing operating functions on the president or downgrading the position of director by also providing for a special assistant to the president. Within the Congress, opponents of the antipoverty bill repeatedly alleged that it would create a "czar," but observers of administration well knew that czardom was easier to attribute than to establish.

The third organizational decision was fixed in part in the act. Although located in the Executive Office, OEO would be an operating agency. Shriver has said that when he read materials the president handed to him when he was asked to be director, he saw that all he had was a community action program. He saw in the Job Corps the opportunity to achieve quick results, and as an operator by nature he wanted the responsibility for its establishment.[27] In pursuance of his desire, the act "established within the Office of Economic Opportunity . . . a Job Corps."

Location of other operating functions was not determined in the act. It was assumed that direct administration of the planning and coordinating

Title	Program Authorized or Directed	Expenditure Authorization for First Year
I	Job Corps (rural and urban residential centers) Work-Training Programs (for unemployed youth) Work-Study Programs (in institutions of higher education)	$412,500,000
II	General Community Action Programs Adult Basic Education Programs Voluntary Assistance Program for Needy Children (Solely an information center)	$340,000,000
III	Special Programs to Combat Poverty in Rural Areas Assistance for Migrant, and Other Seasonally Employed, Agricultural Employees and Their Families	$35,000,000 plus possibility of $15,000,000 from other funds for the Migrant and Seasonally Employed Program.
IV	Employment and Investment Incentives (For small businesses)	_____
V	Work Experience Programs (For unemployed fathers and other needy persons)	$150,000,000
VI	VISTA and Administration	$10,000,000

functions of the Community Action Program would be in the Executive Office agency. While other functions might be retained by OEO, the director, with the approval of the president, could "delegate any of his powers" and "authorize the redelegation thereof."

OEO therefore became an operating agency. Yet inherent from the beginning was the danger that operations would eclipse coordination. Operations are immediate responsibilities, and the immediate always gains precedence. Operations allow initiative for the creation of new programs and

85

procedures. They could be enjoyable, particularly for Shriver and his associates who had a zeal for action and a desire for program visibility. But coordination is almost always pursued against resistance, even obstruction, from old agencies, and with unspectacular results.

A fourth organization decision was inherent in the program planning. Community action would unite, and national action would unite, various programs and organizations in the "war." The president said to Congress, "I do not intend that the war against poverty become a series of uncoordinated and unrelated efforts."[28] Numerous means to coordinate effort in a "war" that sought to use new and old statutory authorizations and agencies of administration were granted in title VI of the act:

1. Allocation of funds. The director could allocate or transfer funds made available under the act to federal agencies (sec. 602h); with the approval of the president, arrange with and reimburse agencies for performance of functions under the act (sec. 602d); and the president could direct that funds of federal agencies be expended, to the extent not inconsistent with law, in support of programs authorized under the act (sec. 611c-3).

2. Policies and procedures; contracts. The director was authorized to establish policies, standards, criteria, and procedures, to prescribe rules and regulations, and to enter into contracts and agreements with public agencies and private organizations and persons.

3. Cooperation. To ensure coordination, cooperation of the director and federal agencies was enjoined (sec. 611).

4. Preference. Heads of agencies were directed to give preference to applications for assistance to community action programs (sec. 612), and the president was authorized to direct that agency programs be carried out in support of programs authorized in the act (sec. 611-a-3), in both cases to the extent consistent with law.

5. Interagency consultation. The act created an Economic Opportunity Council for advice to the director and coordination of antipoverty efforts, chaired by the director and composed of seven cabinet officials and other officials with functions related to the program.

In addition to these authorizations and arrangements, the act included provisions for cooperation and for coordination of activities related to specific functions. Particularly for the Job Corps program, types of interagency aid were specified; and for the Community Action Program the objective of mobilizing and utilizing resources, public and private, was stated.

Thus, following the president's decision for leadership through a new agency located in the Executive Office, the executive planners had obtained legislation that authorized division of operating responsibilities at both local and national levels of activity and provided for coordination by the director of the new agency.

Location of Operating Responsibilities

It was understood within both the administration and the Congress that the director, with approval of the president, would immediately delegate certain of the functions authorized in the act. Delegation was to be the means of resolving the competing claims of departments. Six programs were delegated on 24 October 1964, as follows:[29]

Program	Title	Recipient Agency
Work-Training (Neighborhood Youth Corps)	I-B	Department of Labor
College Work-Study	I-C	Department of Health, Education, and Welfare
Adult Basic Education	II-B	Department of Health, Education, and Welfare
Rural Loans	III-A	Department of Agriculture
Small Business Loans	IV	Small Business Administration
Work Experience	V	Department of Health, Education, and Welfare

Delegation enabled the receiving departments or agencies to coordinate antipoverty programs with their existing programs. To ensure converse coordination with antipoverty efforts, the delegation orders provided for the programs to be administered pursuant to policies and procedures prescribed jointly by the director of OEO and the official to whom authority was delegated. OEO thus sought to retain influence over program administration by agreements and, additionally, by some oversight.

Later, some of the delegated programs were assigned by legislation; the College Work-Study program and Adult Basic Education program to the Office of Education, HEW, in 1965 and 1966 respectively, and the Small Business Loan program to the Small Business Administration (SBA) in 1966. Also, in March 1967—after much negotiation involving the White House, Labor, OEO, and BOB, and concurrently with reorganization within Labor to provide consolidated administration—OEO, with approval of the president, delegated to Labor a number of related job and manpower programs that had been created by amendment to the OEO act.[30] Finally, the Follow-Through Program for elementary education for disadvantaged children was delegated to HEW on 26 June 1967.[31]

For its own direct administration, OEO started with two programs designated for it in the act (Job Corps, Community Action) and two others. The act authorized the director to recruit, select, train, and assign volunteers. This program became Volunteers in Service to America (VISTA), and both by its nature (assistance to any program) and by the experience of Shriver in directing the Peace Corps it was understandable that administration of this activity would remain in the OEO. Links to community action activities also resulted in the program for migrant workers being retained in OEO.

The zeal of a new agency committed to a single objective, and of personnel sharing the drive and enthusiasm of the director, led to the initiation of a number of "packaged" or "national emphasis" programs as part of the Community Action Program, and these then were shortly incorporated in legislative authorizations. The largest of these was Head Start, a program of preschool education established in 1965 for poor children. Other national emphasis programs were Legal Services, Emergency Food and Medical Services, Senior Opportunities and Services, Head Start Follow-Through, Family Planning, and Upward Bound—a program designed to generate high-school graduates for post–high-school education. All of these were legislatively authorized in succeeding years.

The local Community Action Agencies (CAAs) developed, in addition, their own programs, including programs in manpower, education, health, and housing, and neighborhood service centers. Many of the local or national emphasis programs were in areas where other agencies were engaged in parallel activities, and sometimes indeed in the same activity.

The administrative pattern that developed is partially displayed by the estimated obligations of funds for programs in fiscal year 1968. Of the total for OEO of $1,771.1 million, delegated programs were allocated $545.6 million and direct operations $1,225.5 million. Of the former, Labor received $462.1, HEW $44.3, Agriculture $35.4, and the Department of Commerce $3.8 million. Among the directly administered programs Head Start was the largest with $316.2 and the Job Corps next with $282.3 million.[32]

THE PROBLEM OF COORDINATION

Those who believe that imagination and drive for new program development can be best obtained through a new agency, independent of existing bureaucratic structures, find much support in the history of OEO as an operating agency. It established the Job Corps, VISTA, and a migrant workers program. It initiated and pushed vigorously new programs that have endured in some form. It moved energetically to the successful creation of community action agencies. Moreover, a provision of the Economic Opportunity Act, not well understood or much discussed at the time of its enactment, provided that the community action programs should be "developed, conducted, and administered with the maximum feasible participation of residents of the areas and members of the groups served."[33] This goal was sought with sufficient vigor to activate new representation of the poor in communities and even to upset or threaten power balances in many. Nevertheless, the greater significance of OEO in viewing executive structure is the experience in seeking leadership for program coordination. For, while the experience in OEO is instructive in itself, it also reflected the new dimensions of leadership for coordination created by the Great Society legislation. Its significance can best be illuminated in the setting of the larger problem of leadership it illustrated.

The New Dimensions of Coordination

With the passage of Great Society legislation, the problem of coordinating administration of domestic programs attained dimensions and complexities undreamed of in previous periods of American history. On the one hand, segmentally considered legislation set up numerous categorical programs that were difficult to mesh in administration. On the other, legislation often expressed broad objectives that could be achieved only by the collaborative use of a variety of legal authorizations, often carried into effect by different organizations. Urban development, rural development, mass transportation, youth and adult employment, regional development, civil rights enforcement, crime reduction, water development, the War on Poverty—realization, indeed, of "the quality of life"—all had two things in common. First, they could be realized only by putting together at the administrative level what specific legislation had separated, in policy direction or in administrative structure or in both. This changed substantially the problem of national administration: no longer was it administration of single programs or parallel ones that could be put together in unitary organizations; it was a problem of interorganizational collaboration. Second, the programs had to be put together at the local level. National programs reached into communities and became intertwined with independent local administrations; this too created problems of collaboration, both horizontally at the community level and vertically with state and national structures. Coordination, once a word treasured in academic discussions, was now a necessity for program achievement.

Coordination is not a goal to be pursued by structure or process alone. On the contrary, coordination may be achieved by a range of behavioral or structural methods that can be placed on a scale: adaptation arising from mutual understanding, consultation, cooperation, leadership, integration within organization, fusion of programs. A task force reporting during the Johnson presidency condemned the lack of arrangements for coordination and then suggested in a covering memorandum that coordination was largely a problem of cooperative behavior.[34]

Coordination is, moreover, achievable by activity at various levels of administration. Above the lowest level where two people coordinate their related activities, coordination merges into the problem of leadership. At the presidential level, leadership can include motivation for cooperative behavior to achieve shared purposes among those who can be reached by such motivation. But inevitably top-level administrative planning for coordination turns to structural arrangements that promote coordinative behavior at successive levels.

A structural problem was perceived during the Johnson presidency, and structural solutions were sought. One of the devices was assigning responsibility to coordinators. In an authoritative discussion James Sundquist summarized this technique as follows:

> At the Washington level the government designated coordinators— not one but several, each with responsibility for coordination in a particular field but without power to enforce coordination. Two of the coordinators were assigned on a geographical basis; the Secretary of Housing and Urban Development was made responsible for coordinating urban development programs and the Secretary of Agriculture for coordinating rural development programs. The Appalachian Regional Commission and the five other regional commissions subsequently established had responsibility, however, for coordinating development programs in their designated regions, and the Secretary of Commerce was charged with coordinating their work and regional development in general. Beyond that were functional coordinators in a series of fields—the director of the Office of Economic Opportunity for antipoverty programs, the Secretary of Labor for manpower programs, the Secretary of Health, Education, and Welfare for programs in those fields insofar as other departments or agencies were involved. In 1965, coordinators were being designated with such frequency and regularity that one of them referred to the group irreverently as "the coordinator-of-the-month club."[35]

There was also designation of Vice-President Humphrey as liaison officer with mayors, and the director of the Office of Emergency Planning as the principal contact with governors. By legislation or executive order, heads of departments or agencies were told to "coordinate," to "convene" meetings, or to "advise" or "assist" the president. Sundquist concludes that there was an "unavoidable overlapping of coordinating spheres" but no "system of coordination."[36]

Similarly at the local level, planning, coordination, comprehensive program development was sought through numerous organizations. Secretary Orville Freeman summarized the result:

> Of these, the most significant are those Federal programs which stimulate or encourage other types of community action which complement,

overlap, or compete with CAP. At the present time OEO is encouraging the formation of Community Action Organizations to prepare Community Action Plans, the Economic Development Administration (Commerce) is encouraging citizen economic development groups to prepare Overall Economic Development Programs, the Housing and Home Finance Agency is providing funds to local public planning bodies for public facility planning and to local public agencies for urban renewal, the Appalachian Regional Commission is sponsoring the formation of Economic Development Districts, and the Department of Agriculture is encouraging the formation of Rural Areas Development Committees to prepare comprehensive rural community development plans. To this list might be added certain limited purpose bodies like the Councils on Aging sponsored by the organizations assisted by HHFA.[37]

The Special Significance of the War on Poverty

In no earlier program, or set of programs, in the domestic affairs of the nation was the vision of unified effort equally affirmed or as urgently sought as in the War on Poverty. The president prescribed it; the legislation gave it legal support; administrators sought to achieve it; the word became common among the doers and the critics. The program objective was stated in terms of coordination of all efforts that could contribute to its achievement. The core was "coordinated community action."

The difficulties to be overcome were great. Specific areas of program development were, in large measure, areas in which government was already active and had established organizations. Manpower and educational programs, with their varied components and their complementary and overlapping purposes, dominated in the War on Poverty. Health centers ultimately added another entry to old areas of public policy. New purpose would be overlaid on old purpose, with the warriors against poverty seeking revision of the objectives and habits of established organizations and units of government. Fervor and imagination among the warriors would disturb the relations with the established units. The activation of CAAs that were independent of local governments would seriously aggravate the problems of coordination at the local level. Finally, the drive to give "maximum feasible participation" to the poor, mandated in the antipoverty act, often disturbed balances in community power and everywhere fostered new components in community activity to be coordinated politically or administratively with the existing structure.

Yet the impact of OEO on coordination was limited by the fact that the size of the antipoverty effort never matched the vision of an "unconditional war on poverty" "wherever it exists." In the last full year of the Johnson administration—fiscal year 1968—the funds from OEO amounted to only $1.8 billion in the estimated total expenditures of $22.1 for assistance to the poor from the federal budget.[38] Moreover, since the War on Poverty concentrated on improving human capabilities rather than on ameliorating the current human condition, it generally avoided any problem of coordination with financial assistance and income maintenance programs of the federal government. Had the dimensions of the program been larger, or its spread wider, the problems of coordination would have been more compelling. As it was, administrative assimilation of new program activity was a serious concern in Washington, though less intense than the concern with complaints from cities about the way the stimulated representation of the poor affected distribution of political power.

Techniques for Coordination

In the setting of delegated and direct operations, both related to preexisting areas of government activity, some techniques of collaboration appropriate to the requirements were developed. Notable among these was the formal interagency agreement. At least twenty of these were signed between OEO and five departments and one agency, marking OEO as the agency historically making most use of this device. Their purposes varied. A number of these arranged, particularly for the Job Corps, for reimbursable services in the form of facilities or personnel. Two departments, Interior and Agriculture, operated Job Corps centers as conservation centers in accordance with statutory authorization for this purpose. An umbrella agreement with HEW set the stage for cooperation as new programs, such as provision of health services to the poor, were adopted. In addition, separate agreements provided for collaboration in separate programs, such as Foster Grandparents, Home Health Aides, and Education of the Disadvantaged.

An example of the use of the agreement was in the troublesome relations of the Job Corps with the United States Employment Service (USES), where agreements were made on recruitment and on placement. OEO officials were irritated by what they thought was unresponsiveness of USES to the special need for service to the poor. They were able, however, to obtain the agreement of USES to place personnel in ghettos, and according to some participants more accommodation of USES personnel to the purpose of the War on Poverty.[39]

A unique arrangement, adapted to correcting the confusion arising from creation of program activity by the CAAs, was the checkpoint procedure. OEO instructions prescribed that CAA projects be submitted for comment to local elected officials and other relevant officials, such as the local director of the state employment service, the school superintendent, and the director of the county welfare agency. Conversely, OEO negotiated arrangements with HEW, HUD, and Labor to submit their poverty-related projects to affected CAAs for comment.

As might be expected, miscellaneous means of cooperation between OEO and other departments or agencies were developed. Annual allocations of OEO funds gave opportunity to consider interagency relationships, though with less effect than would have been possible with larger appropriations. The staff of the OEO Office of the General Counsel reviewed policy documents of delegate agencies to determine their consistency with the act and OEO policies. OEO placed its own representatives in HEW regional offices. It prepared a catalog of federal assistance programs and arranged for establishment of community information centers to provide, with the cooperation of different agencies, information to the poor on the forms of government aid available. Numerous operating relationships were necessary—as, for example, for dual instruction from OEO and Agriculture to operating personnel in the Forest Service administering Job Corps units. Reports of participants, however, give no evidence that departments of government gave preference to OEO programs, as commanded by the act, and it is difficult to understand how this could have been expected.

Coordination through Community Planning

The primary technique for coordinated activity contemplated in the initial planning in the subpresidency in 1963 was community planning by the CAAs. The president embraced the idea of "long-range plans" that would call "upon all the resources available to the community—federal and state, local and private, human and material."[40] The administration's bill, though providing that community assistance without comprehensive planning could be "extended for a limited period," contained strong supports for comprehensive planning. While these requirements were greatly weakened in the provisions of the act, it still stated the purpose of mobilizing community efforts.[41]

Mobilizing community resources under a comprehensive plan was a lofty concept in a setting of separate government programs and often of dispersed community government structures. If pursued persistently with vigor, it might over a prolonged period present a complement to, and partial reduction of, national responsibility for coordination. It was not pursued with vigor. With the permissiveness allowed by the act, OEO concentrated effort toward quick results, and in the absence of preexistent planning it approved individual projects. Later, as national emphasis programs were pressed upon the communities, the objective of comprehensive planning was crowded out. A competent study of selected CAAs in eight states in 1967 concluded that not one had succeeded in achieving, or was even attempting to achieve, the "unified approach" promised by the president.[42] As the end of the Johnson presidency was nearing, the Congress had completed a circle and was seeking to impose the requirement.[43] In 1967 amendments to the act, it prescribed, with qualification:

> After July 1, 1968, the Director shall require, as a condition of assistance that each community action agency has adopted a systematic approach to the achievement of the purposes of this title and to the utilization of funds provided under this part.... The Director, may, however, extend the time for such requirement to take into account the length of time a program has been in operation.[44]

The dream of unified community effort toward eliminating poverty had not been attained.

The ability to coordinate community efforts was further complicated by the inauguration of the Model Cities program in 1967. The objective of a "unified" approach, declared by the president in 1964 for the War on Poverty, was reasserted by him in January 1967 as he presented the Model Cities program as "now the primary incentive provided by the Federal Government to accomplish" "concerted attacks on city problems." To receive grants, the cities would be required to develop "comprehensive plans" and "enlist Federal, State, local, and private resources" to bring them to fruition.[45] The Model Cities organizations in the cities would start with advantages over the CAAs, for they were, under instructions from HUD, to be an "integral part" of the city government and would thus avoid the threat to the institutions of local government that had sometimes resulted from CAAs. Here, then, were two structures in the same geographical areas attempting to coordinate a concerted attack on local problems.[46] It is not surprising that the transition report on OEO, made by the Johnson administration to its successor, should state that there would be a need to work out complementary relationships between the two local structures.[47]

The National Structure for Coordination

The act created an Economic Opportunity Council to advise the director of OEO. Its membership included the director as chairman, eight cabinet secretaries, the housing and home finance administrator, the administrator of SBA, the chairman of CEA, the director of the Selective Service, and other agency heads designated by the president. The president promptly added the director of BOB and the federal co-chairman of the Appalachian Regional Commission.

After nearly a year and a half, the vice-president reported to the president that he had attended two of the council's three meetings and that "on the whole, it has not functioned effectively. You have referred to the Council as the domestic counterpart of the National Security Council, but it has hardly lived up to this important function "[48] Much later the Senate Manpower Subcommittee concluded that it had "not served as an effective tool for concerted action with coordinated followthrough."[49] The transition report to the Nixon administration claimed some success for the council as a top-level medium for interchange of ideas and information and for the studies it initiated; but it said also that it was not an "unalloyed success." Humphrey thought it needed a "more precise agenda," and the transition report noted its lack of a permanent staff. A fuller estimate of the reasons for the council's ineffectiveness has been given by Robert Perrin, the man on Shriver's staff who was responsible for liaison with it: its chairman was not a cabinet member; it had no full-time staff; Shriver neither planned nor accepted stable agendas; cabinet members ceased to come, and representation moved down to third- or fourth-level officials in hierarchies. Perrin recommended and Shriver concurred in its abandonment after about twenty meetings.[50]

Congress in 1967 provided for a new council, with full discretion to the president on its constitution and with authorization for an executive director and staff.[51] It had not been established when the Johnson presidency ended.

In 1968 OEO had representation on sixty interagency committees. There were, however, great differences in the extent to which these were important to substantive performance of antipoverty functions.[52]

Within OEO an Office of Interagency Relations was created in the Office of the Director in October 1964 to carry the primary responsibility for coordination with other agencies. In 1967 this became the Office of Governmental Relations, as it was also given the function of coordinating relations with the states. This office functioned, however, within an organization where the sizable units conducted their own program operations, and where coordination unavoidably was thought of in terms of their specific programs. Intraagency coordination in a setting of operating bureaus is itself difficult—indeed, with lack of strong administrative leadership, it may be as unattained as interagency coordination.

Coordination with other agencies was complicated somewhat by the lack of correlation between the regional boundaries and regional office locations of OEO and the departments to which its work was related. As will be explained later, efforts to correct this deficiency were initiated late in the Johnson presidency, but without action during that period.[53] The relationships between headquarters and regional offices showed the characteristic difficulties of national administrative organizations generally: failure of program planners to give adequate attention in the developmental stages of an organization to these relationships, followed by regional office complaints of overcentralization and conflicts over the respective authorities of regional directors and the heads of operating divisions at headquarters. Rather late, in a major document of 23 October 1968, after several inside and outside studies of the problems, the deputy director sought to establish clearly the delegations to the regional offices and the role of the regional directors. Yet the transition papers set forth a list of problems that would deserve attention from a new administration.[54]

The focal point for coordination was, of course, the Office of the Director itself. The zeal, enthusiasm, and drive of the director and his unabated push for program results were, however, according to reports from numerous participants, unmatched by concern with administrative orderliness. The novelty of the program, its inspiring goal, and the energy and dedication of the director drew to the program people with strong purpose and impatience with bureaucratic obstructions. In a setting of aggressive pursuit of operating programs and numerous relations with other agencies and governments, and zealous pursuit of program objectives, the position of deputy director might have served as the coordinating center. Yet this position remained open for almost a year and was filled in midcourse by a man who has recorded his difficulties in operating under Shriver in the position.[55] Not until 1966 was the position occupied by a person whose career had equipped him particularly for the task of administrative direction and coordination.[56]

Shriver's position as "chief of staff" to the president had limited utility. Success in administration must be achieved without burdening the president with operating relationships. Executives will not want their differences aired, or even known, at this level. The subpresidency will intervene to prevent the business of administration from rising that far. The president will move reluctantly to embrace correctives that have uncertain administrative or political consequences.

All in all, the experience of OEO does not provide the administrative planner with a structural model for successful coordination of interagency activities.

Coordination with State and Local Governments

The War on Poverty was conducted primarily through federal agencies and federally sponsored CAAs. The states were not given a significant position in the "war." Yet their participation was present in several ways. On the negative side, the governor of a state was given at the outset a veto over Job Corps contracts, use of VISTA volunteers, and Community Action projects within the state. After a provocative use of the veto by Governor Wallace of Alabama, which carried anti–civil-rights overtones, the veto provision for community action projects was modified to allow the director of OEO to override the governor's veto.[57] On the positive side, the act enjoined the director of OEO to establish procedures for effective participation of the states in the community action program and authorized grants and contracts to the states for this purpose. With OEO encouragement, technical assistance offices were established in each of the states to provide assistance to communities on community action programs. Moreover, the cooperation of state education agencies and state employment offices was particularly important for the OEO program.

Whereas the states were largely bypassed, the established local governments were often antagonized. The act provided no veto for mayors and initially contained no requirements for city and county collaboration. About three-fourths of the CAAs were nonpublic organizations. In many cities effective official leadership was able to integrate CAA program activity with city functions and to avoid confrontation with new political forces. But the fervent effort of OEO to provide, as the act specified, "maximum feasible participation of the poor" sometimes led to open conflict with the control elements in the city, even to what was sometimes called "war on city hall." Dissatisfaction ultimately led to the passage in the House of Representatives, and acceptance by the Senate, of the amendment to the OEO Act, sponsored by Congresswoman Edith Green, that provided that the CAA be a state or local government, political subdivision of a state, or a combination of such subdivisions, or a public or private nonprofit organization designated by the state or local government, subject only to a provision that other public or private agencies could be designated by the director if no organization had been created pursuant to this provision or if the organization was failing to meet its responsibilities.[58] The amendment also required that one-third of the members of CAA boards be public officials. These provisions, coming late and from outside the administration, enhanced the possibilities for coordination of the activities of the federally sponsored CAAs with those of local governments. Yet, with the amendment adopted three years after OEO's formation and with perhaps 80 percent of the CAAs already in conformity with its provisions, no substantial change occurred after its passage.

Reconsideration of Organization

Favorable to the War on Poverty at its initiation were the vision and hope of the president and the zeal and energy of Shriver and his associates within OEO. Yet some factors were uncertain or inauspicious. Two concepts, community action and "maximum feasible participation of the poor," had come from the intelligentsia, but neither had benefited from either clarity of intent or strong interest-group support. The proposal for the poverty program ran into strong Republican opposition and passed Congress by decidedly partisan ballots. The act was carefully framed to give the director powers essential for a unified attack, but it is doubtful whether anyone had thought constructively about the operational aspects of coordination. And the logic of administrative theory was violated by the union of operating and coordinating responsibilities. Because the White House staff itself lacked coordination during the presidential transition, decisions on the structure for administration were made as departments struggled for jurisdiction, and the advice of BOB was not dominant.

Emergence of Discontent

In such a setting it is understandable that questions about the structure and operation of the program surfaced even before it was on a solid footing. As early as January 1965 a BOB staff member was recording questions about duplication in assignments to Labor and HEW and about whether operating responsibilities should be assigned to CAAs, for which the rationalizing concept was planning and coordination.[59] At the same time, Shriver was asking that the Peace Corps, VISTA, and certain other activities be combined and was seeking broader coordination of antipoverty efforts through a consolidated poverty budget or through giving the director statutory authority to direct specified poverty-related efforts.[60] Also, Shriver, already planning the Head Start program, was opposing transfer of the preschool program to HEW. Within seven months after creation of OEO there was some discussion in BOB about a comprehensive review of executive branch structure for the antipoverty program, and some months later there was talk about a CSC-BOB study.[62]

But it was protest from the cities that generated soul-searching within the administration. In June 1965, at a meeting of the United States Conference of Mayors, discontent was expressed over establishment of community action projects that were independent of city hall, and over organization of the poor in militant, politically active groups. A committee, with Mayor Daley as chairman, was appointed, and it proceeded at once to a conference with Vice-President Humphrey.[63] After consulting with representatives of ninety-three cities, the conference published a report that set forth many deficiencies in OEO operations, particularly stressing lack of coordination in the program.[64]

Report on the attitudes of governors was also critical. Buford Ellington, director of the Office of Emergency Planning, who was responsible for liaison with the governors, reported to the president in June "a lack of understanding at the local level as to which department or agency is responsible for each individual program,"[65] and in August, after a governors' conference, he reported:

All are in favor of the program, but I didn't talk with a single Governor who approves of the way it is being handled in Washington or at the State level. Our closest friends are very much upset by the way it is being administered.[66]

Dissatisfaction was mounting in Washington too. Secretary Freeman thought the Department of Agriculture was not being used sufficiently;[67] Secretary Wirtz, while concluding that "working relations are extremely good," was unhappy with the lack of concentration of manpower functions in Labor and thought "some procedure for inter-agency cooperation and participation in the decision-making" was imperative. He suggested a program control center for the entire federal economic opportunity/education/manpower program, so far as it involved the financing of state and local projects.[68]

These were faint-sounding intimations of stronger opposition to come later; but the concern of BOB was heard within and outside the government. In September 1965 Schultze sent a long but pungent statement to the president: "we ought not to be in the business of organizing the poor politically"; "we ought to involve them at the actual working level in the poverty program"; OEO should "be requested to emphasize the development of comprehensive anti-poverty plans as a condition for CAP grants." Schultze added, "If you think this approach makes sense, I'll take it from here." The president responded, "O.K. I agree."[69]

Shortly thereafter, Schultze discussed with Shriver the dual objective of less emphasis on representation and more emphasis on employment of the poor. Also, a member of the staff of BOB "indicated forcefully to a group of OEO officials," as Shriver recorded the events, that OEO should restudy and modify its public stance on maximum feasible participation of the poor. A story of dissension broke in the press, chiefly the *New York Times*, and the president instructed Schultze and Shriver, through Califano, "to stop fighting each other through the press." This led each man to make lengthy face-saving reports to the president on the events, their lack of personal responsibility for a leak, and the existence of friendly relations despite some differences.[70]

Structural Revision Recommended and Rejected

Much more significant than this episode was the consideration that would shortly be given to revoking the organizational decisions that gave birth to OEO. The White House Task Force on Urban Problems, reporting on 21

December 1965, recommended transfer of the community action programs from OEO to the newly created HUD.

> Such programs could and would add important "human" dimensions to a Department that would otherwise be preoccupied with the physical environment alone. Moreover, the Department with its funds, programs and new status would lend strength to the Community Action Programs.[71]

A report to the president stated that the move was sponsored by Walter Reuther and Ben Heineman, members of the task force, "for two reasons: to give HUD an active social agency that would challenge the rest of the department, and to give Community Action a strong base of organizational support." Kermit Gordon stated in writing his dissent to the task force; and the president was told that Gordon thought it would be placing too much in the new department[72] and that "CAP would probably be swallowed in H.U.D.," adding "the poor to a lengthy roster of H.U.D. clientele groups with whose interests the needs of the poor will sometimes conflict."[73] But while Gordon was concerned about placing representation of the interests of the poor in a department likely to be dominated by financial interests in housing, Whitney Young of the National Urban League feared the adverse effects on the consideration of a fellow black, Robert Weaver, for secretary of HUD. Though not dissenting in the task force report, he asked that his reservations be reported to the president: the timing was poor because of lack of knowledge about who would be secretary of HUD, and he was not convinced that the present CAP program was doomed or would be ineffective or watered down.[74]

Plans for full-scale reorganization of the War on Poverty and abolition of OEO were promptly developed. Attorney General Nicholas Katzenbach and his aides drafted, with Califano's detailed attention, two orders: one to delegate OEO's functions to departments, the other to abolish OEO in a follow-up and clean-up reorganization plan.[75] Califano reported to the president his support for a "typically dramatic Johnsonian move":

> The reorganization of the War Against Poverty is potentially the most politically explosive act the Administration could take, even though it makes good organizational sense. There is at least one way to make it a plus. If the reorganization were coupled with the delegation of the HUD Secretary as the recipient of the coordinating functions of the War on Poverty, Chairman of the Economic Opportunity Council and Director of the Community Action Program and if you named Shriver as Secretary of HUD (with a Negro like Weaver of Sam Proctor as Under Secretary), I believe you would not only get little, if any, adverse political comment from civil rights groups, liberals, and others. You could also get a tremendous plus from the liberals, as well as the con-

servatives, and the mayors and the city organizations who would like to get this program in more formal channels.[76]

Another staff aide, however, advised the president to hold the CAP question open pending appointment of the secretary and the views of Congress, mayors, and civil rights leaders.[77]

The president did not approve Califano's ingenious proposals. He appointed Robert Weaver secretary of HUD. As for OEO, discussion of abolition was followed by two things that were quite different.[78] They reflect Johnson's desire to shore up the internal administration of OEO. First, Shriver's ability to devote attention to OEO's problems was furthered by Johnson's appointment in January 1966 of a replacement for Shriver as head of the Peace Corps. Second, Bertrand Harding, distinguished by management experience in federal service, was asked in February by Schultze and John Macy, chairman of the CSC, to make a management study of OEO. As the study was being completed, Harding was appointed deputy director of OEO and brought his talents to the improvement of internal management, field administration, and relations with other executive agencies.

Survival of Structural Issues

During 1966 the OEO program received strong expressions of support from mayors, but criticism was mounting in the Congress, where the Republicans pushed unsuccessfully their plan for an "opportunity crusade" that would have stripped OEO of all its operating functions except Community Action and VISTA. For the first time, Congress earmarked appropriations for all major programs, favoring some but materially reducing appropriations for the Job Corps and "versatile" Community Action programs, a category that included locally developed and experimental programs. Shriver saw a "great and grave" impact on the less-favored programs.[79]

At the end of the year, new recommendations were made to the president on revising the structure of the antipoverty program. Shriver himself sent a message to the president on 13 December 1966 recommending the creation of a "Social and Economic Development Council," similar to NSC, which would focus responsibility for the Great Society program and absorb the planning and coordination functions of OEO. Meanwhile, the distinguished members of the Heineman Task Force on Government Organization had initiated their work of considering, on White House request, the organization of OEO functions. Heineman held extensive conversations with Shriver, and a task force report was sent to the president on 15 December. While praising OEO for its "extraordinary record of innovation and program development," the task force concluded that "the machinery in the Economic Opportunity Act of 1964 for coordination of federal government activities and programs affecting the poor has not proved workable."[80] Its central recommendation for change was to "establish the expectation that antipoverty programs by OEO will be delegated to Executive agencies when their focus and character is secure, and they become national in scope." Particularly endorsed was early transfer of the Job Corps to Labor and the ultimate delegation of Head Start to HEW. OEO itself would be set up outside the Executive Office to run CAP, to develop and demonstrate new programs for ultimate delegation to departments, and, by delegation rather than transfer, to maintain surveillance and budgetary influence over departments administering the programs. For coordination of poverty operations, it was recommended that a special assistant be designated in the White House, though Schultze dissented on the basis that study of other Great Society programs should be looked at by the task force and though Gordon preferred that the special assistant also be director of OEO. Shriver's proposal for a domestic NSC was rejected for the moment.

Again, as a year earlier, the president did not follow the recommendations of a task force for reassignment of OEO functions. Instead, the administration was shortly involved in a struggle with Republicans and opposition Democrats in Congress to save OEO from dismemberment through spin-off of its programs. Administration forces were cognizant of the threat and prepared a strengthened OEO bill to meet it. Preparations for the year 1967 have been summarized as follows:

The OEO bill and budget
—More time was spent by the President and his staff on this legislation than on any other single item in the 1967 legislative program.
   The policy decisions relating to the OEO bill were made at the highest levels of government. Extensive preliminary discussions were held during October, November and December by Califano, Schultze and Shriver. Ultimate decisions were made during extended discussions between the President and Shriver (including a full day meeting at the LBJ ranch on December 29, 1966) and between the President and Director Schultze.[81]

There was sentiment in some places that the administration's support was not enthusiastic. But the president's commitment to the antipoverty effort in his messages was unequivocal,[82] and his attention to the program was unusual:

From November 1966 through August 1967, the President meets 6 times with Shriver and has 3 other telephone conversations with him. This includes a full day meeting in Texas at the LBJ ranch to work out the final details on the OEO bill and budget.[83]

The White House staff was especially active:

Califano meets with Shriver more than 50 times during this 9 month period and has about 15 telephone conversations with Shriver each month (and as many as 26 in February).

Califano meets on several occasions with Senator Clark on the OEO bill and on August 10, Califano and Gaither [White House aide] spend two hours with Senator Clark urging quick action and support for the Administration's OEO bill.

Gaither meets with Shriver and other top OEO officials more than 11 times during that period, and has more than 95 telephone conversations with them concerning OEO matters. In addition, Gaither spends about 1 hour each day on OEO legislative and operational matters, maintaining constant liaison with OEO officials and assisting in the coordination of poverty programs.[84]

It is obvious that the special assistant function contemplated for the director of OEO was dispersed among the White House staff with some concentration on Califano.

The OEO survived the 1967 attack, saved largely by the Green amendment, and respite was gained for the administration by a two-year authorization, the first for the program. Yet consideration of the administrative structure was not dead. In February Califano wrote to the president, "Attached is the way Zwick and I would distribute the OEO program, should such a decision be made." All functions were listed for transfer, with community action, VISTA, and general direction going to an "HEW-OEO Unit."[85] The new consideration was concurrent with the appointment of Shriver as ambassador to France and the appointment as acting director of OEO of Harding, who it may be noted was much more sympathetic than Shriver to spin-off of established programs to other agencies.[86] Again, the Department of Justice was asked for a report on legal requirements for reorganization of OEO, and it reported that, while operating functions could be delegated by the director with approval of the president, OEO could not be abolished or its functions transferred out of the Executive Office without a statute or reorganization plan. Also, if OEO were to be maintained as merely a planning and coordinating agency, none of the seven top officials of the OEO could be transferred without a reorganization plan or statute.[87] At about the same time, the president was interested in discussing the relation of proposals for a "domestic security council" or the newly legislated Economic Opportunity Council to the "questions regarding HEW and OEO."[88]

As for transfers to HEW, Cohen reported to the White House that he supported transfer to HEW of eleven OEO programs (not including

103

Community Action or VISTA). He favored the transfer of Head Start to the Children's Bureau, and the administration opposed the Dominick amendment in the House that would have transferred it to the Office of Education.[89]

Finally, as the administration neared its end, Congress provided in amendments to the Vocational Education Act that the president should make a special study of whether the Head Start program should remain in OEO or be delegated to another agency, and that the commissioner of education should make a study on whether the Job Corps should be transferred to "State or joint Federal-State operation," both reports to be made by 1 March 1969.[90] Task forces reported on both studies early in December 1968. Following this, at a meeting of Califano, Cohen, Wirtz, Harding, Zwick, Harold Howe (commissioner of education), and James Gaither (White House staff) there was consensus on a recommendation to the president, as the "ideal solution," that he delegate Head Start to HEW and the Job Corps to Labor. If a decision were made against this action, then the president would express the view that once programs were "tested and proven in practice" they should be delegated and that, though he felt these two programs were ready for such delegation, that action would be left to the new administration and Congress. The president asked that this be checked out with Congress.[91] White House staff checked the issue with Senator Ralph Yarborough (D–Tex.) and Congressman Carl D. Perkins (D–Ky.), and both recommended that the president not submit either of the reports required by Congress, but that he make a strong statement in support of OEO and the War on Poverty.[92] The president, after requesting conference on some of the language of a report to Congress, ultimately approved statements on the antipoverty program for his final messages that included the following:

> The Economic Opportunity Act has been successfully administered by the Office of Economic Opportunity, and should be extended for two more years.[93]

> The past few years have necessarily involved considerable experimentation. We have had many successes and some failures.[94]

> I believe the Congress this year will want to improve the administration of the poverty program by reorganizing portions of it and transferring them to other agencies.[95]

CONCLUSION

The War on Poverty illustrates the problems of organizing for coordination within the federal executive structure when a novel objective is to be achieved by programs crosscutting established programs in other departments and agencies. It illustrates problems that characterized the administration of Great Society programs in general and the problems that can be anticipated as new programs are instituted in the future.

One issue in organization was whether to place administration within an existing department. Arguments on the advantages of freedom of initiative against those of support from an established organization will recur as vast new programs are undertaken that are somewhat different from those already in place. In this instance there were many special factors that may have influenced the president to choose a person, give him the prestige of the presidency, and allow him to create his own organization.

The choice of this person was the president's most influential decision with respect to the antipoverty program: appointment is the president's most powerful administrative weapon. In the case of OEO, the decision released imagination, energy, and enthusiasm that drove an organization toward goal achievement, but it also resulted in an administrative structure that was questioned repeatedly throughout the Johnson presidency.

Whether support gained by its location within the presidency can be more significant for the success of a new program than support from a department will almost certainly depend upon a variety of factors, but especially significant in this case was the type of function that became central. BOB's opposition to placing operating responsibilities in the Executive Office was not heeded by Shriver as he planned for quick and visible results. As operations crowded out coordination in the daily work of the agency, the advantages of the presidency were lost. OEO thereby became an agency itself, not primarily an aide to the president in guiding and coordinating other agencies.

Similarly, operating responsibilities diverted CAAs from the coordinative task initially set for them. Although their efforts were significant in program development and in stimulating participation by the poor, the opportunities for coordinated planning and action were weakened. Combined with the lack of coordination with local and state governments and of federal field structures, this diversion from core purpose led to serious impairment of a great opportunity to develop coordination at local, state, and regional levels of government.

Within the federal structure, there was an extraordinary development of coordination techniques. The interagency agreement, the arrangements for monitoring action, the checkpoint procedure, the establishment of neighborhood centers, and the development near the end of the Johnson administration of plans for regional decentralization and for common field locations and boundaries for social service programs are cumulatively significant developments in administrative technology. Supplemented by informal cooperation—encouraged by pressure and sometimes by intervention from the White House—and the sharing of purposes, these devices undoubtedly contributed toward coordination. But undoubtedly also there were delays and failures in attainment of the objective.

What does the history of this program show about organizing for coordination at the agency and presidential levels of executive action? It appears that at the agency level coordination suffered not only because subordinate staff were engrossed in operating programs, but also because of the director's lack of attention to administrative coordination and his failure to complement his remarkable and distinctive capabilities in program development with continuing strong administrative direction and interagency coordination from the deputy's office. At the presidential level, the failure of an interagency council to operate successfully deserves special attention. The director seems to have made little effort to make it a strong influence; and, after congressional effort to strengthen it, the president seems to have sensed that it would not be possible to make it effective. Shriver proposed the creation of a domestic NSC, which would have the effect of presidential chairmanship. This kind of structure had other supporters during the Johnson presidency, as we will show in the subsequent chapter on presidential guidance and coordination.

As for Shriver's location in the Executive Office, as the president's special assistant or chief of staff for the antipoverty program, we have seen no evidence that location in the Executive Office made his relations with the president any different from those of an independent (nondepartmental) agency head located outside the office. In either position a person may have a close relationship with and strong support from the president. The evidence does show that advice to the president on antipoverty matters was dispersed among several actors in the subpresidency—particularly Califano, Schultze, and McPherson—as in the case of other programs developed and administered in the Executive branch.

FIVE

REORGANIZATION PLANS
Continuous Adjustment of Structure

By the time of the Johnson administration, reorganization plans were an accepted mode of changing the structure of the executive branch. The authority granted to the president in the Reorganization Act of 1949 to propose reorganization plans had been kept alive, except for brief periods, by statutory extensions. It had expired on 1 June 1963, but Congress granted President Johnson a renewal on 2 July 1964, to extend to 1 June 1965, and on 18 June 1965 it gave a further renewal to 31 December 1968. Johnson, in consequence, possessed the authority of the act for most of his presidency.

Johnson—like Truman, Eisenhower, and Kennedy before him—lost on a recommendation that the authority be granted permanently. Indeed, when the Johnson administration sought an extension of the authority after its lapse during 1963, Senator McClellan (D–Ark.)—who except for two years had chaired the successive Senate committees that had jurisdiction over reorganization plans after 1949—was reluctant to go along, believing that the technique had yielded meager results,[1] and the Congress granted only an eleven-month renewal to 1 June 1965. When Johnson submitted a draft bill for removal of the time limit the next year, the tender feelings of members of Congress on the subject surfaced, and the renewal was again for a limited period.[2]

The reorganization plan procedure reverses the sequence of legislation. It has been called "a genuine problem-solving institution innovation."[3] The president initiates and the houses of Congress possess veto power—either house being able to veto if a majority votes for a resolution of disapproval. The president's position is further strengthened in the act by limitation of the veto period to sixty days and by exclusion of amendments by Congress.[4] Also, the president has been favored by the procedures of the houses, which have assigned reorganization plans to the Government Operations committees or a similar nonprogram committee,[5] thereby circumventing the program committees' biases toward the status quo and against changes that impair their jurisdictions. Yet there is no delegation of legislative power to the president; procedure is altered, but each house retains its powers.

Within the executive branch, the Bureau of the Budget (BOB) coordinates the activity on reorganization plans. These may be initiated within departments or agencies, by the White House, or within the Bureau; but the Bureau ensures their orderly and careful consideration and oversees the preparation of plans. The Bureau's files contain the history of reorganization proposals and lists of reorganizations that might be considered, and its staff can produce analyses of current proposals on short notice. From the Bureau, plans go to the Justice Department for checks on legality, and from there to the White House for its approval on substance and determination of prospects of avoiding disapproval in Congress.

Within Congress the mode of opposing a plan is to introduce a simple resolution of disapproval. Whether or not such a resolution is introduced, a subcommittee of the House Committee on Government Operations will usually hold hearings on the plan, and a corresponding Senate subcommittee may also do so. A program committee with jurisdiction over an affected agency's programs may also hold hearings, but it rarely does. Votes on the plan may or may not be taken in committees or in the houses, and many reorganization plans go into effect without any votes within Congress.

While the adoption, and the grudging renewal for limited periods, of the authorization for reorganization in the act of 1949 indicates Congress's recognition of the need for presidential leadership on structure of the executive branch, the terms of the grant are restrictive. The substance of legislation cannot be changed, and change in directions of policy is not recognized as legal basis for a plan. The legal bases are managerial. The purposes stated in the act include "better execution of the laws," "more effective management," "expeditious administration," to "reduce expenditures," "increase the efficiency," "group, coordinate, and consolidate . . . according to major purpose," "reduce the number of agencies," "eliminate overlapping and duplication"; and the president is required to specify any probable reductions of expenditure. A finding of conformity with one or more of these purposes is included in the presidential message transmitting a plan. The Reorganization Act exempts from its processes the courts, the Comptroller General, the transfer of District of Columbia government or all its functions, and the abolition or transfer of an executive department or all its functions or consolidation of two or more departments or all their functions. The act originally allowed the creation of new departments by reorganization plan, but after Congress rejected a plan submitted by President Kennedy for a department of urban affairs—use of the plan that was political (to out-maneuver the House Rules Committee), not managerial—Congress amended the act to exclude "creating any new executive department."[6]

What, we ask, was the significance of the reorganization plan in the Johnson presidency? Seventeen plans were sent to Congress, and sixteen became effective. One can discern immediately that they dealt with mis-cellaneous subjects. Examination shows that there was no characteristic central policy or management purpose, as there was in the Truman adminis-tration when two management themes advanced in the Hoover commission reports ran through numerous reorganization plans.[7] We have looked at the nature of the reorganization in each of the Johnson plans. Six were internal reorganizations within a department or agency, or in one case within a government (District of Columbia). While one of these involved presidential appointment power (Customs Bureau), one involved arrangements affecting the governing board of an agency (Tariff Commission), and one reorganized government for an area (District of Columbia), the other three were of the kind a department or agency head could have effected if he had been granted complete power to reorganize and delegate functions. Nine of the seventeen plans effected interdepartmental transfer of an agency or function. Two reorganizations abolished agencies. At least one (Water Pollution Control Administration) was regarded by the president's staff aide as significantly related to a specific policy objective of the president. One (District of Colum-bia government) made a major change in the administrative pattern of a government.

Such distinctions indicate that the need for presidential reorganization plans could be reduced by legislation that was less detailed or that vested more authority in agency heads. They also indicate the small utility of reorganization for some of the congressional purposes stated in the Re-organization Act. On the other hand, many of the changes could not have been consummated by processes other than legislation or reorganization plan.

It is readily apparent that many of these reorganizations are minor house-keeping changes in the executive branch. Examples under President Johnson include:

Consolidation of locomotive inspection functions in the Interstate Com-merce Commission.

Elimination of certain interdepartmental committees (though some of these were important).

Abolition of committees of the National Science Foundation.

Transfer of functions relating to construction at the District of Columbia Zoo.

Abolition of the National Capital Regional Planning Council (because of the rise of other agencies).

Transfer of authority to surrender certain documents.

Transfer of certain recreation functions to the commissioner of the District of Columbia.

Transfer of functions with respect to the District of Columbia Redevelopment Land Agency to the commissioner of the District of Columbia.

The authority to make such changes without statutory procedures is not unimportant. In this chapter, however, we discuss only some larger changes that were effected. The discussion is here in part because the changes had some substantive significance. Yet the main purpose is to reveal the ways these changes occur, the extent of the president's participation, the role of the subpresidency, the perspectives of Congress, and the function or utility or reorganization plans in restructuring the executive branch.

CUSTOMS BUREAU

Reorganization Plan 1 of 1965 to abolish fifty-three presidential appointees in field offices of the Customs Bureau of the Treasury Department was Johnson's first reorganization plan.[8] In his State of the Union Message of 4 January the president had stated the administration's intention to "reshape and reorganize the executive branch." Plan 1 was submitted with a presidential statement of traditional management objectives: part of a program "on new economies we are planning to make"; "tightened management controls," making possible nine million dollars savings a year; "a more effective administration of the customs laws."[9] Improved management was an appropriate objective to state, for this was the purpose of the Treasury Department in proposing the plan, and the plan had no relation to any of the president's policy objectives other than good management. It was, moreover, an example of adjustment of organization to conditions and practices of a new period, for the organization to be superseded had been created before the federal income tax, and positions as collectors of customs were prime patronage appointments.

The plan was proposed to aid an internal reorganization of a bureau. Also, it was generated within the Treasury Department. An exhaustive Treasury Department–Bureau survey—conducted under the chairmanship of James H. Stover, director of Treasury's Office of Management and Organization—had culminated in a large report recommending radical structural changes in the bureau. Included in its 230 recommendations for changes at headquarters and field levels was a revision of field structure that would establish 6 regional offices and about 25 subordinate district offices to replace 113 independent field activities reporting directly to headquarters. Such a structure would provide the clear lines of hierarchical authority upward to the director of the bureau that organization theory mandated.

An obstruction to this change was the requirement that the president, with the advice and consent of the Senate, appoint fifty-three officers serving as collector of customs, comptroller of customs, surveyor of customs, and appraiser of merchandise. These officers reported to a director whose status was inferior to theirs in that he was appointed by the secretary of the treasury. Responsibility was divided by the existence of these positions, and their occupancy prevented the development of a corps of technically qualified administrators. The Stover Report recommended their abolition.

While most other parts of the management plan of the Stover Report could be implemented by orders of the secretary or the bureau director, abolition of presidential appointments could be achieved only by statute or reorganization plan. Secretary Conley Dillon pushed vigorously for presidential submission and congressional acceptance of such a plan.

The plan moved expeditiously and in the usual ways through the substructure for presidential operations. Within the Treasury Department the attorneys advised on 18 December 1964 that a reorganization plan would be necessary and also that abolition of the positions could legally be affected by a reorganization plan—an issue raised because of a limitation in the Reorganization Act.[10] The plan and a rationale for it were prepared in the department and sent to BOB on 11 January 1965.[11] The rationale was revised later in the month to show the relation of the abolition of positions to the broader purposes of the anticipated restructuring of the Customs Bureau.

Within BOB there were several concerns. The director of the bureau originally preferred an omnibus submission by the president with an accompanying "Reorganization Message."[12] James Stover prepared an analysis of the experience with a package submittal of three plans by President Truman in 1952 proposing abolition of presidential appointments to field positions. The package was defeated.[13] BOB prepared an analysis of possible objections to the plan.[14] Finally, BOB was concerned, since reorganization orders could not at that time be revised after submission to Congress, that the plan and the president's message transmitting it be carefully prepared and not changed after approval by BOB and by the Department of Justice. Yet in this instance changes were made by White House staff and not cleared again with BOB and Justice, leading Harold Seidman, BOB's director of the Division of Management and Organization, to send a letter of objection to the director of BOB.[15]

As could be expected, the president's participation in a matter of this kind was minimal, but it supplied what was necessary for the result. Dillon had obtained his assent to the concepts before moving to BOB.[16] Recognizing that Johnson would be interested in senators' reactions to proposals for reducing their patronage before determining to send forward a plan, Dillon reported his conversations with senators to the president, then alerted him to the need for help by Lawrence O'Brien, congressional liaison official in the White House, after the plan went to Congress.[17] Dillon's chief concern was to obtain a quick approval from the president, because he feared the Stover Report might be leaked to the press before announcement by the White House.

The president sent the plan to Congress on 25 March 1965. Resolutions of disapproval were introduced by Senator John Pastore (D–R.I.) and Congressman Albert Thomas (D–Tex.), hearings were held in both houses, and a resolution for disapproval was carried by Senator Spessard L. Holland (D–Fla.) to the Senate floor. Arguments pro and con were diverse; and there was, as expected, some support for retaining senatorial confirmation, to provide in the senators—as Senator Holland said—"a buffer between their people and the bureaucracy in Washington." But, surprisingly to sponsors and revealing of the perspectives of congressmen on reorganization, the chief objection to the plan concerned the location of offices. Pastore did not want Providence to be a subport instead of a district office, and Thomas apparently wanted a regional office in Houston, in which his district was situated. Congressman Chet Holifield (D–Calif.), member of the House Committee on Government Operations, wanted a regional office in Los Angeles. The Stover Report recommended a regional office in Baltimore, but Secretary Dillon had substituted Miami in the subsequent plans; the entire Maryland delegation appealed to President Johnson. There was support for other cities. In addition, there was support for changing certain cities from subports to district sites.

Motivations of members of Congress, like those of other persons, are difficult to discern, but efficiency and economy were not the moving forces. This is indicated by an interchange in the Senate Subcommittee on Executive Reorganization on 12 May between Senator Claiborne Pell (D–R.I.) and Secretary Henry Fowler, who replaced Dillon:

> Senator Pell: I wonder if, in connection with this point, since it would have the functions of a district, why an administrative determination could not be made by you to call it [Providence] a district?

> Secretary Fowler: I think we are dealing somewhat here, to a considerable extent, with problems of semantics.

> Senator Pell: And pride.[18]

Neither resolution for disapproval was reported favorably from committee, and Senator Holland's resolution was defeated in the Senate 64 to 17. Victory for the plan was aided by several things. Unlike the case in 1952, the plan went to Congress alone and with assurances that efforts would be made to find jobs for those whose positions were abolished. The decision to present the plan as part of the larger reorganization purpose for the Customs Bureau undoubtedly was necessary for effective consideration and favorable reception. Most important, however, was the willingness of Secretary Fowler to consider congressional viewpoints and to compromise on locations. The New York Times reported on 9 May with respect to the clamor on office locations: "Hoping to calm the furor over reorganization, the Secretary disclosed on Wednesday (May 5) that he had ordered a study of this phase of the plan."[19] And on 22 May the Times reported that Los Angeles, Baltimore, and Houston would be designated regional ports.[20] There were also revisions on districts, with Providence becoming a district.

The reorganization plan in this instance provided a technique for restructuring a bureau to provide, in the judgment of the executive establishment, for improved management. The plan came from a department and was approved by BOB. It had the president's approval, and it was presented to conform to the congressional purpose of economy and efficiency in the act of 1949. The effect of constituency viewpoint, particularly when held by congressmen strategically placed, is apparent; but in this instance the compromises required did not seriously impair the purpose of the plan's proponents.

PUBLIC HEALTH SERVICE

Reorganization Plan 3 of 1966 accomplished an internal transfer of functions from the surgeon general to the secretary of the Department of Health, Education, and Welfare (HEW), accompanied by abolition of existing offices and authorization for reassignment of functions. It conformed with the concept of the first Hoover commission that full authority and responsibility for administration of departments should be vested in the secretaries of departments by transferring to them all statutory authority of subordinates. The practical effect in this instance was escape from rigid statutory prescription of structural detail.

Reorganization Plan 1 of 1953 establishing the Department of Health, Education, and Welfare had left education functions with the commissioner of education and health functions with the surgeon general, who directed the Public Health Service. Moreover, a statute of 1944 prescribed four units of internal structure through which the functions of the Service were to be performed. By 1962 the view prevailed in the Kennedy administration that this structure was rendered obsolete by new and enlarged functions. Revision of the structure by reorganization plan was considered in BOB and the Department of Justice; but legislation, which was not enacted, was proposed instead.[21]

In 1965 and early 1966, BOB, which was committed to the concept of the first Hoover commission, was asking Califano to consider including among reorganization plans one that would transfer the functions of the commissioner of education and the surgeon general to the secretary of HEW.[22] There was some fear that such a plan would be opposed by those who favored creating a separate department of education, since it would lessen their chances of success. Secretary Anthony Celebrezze declined to support such a general reorganization in the 1965 congressional session.[23]

By January 1966 several elements in the situation had become clear. Dr. William H. Stewart, surgeon general of the United States, and a committee chaired by John Corson of Princeton University had reached similar conclusions on the desirable internal structure for the Public Health Service (PHS). While the new secretary of HEW, John Gardner, was toying with ideas for creation of a department of human affairs organized as a "superdepartment" on the Department of Defense pattern, his immediate concern was centered on correcting the organization within PHS. As a result, Douglass Cater of the White House staff reported to the president on 25 January that a meeting of principals revealed a difference of opinion between Gardner, supported by under-secretary Wilbur Cohen, and BOB. Gardner desired a reorganization plan only for PHS, accompanied by legislation on related personnel changes, while BOB wanted to avoid setting a precedent for less than transfer of all departmental functions to the secretary.[24]

This issue was promptly decided in favor of Gardner's position. Immediately, the administration's position was embodied in Cohen's draft of the president's message on domestic health and education, circulated on 2 February. In this message, sent to Congress on 1 March the president said, "I will shortly submit to Congress a proposed reorganization of the health functions" of HEW.[25] The method of reorganization was not stated; but the staff of BOB, alerted by Cohen's draft, began work on a reorganization plan. Charles Schultze, director of BOB, also asked Cohen to get in touch with the appropriate congressional leaders. These and other contacts satisfied Cohen and others of general approval. One change was made in the plan as the result of these contacts—the exemption of the statutory committees of the National Institutes of Health (NIH), as, for example, for heart and cancer. The plan was sent to Congress 1 April; submitted also for Congress's information were the department's plans, based on the Stewart-Corson studies, for bureau organization of PHS.

The plan proposed the transfer of all functions of the surgeon general and PHS, with the exception noted above, to the secretary, authorization to the secretary on a continuing basis to arrange for administration of the functions, and abolition of the existing bureaus within PHS. The plan aroused no substantial opposition within Congress. Hearings were held in both houses, but no resolutions of disapproval were offered. Senator Lister Hill (D–Ala.), a powerful influence on health matters as chairman of the Senate Committee on Labor and Welfare, approved readily. Congressman John E. Fogarty (D–R.I.), influential as chairman of the Labor-HEW subcommittee on the House Appropriations Committee, stated to the House committee his disagreement with the president's concepts on restructuring PHS.[26] Congressman John Erlenborn (R–Ill.), members of the House Committee on Government Operations, accompanied his questions with the explanation that it was desirable to have a "devil's advocate," since the majority party might not ask embarrassing questions.[27] There was some dissatisfaction, from Senator Abraham Ribicoff (D–Conn.) and from private individuals, because a separate bureau on environmental health was not included. The most significant effect of discussions was to reveal the deep interest of members of Congress in the details of organization for health administration, presaging—as Secretary Gardner reported—the need for close cooperation of the department with Congress in implementing the changes.[28]

The escape from rigid statutory prescription was accomplished without the need for active presidential intervention. The subpresidency guided the decision process: Gardner and Cohen from HEW, Schultze from BOB, Cater and Califano as channels of communication to the president, O'Brien reporting on the acceptability of congressional assurances, and the entire process supported by backup assistance from BOB staff, Stewart and the Corson committee, and congressional liaison personnel in the White House and HEW.[29]

DRUG ABUSE AND NARCOTICS

Reorganization Plan 1 of 1968 is a clear illustration of the use of the reorganization plan as a convenient and expeditious means of realigning the structure of the executive branch in response to growth in functions of the national government. In the Harrison Act of 1914 the national government embarked on the control of traffic in narcotics. Punishing crime was traditionally the role of the states, and the commerce clause of the Constitution had been little used as a base for national control over crime. Consequently, a system of control based on the taxing power was constructed, in which controls were attached to a requirement that dealers in narcotics pay an occupational tax. The logical choice for location of enforcement seemed to be the tax-collecting agency. As additional drug control statutes were passed, including the Marihuana Tax Act of 1937, the enforcement of these was also placed in the Treasury. Within the Treasury the primary enforcement functions were placed in a Bureau of Narcotics, though tax collections were made by the Internal Revenue Service and cooperation in import controls was provided by the Bureau of Customs.

In 1965, responding to the immense spread of drug use, Congress extended national legislation to control of dangerous drugs generally, including depressants, stimulants, and hallucinogens such as LSD. The responsibilities under this act were vested in the secretary of HEW and were exercised primarily through a Bureau of Drug Abuse Control, but with research and educational aid provided by other parts of HEW. Thus there came to be two agencies—the Bureau of Narcotics and the Bureau of Drug Abuse Control—for enforcement of drug control statutes, in some cases producing an anomalous situation. "For example," said the president in recommending to Congress consolidation of the two, "more than nine out of ten seizures of LSD made by the Bureau of Drug Abuse Control have also turned up marihuana—but that Bureau has no jurisdiction over marihuana."[30] The consideration of his reorganization plan, particularly in the debates over it in the House of Representatives, showed virtual unanimity that consolidation was desirable.

In the meantime, another development had occurred in national policy. The national government, under the commerce power, had developed a national criminal law, much of which was enforced through the Department of Justice. The department became the nation's primary center for combating organized crime. By the late 1960s there was deep concern over the effective exercise of this function, and also perception that the drug traffic was significant in the expansion of organized crime. As a result of these developments, the location of consolidated drug control functions in the Department of Justice appeared as a solution. On this solution, however, there was disagreement.

The first Hoover commission recommended that the Bureau of Narcotics be transferred from Treasury to Justice. In 1963 a President's Advisory Commission on Narcotic and Drug Abuse recommended that its enforcement functions be transferred to Justice, its regulatory functions to HEW. Then, with the extension of national controls to all dangerous drugs in 1965 and the deep concern over organized crime, the President's Task Force on Crime, reporting at the end of 1967, recommended five kinds of action on drug control, including the transfer of the functions of the Treasury and HEW over drug abuse to Justice.

The initiative for this step seems, however, to have come from HEW and White House staff. A representative of HEW testified that the department had been a prime mover because of "the involvement of organized crime in the trafficking."[31] BOB learned only incidentally at the end of 1967 that transfer of the two bureaus to Justice was under active consideration.[32] It moved in January 1968 to staff work on the proposal, as Califano was reporting to the president on the matter. As could be expected, there was opposition within the Treasury Department. Secretary Fowler took the position that it "would presently be politically inadvisable" to make the change because "the Bureau of Narcotics is known as a hard line enforcement agency, and we should not tamper with this image." Califano concluded that "Fowler does not feel strongly about this and is reflecting memoranda from his own staff, rather than even the Bureau of Narcotics." The Justice Department and the Federal Bureau of Investigation within it had traditionally opposed the transfer to the department of the Bureau of Narcotics, and Fowler reported to the president that Justice preferred consolidation within the Treasury Department. Califano, however, reported to the president that Fowler was in error on this, that the Justice Department preferred transfer to itself, and that both BOB and Justice were working on a reorganization plan. Califano, in detailing these things to the president on 29 January 1968, asked for approval to tell Fowler that his "tentative judgment" was to move the bureaus to Justice, to ask Fowler to hold his people in line until the final decision was made, and to ask BOB to join in reviewing the proposal with congressional committees. The president signified approval.[33]

Califano thus became the instrument for interpreting to the president the positions of the departmental actors, in a situation where lack of communication among these had produced some confusion. The administration's position quickly took shape, and a reorganization plan went to Congress on 7 February 1968. No resolutions of disapproval were introduced in the Senate, and no hearings were held there. In the House two Republican congressmen filed a resolution of disapproval, and after intense probing of administration witnesses, opposition crystallized by the time of debate in the House in favor of the alternative of locating the consolidated functions in the Treasury. The opposition found that the witness from the Treasury Department revealed delayed and unenthusiastic consent for the transfer of the Bureau of Narcotics away from the department and agreed that coordination between that bureau and the Bureau of Drug Abuse Control could be achieved within the Treasury Department. The witnesses from HEW emphasized in the hearings that their support for location in Justice was the "organized criminal elements involved in the trafficking in dangerous drugs," and the same theme ran through the attorney general's statements. The opposition's arguments were less simple. On the one hand, it saw a need for relating enforcement to a broader context of research and education, and in the reorganization plan a lessening of coordination with the research and educational functions of HEW, particularly the Food and Drug Administration, of which the Bureau of Drug Abuse Control was a part, and NIH. In partial response, the administration filed a statement with the committee on the arrangements that would exist for the Department of Justice—which would decide what drugs were "dangerous" and thus within its enforcement responsibility—to use the research capabilities of HEW staff. On the other hand, the opposition stressed the opportunities within the Treasury for coordination with the Bureau of Customs and the Internal Revenue Service. The response from BOB at the hearings was that "one of the facts of organization life is that no matter how we organize . . . problems of coordination of interagency relationship will remain." The opposition also saw disadvantages in combining the regulatory functions in the narcotics area with enforcement, thereby bringing agents of the Department of Justice into the offices of legitimate manufacturers and dealers. The strong record of the Bureau of Narcotics in its existing location was also noted.[34]

The issue was decided by a close vote in the House. The resolution of disapproval was voted down by 200 votes against 190. The opposition to the plan was led by the Republican members of the House Committee on Government Operations, with some support from the persons historically connected with narcotics control functions, such as members of the Ways and Means Committee and the appropriations subcommittee for the Treasury. The members of the Government Operations Committee split in the ballot strictly along party lines.

The most significant revelations of this episode, perhaps, are the promptness with which the White House staff could respond to a task force recommendation and obtain a structural change of importance by approximately three months after the recommendation; the change of structure in response to development of policy, in this instance the administration's attack on organized crime; and the continued necessity of interagency collaboration after reorganization.

FEDERAL WATER POLLUTION CONTROL ADMINISTRATION

Reorganization Plan 2 of 1966 made an uncomplicated shift of an agency from one department to another—a "lock, stock, and barrel" transfer of the Water Pollution Control Administration from HEW to Interior. It followed another organizational change accomplished by statute only a few months before. It reflected a broadening of presidential objectives as these affected water pollution, but with the president himself virtually outside the decision process and consenting reluctantly to Califano's determinations.

Water pollution had only recently become a matter of serious concern to national policy-makers. Basic statutory authority for experimental federal activities was provided in the Federal Water Pollution Control Act of 1948. After being extended to 1956 and then made permanent, the federal program was strengthened and extended in the Federal Water Pollution Act Amendment of 1961 and the Water Quality Act of 1965. As the program had evolved, it included comprehensive, permanent federal activities for prevention and abatement of water pollution by technical and financial assistance to state and local governments, grants to communities for assistance in constructing sewage treatment works, the establishment of water quality standards, the operation of research facilities, and the development of comprehensive river basin programs. The responsibility for administration was centered originally in the surgeon general; but increasingly, particularly in 1961, Congress had enlarged the responsibilities and functions of the secretary of HEW. Then, in the Water Quality Act of 1965, Congress sought to strengthen the administration of water pollution functions by concentrating all operating functions in a new Federal Water Pollution Control Administration, operating under the direction of the secretary, assisted by a new assistant secretary.[35]

The initiatives in these structural changes lay within the Congress, and the president accepted them in signing the act on 5 October. Then, surprisingly to many in Congress, a new idea, not a subject of deliberation in creation of the new pollution control administration, surfaced in the White House in December. As a result of a request by Elmer Staats in BOB, arising from an oral inquiry by Gardner Ackley of the Council of Economic Advisers, an analysis of the issue of transfer to Interior was presented in BOB on 17 December, with a conclusion, however, by the person who made the study that HEW was better prepared than Interior to exercise effective control and that HEW "should be permitted full opportunity to proceed under its new authority."[36]

The idea was also opposed or questioned at higher levels. Schultze laid before the president his "serious reservations," outlining at length six reasons: public health was a major rationale for enforcement; fragmentation by separation from certain other functions affecting health; conflict of interest between water pollution control and certain functions of Interior; weakening of research on the health aspects; conflict with the administration's position in failing through three sessions of Congress to make a serious move toward transfer to Interior; loss of momentum in control of water pollution.[37] Secretary Gardner had stated to Califano the problems posed by a transfer but stated that he would not object if the president favored the transfer.[38] But the strong opposition came from Senator Edmund Muskie (D–Maine), who had been prominent in gaining passage of the Water Quality Act. In a long letter to Secretary Stewart Udall, Department of Interior, he stated his position that, though the evolution of present policies might lead to new answers on organization, the time was not "now." There would be disruption and delay in implementing the changes Congress had just enacted. Moreover, he had given assurances to critics that the move out of the Public Health Service was not "an interim step on the way to the Department of Interior."[39]

But the idea was persistently supported by Udall and Califano. It was

119

presented to the president on 14 January by Califano, when transmitting Schultze's reservations. Califano said, "I think Interior and Udall are the right people to take water pollution at this point especially with your program to attack water pollution on river basin basis." Yet the president was told that decision could await Lee White's "soundings on the Hill."[40]

The record shows five replies by the president. In a memorandum reporting the reasons for Muskie's opposition, White said Muskie would discuss it with other people and report to him. The president marked, "OK."[41] In a later memo to the president, White reported the continuance of Muskie's opposition and advised that an effort be made to get the new HEW organization off to a good start and to try during the following year to build support for a transfer. The president marked the "approve" blank and added, "subject to your getting Joe C. to approve."[42] The president then approved suggestions from Califano that the change be included as part of the river basin plan in the forthcoming pollution message and that Udall bring Muskie around on their forthcoming trip to Germany.[43]

The next two replies illustrate a president's need to rely on the presidential substructure for managerial matters and the possibility that staff operations will skip beyond advice to decision. On 18 February Califano summarized Muskie's objections for the president, restated his support for the transfer, and suggested that, "While you have already approved the move of the Water Pollution Administration to Interior," Muskie's potency as an adversary was a problem. He asked whether the president wanted to see Muskie or whether he should do so. The president wrote on the memo: "Joe—I can't spend my year on these matters. I wouldn't start something I couldn't pass. I agree on Muskie. If Udall can't convert him then too bad."[44] Eight days later—after the president had sent a message to Congress proposing a clean rivers demonstration program and stating that he would soon send a reorganization plan to transfer the Water Pollution Control Administration to Interior—Califano sent the proposed plan to the president for his signature, with the accompanying message. The president now wrote two notes: "This needs some good editing but I find it is too late." "Joe. I'm acting against my judgment without knowledge as to Committee votes but I'll ride with you on this one. Let's go over these 2 or 3 days in advance and get Larry's certification that we are OK with votes before moving on other legislation."[45]

The plan went to Congress 28 February two months after the effective date of the Water Quality Control Act, the president stating that "It should be carried forward as an integral part of comprehensive planning for the development of river basins."[46] A relatively small amount of interest in the plan was generated outside the government. This was probably due to the extensive airing of the issues over transfer of the pollution functions from

PHS to the new administration in the preceding year and to the acceptance of defeat by those who favored retaining pollution control in the health agency. The substantial opposition of state health departments and other state interests to transfer to Interior that had been present in preceding years did not appear in 1966. Moreover, the act of 1965 had settled the issue of rights for commissioned officers of PHS whose functions were transferred, giving them the option of transfer and accepting the status and benefits of the general Civil Service.[47]

Within Congress, all the questions raised by BOB and by Gardner in Executive Office consideration surfaced in committee hearings. These were held first on 30 March in the House in a subcommittee of the Committee on Government Operations.[48] Secretary Udall and James M. Quigley, commissioner for the new Water Pollution Control Administration, carried the burden of presenting the case for the plan. Udall emphasized the need to unite the functions of conservation and use with pollution control and sought to answer the fears of dominance of other interests over health in an Interior operation, particularly emphasizing his own devotion to pollution control. With full loyalty to the president, Secretary Gardner—despite reservations expressed earlier—and Harold Seidman of BOB—despite BOB's initial opposition—supported the plan. Seidman sought to placate the fears that too little attention would be given to health in pollution administration by pointing out that new coordinating arrangements would undoubtedly be made, now at the presidential level, in place of the secretarial ones. He even, in response to questions, saw economies in the move. Hearings in the House were renewed on 4 May as a result of a resolution of disapproval of the plan submitted by Congressman James C. Cleveland (R–N.H.) of the Public Works Committee. Congressman Cleveland noted that his attention was directed to the plan by a *New York Times* article that suggested that the battle against pollution was imperiled by the threat of exodus of public service personnel who feared that fish and wildlife interests would predominate over health; but he stressed the premature nature of the proposal for transfer, following so closely on the heels of exhaustive consideration of organization in 1965.

Hearings were held in the Senate on 6 and 7 April with Senators Ribicoff, Joseph S. Clark (D–Pa.), Ernest Gruening (D–Alaska), and Muskie probing deeply and reflecting concern over coordination with health functions in HEW, and with Muskie still opposed to the loss of momentum and delay in transfer of administration so soon after new concepts had been initiated.

But the plan was not rejected. Congressman Cleveland's resolution of disapproval was reported by the House committee on 5 May, but no action was taken on it.

With respect to presidential participation in decisions on administrative

121

structure, the details of this episode are revealing. The president was committed to policies of pollution control and specifically to the river basin approach.[49] Yet he could not spend *his* time on important issues of administrative structure to implement these policies. On issues of execution of policy, he was dependent on the subpresidency. Illustrated, in addition, was President Johnson's usual insistence on prospects of success. He wanted no defeats, and his persistent requirement of staff work was that it ensure that none occurred. In this instance, the president seemed less concerned with staff position on policy implementation than with loss of strategic position.

COMMUNITY RELATIONS SERVICE

Reorganization Plan 1 of 1966 transferring the Community Relations Service (CRS) from the Department of Commerce to the Department of Justice did not follow the pattern of BOB analysis and recommendation that normally characterizes reorganization plans. Staff work centered in the Department of Justice. Moreover, while the transfer of CRS itself was comparable in significance to other interdepartmental transfers discussed here, it reflected and was part of a large and encompassing restructuring for effectiveness in civil rights administration.

By 1964 the functions in enforcement of civil rights legislation were vested in various departments and agencies, with some coordination provided by a set of committees created by presidential action. There were two creations by statute in 1957—the Commission on Civil Rights and the Civil Rights Division of the Department of Justice—and two additions in the Civil Rights Act of 1964—the Equal Employment Opportunities Commission and the Community Relations Service. Beyond these, the various agencies administering grant, loan, and contract provisions were vested with responsibility for preventing discrimination by section VI of the Civil Rights Act of 1964.

A President's Committee on Equal Employment Opportunity, created by executive order in 1961 and chaired by the vice-president, had governmentwide jurisdiction to prevent discrimination in employment in government, by federal contractors and subcontractors, and in employment in construction financed totally or in part by federal grants. Two additional committees created by President Kennedy were the President's Committee on Equal Opportunity in Housing, whose duties overlapped with those of CRS, and the President's Committee on Equal Opportunity in the Armed Services. There was finally a Subcabinet Committee on Civil Rights that brought a large group of officials together in monthly discussions.

Structuring for improved coordination of civil rights enforcement took place in two phases under President Johnson, each of which represented different but frequently used management methods. Immediately after the election of 1964 the president asked Vice-President-Elect Hubert Humphrey "to consider how best we should coordinate the functions of the various federal agencies in the area of civil rights." He said, with respect to coordination, "I would like for you to take it on."[50]

The president also talked with Nicholas Katzenbach, then acting attorney general, requesting that he consult with Humphrey on the matter. Katzenbach prepared for Humphrey a long summary of the responsibilities of the several agencies. Katzenbach supported the idea of making the vice-president the focal point of policy in this area.[51]

After extensive conversations with federal officials and with representatives of state and local governments and of private organizations, Humphrey recommended to the president the "establishment by Executive Order of a President's Council on Equal Opportunity, composed of the highest level representatives of those departments and agencies most directly involved in the civil rights field, and chaired by the Vice President." By executive order on 5 February 1965, the president created the recommended council. His letter to Humphrey had an air of tentativeness, for the vice-president was told, "as we gain experience" in implementing the civil rights program, "I trust you will make such suggestions and recommendations for changes and improvements as occur to you."[52] It has been stated that the president created the council "with considerable reluctance and indicated to the Vice President that it was to be a temporary body."[53]

The council itself was not an operating agency, and the chief instrument through which the vice-president could exert influence was the President's Committee on Equal Employment Opportunity, which through investigative units in the several departments could determine noncompliance with equal employment requirements for government contractors. The committee's aggressiveness antagonized opponents of vigorous enforcement of civil rights legislation, who sought to cripple it by trimming its funds from other agencies' appropriations. In a struggle with the Senate Appropriations Committee, the vice-president had been able to arrange a moratorium on fund-cutting.[54] Within the administration, consideration of changes in the council system were considered, such as the transfer of functions of a Committee on Government Employment, relating to government employees, to the Civil Service Commission, or the transfer of all its functions to the council.[55]

The administration moved instead to abolish the council and to coordinate through key departments or agencies. It was reported to the president that "by and large, interagency groups are not nearly as effective as the traditional departments with considerable strength and muscle behind

123

them."[56] In line with this idea, two executive orders reassigned responsibilities previously vested in the President's Committee on Equal Employment Opportunity and the President's Council on Equal Opportunity. One order "placed responsibility for the Government-wide coordination of the enforcement activities of executive agencies in the Secretary of Labor with respect to employment by Federal contractors and in the Civil Service Commission with respect to employment by Federal agencies." The other "directed the Attorney General to assist Federal agencies in coordinating their enforcement activities with respect to Title VI of the Civil Rights Act of 1964, which prohibits discrimination in federally assisted programs."[57] A third change, requiring a reorganization plan or legislation, was the transfer of CRS.

The processes through which changes were effected reflect the significant role of the attorney general, the willingness of the vice-president to concur, the smoothness of White House operations, and the political acumen of the president. The steps were as follows: (1) preparation of suggested consolidations in authority by the attorney general, assembled without the knowledge of the vice-president and without the usual staff work in BOB; (2) a conference of the president with the attorney general, Califano, and White; (3) a conference with the vice-president to present the changes and give him the face-saving opportunity to formally propose them; (4) transmission by the vice-president to the president of the proposed changes; and (5) two executive orders and a decision for a reorganization plan. From a staff report to the president outlining these processes,[58] through the conferences in the president's office and the formal submission by the vice-president, to the delivery of executive orders to the president from the attorney general, only four days passed—20 to 24 September—and a new system of coordination was inaugurated.

While the transfer of CRS was not a part of the settlement on the functions of the President's Committee on Equal Employment Opportunity and the abolition of the council, it conformed with the philosophy that justified those changes. With the Department of Justice receiving the coordinative functions with respect to title VI, it was logical to extend its responsibilities to CRS, whose activity was linked to other agencies.

The function of the agency was "to provide assistance to communities and persons therein in resolving disputes, disagreements, or difficulties relating to discriminatory practices based on race, color or national origin."[59] This mediatory function had its own independent history. Senator Lyndon Johnson had favored provision for such a function in 1957, and President Kennedy included it in his recommendations for civil rights legislation in 1963. It was taken out of the civil rights bill in 1964 by the House committee but reinstated by House vote. The provision was restored because no sanction was provided for the public accommodations section of the bill and hence persuasion and mediation appeared attractive, if not essential. Some congressmen thought it should be an independent agency; but apparently several factors influenced its placement in Commerce: the reference of the section to the Committee on Interstate and Foreign Commerce, the ability of a department to provide service functions for it, and a statement in a Department of Justice submission to Congress on the civil rights bill of 1964 that "a mediating agency, separate from the Department of Justice whose duties are chiefly investigation and litigation, would be preferable" to location in that department.

At a press conference arranged to explain the organizational changes, attention was focused on CRS by questions from correspondent Sarah McClendon. The vice-president defended the transfer of CRS to Justice. Although the original purpose was not as important because of sanctions added and greater acceptance for the public accommodations section than had been anticipated, its relations to the functions of the Department of Justice were emphasized, which also sought solutions to disputes. CRS could perform a kind of middle function, coming into the picture to support an agency such as the Office of Education before initiation of enforcement proceedings.[60]

Nearly two months after the press announcement of the proposal, it was reported in BOB that "no staff work has been done" on the draft reorganization plan for CRS. Nevertheless, the bureau did identify several defects in the draft as well as in the message for the plan and obtained some revisions.[61] Thus, the bureau was able to assert its guardianship over the ultimate form of the proposed change.

Both before and after submission to Congress, additional objections were raised to the plan. McClendon's objection that a mediatory function did not belong in the agency of prosecution was the prime one. Further, since the statute provided that conciliation services should be conducted in confidence, the question was raised how this could be ensured within the enforcement agency. Some thought the function of the agency was being downgraded; on the other hand, Senator Sam Ervin (D–N.C.) expressed to the president the southern opposition, stating that they "had excellent relations with and complete confidence in the Department of Commerce."[62] There was some anticipation of objection by civil rights organizations; but this did not materialize, probably because of the president's persuasiveness in a White House conference with civil rights leaders.[63] The president promoted Roger W. Wilkins, nephew of NAACP executive director Roy Wilkins, to be director of CRS, and he strongly supported the transfer during congressional committee consideration.[64]

Katzenbach, Wilkins, and White House staff sought to maintain a Democratic majority in Congress against a Republican-southern coalition. In the House, resolutions for disapproval were introduced by Congressman

125

Robert P. Griffin (R–Mich.) and twelve other Republicans. The Republican policy committee supported their position.[65] Southern opposition reflected antagonism to connection and possible blending of mediation with enforcement activity. In the Government Operations Committee the vote against these resolutions was twenty to twelve—the twenty all Democrats, and eleven of the twelve Republicans. One southern Democrat voted with the Republicans and another obliged the administration by being absent.[66] In the Senate committee opposition was strongly argued by a Republican and a Democratic senator (Javits, R–N.Y., and Philip A. Hart, D–Mich.), both favorable to strong civil rights enforcement, and Senator Ervin's letter to the president was put in the record. On the committee vote on a resolution of disapproval the administration won by eight Democrats voting against four Republicans and two southern Democrats (Senator Hart was not a member of the committee).

In a two-hour debate in the House the arguments on independence and objectivity, and on confidentiality, were repeated; a report to the president said that five to ten Republican votes would be obtained and that the Deep South would be lost.[67] With more support than was expected, the House upheld the administration by a vote of 220 to 163. In the Senate, with similar alignment, the reorganization plan won by a 42 to 32 vote against the resolution of disapproval.[68]

In the transfer of CRS the reorganization plan was used to fit a piece of structure into a larger pattern of organization being developed. The reorganization was achieved by the active participation of the president, the collaboration of the subpresidency, and party support within the Congress.

URBAN MASS TRANSIT

Definition of the respective responsibilities of two departments in implementing major government policies was the purpose of Reorganization Plan 2 of 1968. The development of the plan strikingly exemplifies how the professional service and the pressure of the subpresidency can achieve a solution to a problem and lower demands on the president and Congress.

The background that led to the requirement for decisions on organizational responsibilities lay in two strands of legislative policy. In extension of policies enacted early in the Kennedy administration, the Urban Mass Transportation Act of 1964 provided for grants and loans to states and local public bodies and agencies for improving mass transportation service and for a modest program of research, planning, and training fellowships toward the same objective, a program with projected expenditures for fiscal year 1968 of $139 million. An older strand of policy was embodied in the construction of the interstate highway and urban freeway systems.

The plans for the creation of a department of transportation called for administration of the highway construction funds in that department. As for the Urban Mass Transportation program, Secretary Robert Weaver stated that it had gone into HUD's predecessor agency "simply by a fluke" in 1961, when it was initiated, and had remained there by accident in later legislation.[69] Alan S. Boyd, who was responsible for developing the proposal for a department of transportation and was later to be its first secretary, felt "strongly" that the urban mass transportation program should be integrated with the highway development programs in the Department of Transportation (DOT) bill shortly to be proposed.[70] Robert C. Wood, under secretary of HUD, has said that "Charlie Haar and I noted this, suggested to Califano that we wait a year, and wait to see if DOT was in fact established before we upset the troops. And Joe and the President agreed."[71] In the meantime a task force study had shown the complexities of the problem and suggested ways both departments could participate in mass transportation activities. The jurisdictional conflict was suspended at this stage by the president's message proposing creation of DOT, which stated the need for cooperation of the two departments and his purpose to ask the two secretaries to recommend to him "within a year after the creation of the new department, the means and procedures by which this cooperation can best be achieved—not only in principle, but in practical effect."[72] The act creating the department provided for such a report on the location of urban mass transportation functions to be made to the president and Congress within a year and, anticipating responsibilities for both departments, for joint annual reports.[73]

The deliberations then moved into a second stage. Promptly after the establishment of DOT on 1 April 1967, Boyd, secretary of DOT, initiated discussions with Weaver, secretary of HUD. Each appointed representatives to a task force, but numerous meetings produced no agreement on location of urban mass transportation functions. In this situation, pressure on the two secretaries was exerted from the White House, in the form of a memo from Califano asking for a report by 1 October.[74] But a meeting of the secretaries produced only continued disagreement, and BOB completed a thorough analysis of the alternatives of locating the functions in DOT or HUD. This professional report recommended location in DOT.[75] After this, Califano gave the president a long report on the arguments for both locations and concluded that he and Schultze concurred with Boyd on the "merits of the issue" and that Weaver had said "he would go along." The president signified approval by his check mark.[76]

The discussions now moved to difficult issues of interdepartmental relationships, with much firmness of position on both sides and some emotionalism among participants. The negotiations were between the two secretaries, assisted by their top aides, with a high official of BOB mediating the conflict as he developed the reorganization language. Weaver and

Wood, having lost the battle against unification of project assistance for urban mass transport with other transportation functions, wanted to retain the position of HUD as the lead agency in planning related to broad urban development objectives. Boyd agreed in principle and even agreed on the desirability of strengthening HUD's ability to achieve comprehensive community planning. The importance of HUD's use of mass transportation project funds as a means of forcing broad community planning had surfaced early in the discussions ("the tail wagging the dog"), and Boyd was willing to agree to cooperate through transfer of funds to communities selected by HUD for comprehensive planning. Weaver, however, wanted some reassertion to Congress of HUD's leadership in urban planning, and it was agreed that Wood would prepare wording for the president's message to emphasize HUD's responsibilities in urban affairs.[77]

The sticky point in the negotiations was the role of HUD in determining, before approval of grants by DOT for urban mass transportation projects, whether the grants as required by the Urban Mass Transportation Act, were part of a "coordinated urban transportation system as a part of a comprehensively planned development of the urban area," and in determining criteria for such grants. The major issue was one of procedure. HUD wanted its position safeguarded through legislation, but DOT wanted it to be worked out through a memorandum of agreement. HUD even wanted the same role in determinations for highway construction, which was not covered in the Urban Mass Transportation Act; but Boyd objected that this would trigger opposition among highway interests.[78] Two weeks before the plan went to Congress HUD proposed that it include provision for determination by HUD of the adequacy of urban mass transportation programs as part of comprehensive planned urban development.[79]

The mediated position, as it went to Congress, contained in the president's message assertion of HUD's leadership in "comprehensive planning at the local level that includes transportation planning and relates it to broader urban development objectives." The plan, while providing for transfer of urban mass transportation functions to DOT, reserved to the secretary of HUD authority under the Urban Mass Transportation Act for research, demonstration, and technical studies on the relationship of urban transportation systems to overall urban development; the role of *advising* and *assisting* the secretary of DOT in determining on a project basis whether the requirements for coordination with comprehensive urban planning in the act were met; and the further role of establishing jointly with the secretary of DOT the criteria for such determinations. The details of a memorandum of agreement were still being worked out when the plan was sent to Congress, and Boyd gave assurances in House committee hearings that the secretary of HUD's negative findings on a project's conformity with the requirements of the Urban Transportation Act would be accepted. With this kind of adjustment of positions, Boyd, Wood, and Phillip S. Hughes from BOB were able to present a united front to the committee in favor of the plan.

These three, appearing jointly, were the only witnesses before a sub-committee of the House Committee on Government Operations. No reso-lutions of disapproval were introduced, and no hearings were held in the Senate. In statements filed with the House subcommittee, the National League of Cities and the National Association of Counties endorsed the plan and the United States Conference of Mayors declined to take a position. In the hearings Congressman Benjamin Rosenthal (D–N.Y.) forcefully pressed the concern that Weaver and Wood had had in the tense deliberations. "It is," he said, "a question of philosophy and mission." "I am worried that the type of urbanologists that reside in HUD do not at the moment reside in your [Boyd's] Department." He thought advisory functions for HUD in project determinations would produce a "dance" "for six months to a year, and after that it will be over." His persistence got on the record the emphatic commitment by Boyd that the memorandum of agreement would include a provision for veto by HUD.[80]

The only other significant expressions of concern came from Senator Jacob Javits (R–N.Y.) and Congressman Wright Patman (D–Tex.). Javits's questions were answered jointly by the two secretaries.[81] Congressman Patman, chairman of the House Banking and Currency Committee, joined by two of his colleagues, wrote to the president imploring reconsideration of a "shortsighted and misguided proposal" that would take jurisdiction away from the Banking and Currency Committee and its Subcommittee on Housing that had served with pride on previous urban mass transport legis-lation.[82]

The course of events described above is potent evidence of the utility of conditional delegation of legislative power, as represented in the Re-organization Act. The issue under discussion was not a simple one of loca-tion of primary responsibility, but a difficult issue of interlocking re-sponsibilities. It would have been very cumbersome for Congress to deal with and unavoidably time-consuming for committee members. In the executive branch the institutional mechanisms operated to reduce the need for presidential attention. Except for one moment of presidential decision, made easier by adequate staff work in BOB and Califano's office, the mech-anisms of the subpresidency produced the professional competence and the pressures on the secretaries that, in effect, made the decisions.

DISTRICT OF COLUMBIA

Reform of the government of the District of Columbia was a major objective of President Johnson. Among his purposes were home rule for the residents of the district and the improvement of the machinery of government to strengthen the administration of Great Society programs. A long and hard-fought battle for the first of these was lost, but the second goal was achieved through a major reorganization and subsequent minor changes, accomplished mainly through reorganization plans.

The major success was Reorganization Plan 3 of 1967. It was the middle path among three lines of reform that were considered before and during the Johnson presidency. One was home rule—a transfer of political power, with limitations, from Congress and its committees, and the president, to the adult residents of the district. Another was rearrangement of numerous administrative functions within the framework of the existing commission system of city government. The middle path proposed in Reorganization Plan 3 was to abandon that system through separation of policy and administrative functions and unification of the latter—to adopt what was in effect a council-mayor system with the president appointing the occupants of the two types of positions created. This was a substantial reformation at the top level of municipal structure, designed to improve performance of both policy and executive functions. It was followed by two other reorganization plans and an executive order relocating designated functions.

The problem of reorganization was the result of certain features inherent in the organic act for the district passed in 1878 and other features developed thereafter. The act itself had two features. First, it confirmed the withdrawal of all citizen participation through election of public officials. By acts beginning in 1871, Congress had abolished the substantial elements of self-government in the district that had existed since the creation of the first government of the City of Washington in 1802. Second, it established a commission system of government in which certain functions were placed in a three-person commission and other functions, chiefly administrative, were vested in the commissioners individually. Two of the commissioners were appointed by the president with the advice and consent of the Senate, and the third, the engineer commissioner, was detailed by the president from the Corps of Engineers. A third feature of the government developed over subsequent years: the establishment of boards and commissions more or less independent of the Board of Commissioners, though individual commissioners served on many of these. By 1952 the administration of district government was diffused among numerous separate offices and agencies, large or small, with varying arrangements for independence from or dependence on the board or its members. A fourth feature was intimate control of district government by Congress, through legislation, annual appropriations, and intervention of committees.

The commission system, for which Reorganization Plan 3 sought replacement, was described by Everett M. Dirksen (R–Ill.), while he was chairman of the House Committee on the District of Columbia, as "a crazy quilt pattern poorly suited to the requirements of modern municipal government." It provided "no clear separation of legislative and executive functions which students of municipal government consider essential."[83] In various studies between 1929 and 1939, professionals in public administration recommended abandonment of the system, and the Bureau of the Budget proposed a reorganization plan in 1952 that included establishment of a council-manager system.

But before a change from the commission system would be adopted as presidential policy, the other two lines of reform would be pursued. Rejecting BOB's proposal, President Truman achieved through Reorganization Plan 5 of 1952 the transfer of the functions of ninety-five boards, offices, departments, divisions, or committees to the Board of Commissioners and authorization, with some limitations, for the board to make provision for the performance of these functions.[84] Pursuant to this authorization the board issued some sixty orders creating a new organizational structure for operation under the commission system. The board's authorization to make further changes was terminated by a rider on the 1954 District Appropriations Act. Although substantial consolidations had been achieved, subsequent reorganizations could be achieved by the board only with ratification through the appropriations process. Thus the District of Columbia was governed without elective participation of residents, under a system of government that had been abandoned by most cities in the country[85] and with rigid control by Congress through statutory prescriptions of boards, committees, and other details of organization that could be modified only with congressional approval.

The solution of President Kennedy and President Johnson to the problem of district government was home rule for the residents on district matters. A modern movement for restoration of self-government in the district had been initiated in 1947 by House Resolution 228 for study of home rule and had been sustained by bills in both houses in every Congress thereafter; in the wake of this development President Kennedy proposed to Congress in the summer of 1961 that government in the district be by an elected mayor and an elected seven-man council. Bills were introduced in both houses in the 87th and 88th congresses, 1961–65, and hearings were held by committees in both houses. Such bills were a challenge to the power of congressmen occupying strategic positions on district affairs. Nevertheless, fresh from his electoral victory, President Johnson, on 2 February 1965, sent Congress a message and an administration bill proposing the "restoration of home rule." The bill, with no radical changes, passed the Senate on 22 July with a comfortable 63 to 29 majority, yet history was to be repeated. Five times earlier the Senate had passed a home rule bill only to have it die in the hostile House District of

131

Columbia Committee. This time the Senate measure was brought to the House floor by a discharge petition, which led the president to issue a statement announcing that "the time of fulfillment is at hand."[86] The House, however, voted to substitute and passed a very different bill. The Senate asked for appointment of a conference committee, but the House District Committee on 11 May 1966 voted against conference, and House conferees were never appointed.[87]

The administration bill raised many issues, particularly an issue on federal payments to district budgets, but the basic causes of its failure were cited frankly in a letter to a high-school student from the White House aide most familiar with the struggle: "I suppose that, generally speaking, the problems are two: the reluctance of a few members, particularly in the House, to relinquish their power to govern the affairs of the District and the reluctance, particularly of Southern members of the House, to contemplate a District government of which many persons would be negroes, since they form about sixty percent of the District's population."[88]

Near the end of 1966 the president was being pressed by organizations outside the government to continue the battle for home rule.[89] Charles Horsky, the presidential aide responsible for advice on district affairs, reporting to Califano on 14 November 1966 on a legislative program for 1967 for the district, listed home rule as item 1 and said he saw "no reason to modify radically" the administration's proposals. Nevertheless, attention was also being given to a reorganization that did not involve home rule and could be achieved without legislation. As early as 1964 a BOB study had recommended that the confusion of legislative and executive functions be ameliorated by delegation by the Board of Commissioners of all its executive responsibility to the president of the board, though such action was not to be a substitute for home rule.[90]

In the spring of 1966 there was consideration of accomplishing the objective through a reorganization plan. In considering whether to move forward with appointing an engineer commissioner, Horsky had discussed reorganization in a meeting with several BOB officials. With Seidman reporting complaints from Congress that too many reorganization plans were being submitted, and with fear that such a proposal would be construed as abandonment of home rule, there was consensus that a new engineer commissioner should be appointed.[91] By November, however, when home rule had failed and the view had developed that reorganization could be pursued without abandoning home rule as the ultimate objective, Horsky and BOB officials were focusing attention on a reorganization plan. On 16 November the president approved Horsky's request for preparation of draft plans.[92] After this, Califano, James C. Gaither, and Horsky from the White House staff and officials of BOB decided to constitute an internal task force, with

Horsky as chairman, to prepare a reorganization plan. Reorganization was recommended to the president and accepted by him. In a special message on 27 February 1967, President Johnson again endorsed home rule and urged the current Congress to adopt it. But, apparently without hope for prompt grant of home rule, he stated that he would "shortly transmit" a reorganization proposal for a mayor-council form of government in which "the President, subject to Senate confirmation, would appoint from among District residents a single Commissioner as chief executive and a council of nine members."[93]

It was to be expected that this announcement would encounter pockets of opposition. Since a reorganization plan would be referred to the Government Operations Committee in the House, it would be viewed as a ploy to escape full consideration by the House District Committee, especially by those members who were anxious to maintain control over district matters and whose opposition had been overcome in the earlier instance by a discharge petition. It was obvious that ten appointments from among district residents would include a number of blacks.

The usual canvass of committee members in Congress before submission of proposals had revealed, however, no definite opposition, and general approval.[94] The president seemed surprised, therefore, when Lawrence O'Brien advised him after the February message not to send up the plan because it would not have a chance.[95] The president referred O'Brien's communication to Califano, with a note: "They told me they checked the committee out—get on it and stay on it."[96] Submission of the plan was delayed to allow extensive rechecks with key members of Congress, including members of the two Government Operations committees and the House District Committee. The extent of this consultation, at the direction and with the participation of the president himself, is reviewed in the remarks of Congressman Frank Horton (R–N.Y.), a supporter of the plan:

> I might also say this—in connection with informing the members of the District of Columbia Committee, Mr. Pollak, who is a special assistant to the President in connection with District matters, I understand, and I have heard it stated and never heard it denied, that Mr. Pollak, before this plan was submitted, at the direction of the President, did talk with every member of the District of Columbia Committee to explain what was in mind, and to get their views. This was done over a period of 4 months, at least, talking individually with members of the District Committee on the House side.
>
> I know he talked with me sometime in February or March with regard to this.
>
> Then there were changes made as a result of some of the comments made by members of the committee. Then subsequent to that, there was

an opportunity for the leadership of the District Committee to meet and talk with Mr. Pollak and others who were interested in the reorganization plan, to get their additional views.

There were changes brought about as a result of those meetings. Then Mr. Pollak, as I understand it—and others can testify to this—but I understood he met before the Senate and he has just recently this past week met before the District Committee in executive session to go over in detail the actual written provisions and details of the plan with the members of the District Committee.

In addition to that, before the plan was sent up, the President invited all members—I attended myself—to a meeting at the White House, at which the President was present, and talked again about this, so everyone had an opportunity to talk about it, in general terms, at least.[97]

The consultations resulted in changes in the details of the draft plan, and some, such as provision for a veto power for the commissioner, were substantial. At a meeting with the House District Committee on 2 May, two changes were suggested.[98] One, to change the terms of council members from two years to three-year staggered terms, was accepted by the president's counselors. Another, to delete the requirement for three-year residence for appointment as commissioner, raised serious questions. While members of the committee argued that such a provision was unusual for council-manager systems and would unnecessarily limit the president's choice, the president's advisers readily recognized that this might be regarded by black supporters of the plan as a device to avoid appointing a black resident commissioner. The plan finally submitted provided for a commissioner and an assistant, one of whom would meet a requirement of three-year residence in the district.

Reorganization Plan 3 was finally submitted on 1 June 1967.[99] In the message of transmittal, the president declared that the commission plan was "obsolete" and that the district could "no longer afford divided executive authority." He said that "we must continue to work toward that day" when home rule would become a reality, but it seemed obvious that Reorganization Plan 3 was a present substitute for a further fight for home rule.

Hearings on the plan were held promptly by a subcommittee of the House Government Operations Committee, and hearings were also promptly held on this and other proposals by a subcommittee of the House District of Columbia Committee. The attack on the plan largely circumvented the provisions of the plan itself. Two kinds of objection were prominent. One was on its constitutionality and legality. Those who saw in the plan a diversion of power from the Congress to the president relied on the constitutional provision that Congress should have "exclusive jurisdiction" over the district to be created. The president in his message sought to answer this objection by stating that the plan would not "in any way detract from the powers which the Congress exercises with respect to the District." The legality issue had been raised and answered by the attorney general in deliberations in the Executive Office; the issue was whether a provision of the Reorganization Act of 1949 that prohibited abolition of the district government was violated by the substantial change in the plan. The other objection emphasized the balances favorable to the president in reorganization plans. Reorganization plans cannot be amended in Congress, and hence the opposition argued that it should have been submitted in the form of a bill. This, in addition, would have transferred jurisdiction from the House Government Operations Committee to the District of Columbia Committee.

A bill identical with the plan was introduced by Congressman Ancher Nelson (R–Minn.), ranking minority member of the District of Columbia Committee. Also, disapproval resolutions were introduced by Congressman John L. McMillan (D–S.C.), chairman of the committee, and Congressman Joel T. Broyhill, Republican member of the committee representing Virginia. Nevertheless, the Government Operations Subcommittee voted favorably on the plan, 11 to 2, as did the full committee, 26 to 4. The plan survived in the House vote by a margin of 244 to 160. It had not been seriously challenged in the Senate.

Except for certain business organizations, the plan had received general support from groups within the District of Columbia, and it had strong support from the *Washington Post* and the *Washington Star*. Also, on occasion the president intervened personally in support of the plan, as he had previously done on home rule. "Get on it and stay on it" was his word to Califano. Moreover, the president met in the White House with members of the House District Committee. On 11 July while the plan was being considered in Congress, he made a supplemental statement in its support. Interestingly, as an illustration of the president's attention to detail and alertness to opportunities, his response on reading an editorial in the *Washington Post* revealing the ways Congressman McMillan used his influence in district affairs, was an instruction to "Joe" (Califano) to "get some citizen in town to send this to every member of Congress."[100]

Reorganization Plan 3 was the most significant plan proposed during the Johnson administration, and its success demonstrates the potential for significant change in organization through this device. A change in the basic structure of city government became effective two and one-third months after the plan was presented to Congress. The processes of change were relatively simple. A presidential staff aide, responding to the request for suggestions for the annual legislative program, tapped the resources of BOB, which—as is often the case—had an idea in the files, and made a proposal to the president, who needed a fallback plan after one of the most notable, and unusual, defeats of his administration. The plan's merits were so obvious, as judged from the perspectives of municipal reform and orthodox administrative theory, that bipartisan acceptance came from all except a few of those in the committee structure of Congress. It was success for the president, acceptance on the basis of merits in the Congress, and demonstration of the advantages of statutory authorization of reorganization plans.

ENVIRONMENTAL SCIENCE SERVICES ADMINISTRATION

Reorganization Plan 2 of 1965 achieved an internal reorganization within the Department of Commerce. The plan transferred the functions of the Weather Bureau and the Coast and Geodetic Survey to the secretary of commerce and combined the two agencies to form a new agency called the Environmental Science Services Administration. The identity of the two agencies was retained, with assignment of duties at the secretary's discretion. Accomplished at the same time was the consolidation into the administration, by the secretary's direction, of the Central Radio Propagation Laboratory of the National Bureau of Standards. The purpose of the plan was to provide a single focus within the department for environmental science efforts. It was believed that this could be the nucleus for a broader national effort in geophysics and control of the natural environment and could in this respect advance key concerns of the administration.

The progress of the reorganization revealed the potential for smooth operation of the subpresidency and limited burden on the political officers of the government. The movement was initiated by J. Herbert Holloman, assistant secretary of commerce for science and technology, in budget discussions in 1964. Subsequently, Holloman asked for a study by a committee composed of directors of the two agencies and the Bureau of Standards, with an advisory group of four scientists. When this committee reported in favor of the consolidation, the secretary of commerce recommended a reorganization plan as the means of accomplishment. BOB had been kept advised and had asked for the opinion of the director of the Office of Science and Technology. The usual checks were made with congressional leaders. The documents were transmitted to the attorney general for legal approval. Concurrence of the secretary of commerce, BOB, the Office of Science and Technology, the attorney general, and Bill Moyers of the White House staff, and signals of approval from Congress led to approval of the president on a memorandum from Kermit Gordon of BOB.

Hearings were held by a subcommittee of the House Government Operations Committee, but no resolutions of disapproval were offered, and scant opposition appeared. In the absence of conflicting interests to be reconciled, the mechanisms of the presidency could move promptly for structural change.[101]

TARIFF COMMISSION

Reorganization Plan 2 of 1967, the only plan submitted by President Johnson that was not accepted in Congress, contained no unusual content. Rather, it followed a principle of organization proposed by the first Hoover commission, applied through six reorganization plans during the Truman administration and subsequent plans during the Eisenhower and Kennedy administrations. It proposed transfer of administrative functions from the Tariff Commission as a whole to the chairman, subject to governance by "general policies of the Commission" and commission approval of certain appointments. The president referred to them as "routine" functions, Califano called them "housekeeping," and "noncontroversial."[102] The first two characterizations may have underestimated the potential of the reorganization for making changes in influence and power within the commission and the extent of presidential influence over it; the last one was an erroneous assessment of congressional viewpoint.

The change had been proposed by the chairman of the commission to BOB, but he preferred that the initiative not appear to come from him. BOB, after approval from John Macy, chairman of the Civil Service Commission, recommended the change through a reorganization plan to the president in March 1966.[103] It was put on the agenda in 1967 by the decision to send three "noncontroversial plans" at that time, because Congressman Holifield wanted the District of Columbia plan not to be the first transmitted to Congress.[104] BOB and White House staff made the usual checks with majority members of the two Government Operations committees, and in this instance also with Congressman Wilbur Mills (D–Ark.) and Senator Russell Long (D–La.), chairmen of the committees with jurisdiction over tariff legislation. On the basis of Califano's report that it was noncontroversial, the president approved submission of the plan, and it went to Congress 9 March 1967.[105]

Although Republican congressman Erlenborn submitted one of his frequent disapproval resolutions, the hearings of subcommittees in both houses were brief and showed no strong antagonism. The administration forces were surprised, therefore, when the Senate Government Operations Committee voted disapproval. Senator Ribicoff, chairman of the subcommittee that held hearings on the plan, was normally a dependable supporter of the president's reorganization plans—though he was, of course, consulted in advance and on occasion expressed dissatisfaction with the choice, timing, or substance of plans.[106] His dissatisfaction in this instance was respected by his colleagues.

Phillip S. Hughes, deputy director of BOB, reported to the president that the reasons for disapproval were "not clear," but that they were not related to the "fine print" and included dissatisfaction of Senator Ribicoff with some decisions on tariff adjustments.

Hughes informed the president of consultations with Senator Henry Jackson—who had sought to slow down the committee action, the chairman of the Tariff Commission, and a member of the White House staff and concluded that "we recommend that the matter be dropped." The president approved this recommendation.[107]

CONCLUSIONS

What was achieved through reorganization plans in approximately five years of an activist administration? No implementation of general principles in the structure of government as in Truman's reorganization orders,[108] and nothing so dramatic as Eisenhower's creation of the Department of Health, Education, and Welfare by reorganization plan. Johnson was foreclosed from trying to create HUD or DOT by reorganization plan by a limitation added in the Reorganization Act of 1964. No substantial savings were predicted for any of the reorganizations. It was easy to find, as required by statue, that some of the management purposes of the Reorganization Act would be achieved by reorganization; but this was frequently done by general assertion.

Nevertheless, some specific effects of the sixteen successful reorganization plans submitted by President Johnson can be listed:

1. A number of minor liquidations and changes of a housekeeping nature were effected.

2. A basic change in the system of government of the District of Columbia—from the commission system to an appointive council-mayor system—was achieved.

3. Resolution of the issues in the relationship of two departments in mass transit functions, which would have been exceedingly difficult through the legislative process, was consummated.

4. There was escape from the rigidity of statutory prescriptions on structure for administration of health functions.

5. The structure for drug-abuse control was updated to conform with expansions in governmental activity.

6. An interdepartmental transfer of a bureau was made to facilitate presidential policy on water pollution control.

7. A simple consolidation of bureaus was made for environmental science services, an internal reorganization in the Customs Bureau was made possible, and a presidential plan for coordination of enforcement of civil rights was aided by transfer of CRS.

While not among the great events of a presidency, these changes were not insubstantial and were part of the process of organizational change that is necessary for effective policy implementation. What, then, can be said in conclusion about the processes of government for these changes?

The record of nine reorganization plans presented in this chapter shows the president reacting to staff and departments and agencies, and in general accepting their recommendations. This does not mean he was not a personal participant. Numerous submissions went to him for his night reading and his approval or disapproval. There were conflicts of view demanding his resolution—as in the instances of Gardner and BOB against Udall and Califano on the location of water pollution control and Gardner and Cohen against BOB on the scope of a reorganization plan affecting health functions. And there were questions on how to move in the case of departmental opposition—as with Fowler on transfer of the Bureau of Narcotics. There was decisive action on his part on a matter of importance—coordination of civil rights enforcement, of which the CRS reorganization was a part. There was attention to detail in the sequence of events—with respect to the District of Columbia plan, he said to Califano, "get on it and stay on it," and "get some citizen in town to send this [an editorial] to every member of Congress." But his dependence on staff was large: "Joe—I can't spend my year on these matters." His dominant concern seemed to be political success—"I wouldn't start something I couldn't pass" was a caution to Califano. On the whole, the record of these reorganization plans demonstrates either that management in general is not the main business of the president or that specific structural changes of the kind permitted by the Reorganization Act make low demands on the president's attention.

It does not follow from this alone that the managerial responsibilities defined for the presidency by the Brownlow committee cannot be carried successfully within it. It does follow that the managerial function is substantially in the substructure of the presidency—in the subpresidency as we have described it.

The smoothness of the operation of the Johnson subpresidency on matters that were—as was usually true of these reorganizations—on a relatively low level of controversy, is demonstrated by this chapter. The hard core of the subpresidency for this element of presidential responsibility was BOB. It had the records of past considerations and the professional knowledge to prepare quick and dependable evaluations of proposals; it was alert to development of reorganization suggestions in departments and agencies; it preserved the integrity of the reorganization plan process and the consistency of organization principle; it maintained its purview of the process.

Operating with BOB was the White House staff. Maintaining the coordinating position was Califano. Numerous others participated in the congressional contacts and communicated to the president, sometimes through Califano and sometimes not, and in an internal reorganization within HEW

Douglass Cater seemed to be the primary line of communication. But Califano's integrating and mediating participation was constantly present, and sometimes his pressure was too. Completing the core of the subpresidency on reorganization matters was the Department of Justice, which assisted in draftmanship and cleared issues of legality. While these three—BOB, White House staff members, and Justice—were the constant elements in the process, each reorganization plan brought into the circle different persons from the departments and agencies. Only once did the report of a task force—the proposal of the Task Force on Crime for the consolidation of drug control enforcement—have significant influence. No outside consultants appear to have been influential, except at the departmental or agency level.

Yet the managerial responsibilities of the president were not yielded to others. Califano got ahead of the president on water pollution control administration, and the president, by his own declaration, went along with him against his better judgment. But he warned against further hastiness. The consciousness of the need for the president's approval and support was always present. The complete loyalty of all participants in every case when decision was reached demonstrates that the man at the top was on top. In sum, the president was normally reactive, but he was occasionally active and always in reserve; his powers were never passed to others.

While the burdens on the president in reorganization plan development and adoption appear not to be heavy, the burdens on Congress are conspicuously lighter than in legislative procedure. Amendments cannot be offered for consideration. Legislative hearings and floor consideration are not required. For the nine reorganization plans considered here, committee hearings were held for all in the House of Representatives, for only five in the Senate; there was a vote after floor consideration on three in one house, and for only one in both houses.

The congressional burden was lightened not only by the technique, but by the administration's efforts to avoid submitting plans that would be defeated and by its efforts to reduce controversy on those that were submitted. As a result it was able usually to depend upon leadership and other support within the Government Operations committees. The committee leadership was sometimes unhappy with the kinds of plans submitted, or with the number or sequence of submissions, and sometimes its questions penetrated deeply into the substance of proposals; but, except for the proposal for concentrating administrative powers in the chairman of the Tariff Commission, the majority leadership went with the president. Within the House committee, sometimes forcefully and sometimes with the purpose of presenting a loyal opposition, the probing was usually pushed into the purposes and effects of the proposals. There was usually a substantial degree of party division in the House committee, and in some cases the party division was complete or nearly complete.

There was surprisingly little positive demonstration of the kinds of congressional perspective revealed in some of the larger organizational steps during the Johnson administration. Retention of committee jurisdiction appeared as a factor in the urban mass transit consideration, and it was a central factor in opposition to reform of the government of the District of Columbia. Program interests were present, as, for example, in respect to water pollution control, where some congressmen were concerned that health protection would be downgraded; but the force of this type of objection was not comparable to that which preserved operating autonomy for agencies in DOT.[109] Policy concerns were sometimes revealed, particularly in the case of the District of Columbia proposal (where opposition to black representation in city government was present) and in the case of mass transit (where the fear of insufficient attention to city transportation was strong). Constituency or patronage interests held by strategically situated members of Congress forced compromise on field office locations in the reorganization of the Customs Bureau. But no large cleavages between executive and legislative perspectives ran through the group of proposals.

The final conclusions from this survey are, therefore, that in the use of the technique of reorganization plan there was rational search in the substructure of the presidency for improvement in organization; that the president was primarily concerned with things referred to him and with political support for these; and that the technique itself and the administration's caution in avoiding controversial use of it submerged political objection within the Congress. The usefulness of the reorganization plan as a technique is that it promotes rational consideration of structural change and does so with small or reduced burden on the president and Congress.

SIX

FAILURES OF ORGANIZATIONAL INITIATIVES

It is not political successes alone that reveal the role of the presidency in organizational change. Failures, too, are instructive, showing the political capital of the president at risk, the interpretative and manipulative skill of the subpresidency, and the durability and resistance to change of organizations. President Johnson had been successful in bringing two cabinet departments into being (HUD and DOT), but his proposal for combining the Commerce and Labor departments failed decisively. Less dramatically, the subpresidency's deliberations or the president's recommendations on a department of natural resources, a department of education, and lesser reorganizations were aborted. The reasons varied with the issues at stake and demonstrated the tactical importance of competing interests and perspectives.

THE BRIEF PUSH FOR A DEPARTMENT OF BUSINESS AND LABOR

In his State of the Union Message on 10 January 1967, President Johnson proposed one of his most ambitious reorganization schemes by urging Congress to combine the Department of Commerce with the Department of Labor and other related agencies.[1] Johnson's proposal caught much of Washington by surprise, including all but the highest officials in the Commerce and Labor departments, some of his own staff, and a selected group of leaders in labor and business. Within two months of his speech the proposal was dead, and within a year the president would be jokingly referring to it as "not...one of my better known legislative achievements."[2] The recommendation was nonetheless serious when it was made and was one of

142

Johnson's broad-range reorganization proposals. Its scope was large and, unlike a reorganization plan, not directed to a specific program objective and not an act of bureaucratic housecleaning.

The idea of serving the interests of labor and management through a single department had come to government more than fifty years earlier, but within a decade it had disappeared. In 1903, commercial and industrial interests succeeded after a prolonged effort in moving Congress to create a cabinet-level department serving their special needs. Before Congress acted, however, it included in the new department a preexisting subcabinet department of labor and named the new department the Department of Commerce and Labor. After its creation, organized labor did not like this arrangement, finding its interests subordinate to those of business within the new department. It succeeded in forcing the creation of a separate cabinet-level Department of Labor in 1913.[3]

Fifty-two years after Congress separated the two departments, a presidential task force headed by Don K. Price of Harvard University found that the concept of "conflict between management and labor, and the need to give each a department to represent it" was "obsolete in theory, and has been growing more obsolete in practice." In its report to the president in late 1964, the Price task force urged the creation of a "Department of Economic Development" that would be "the principal Executive Department that is concerned with the general economic development of the Nation." This new department would include the Office of Economic Opportunity, the Department of Commerce (minus its transportation functions), several bureaucracies administering economic development programs, and the Small Business Administration (SBA). The task force believed that "at some later date" it would be desirable to merge the present Department of Labor with the proposed Department of Economic Development.[4] Late the following year, top officials within the Commerce Department gave the merger proposal serious consideration but decided to shelve it. As the acting secretary of commerce, Alexander Trowbridge, later explained, they "did not recommend it at that time because at a casual glance we saw several inherent difficulties which were then . . . involved."[5]

The "later date" that the Price task force wrote about as the time to merge Labor with Commerce appeared to have arrived suddenly in late 1966, but without the prior creation of a Department of Economic Development. The catalyst for the Johnson administration's proposal was apparently commerce secretary John Connor's decision to resign. In a 27 December 1966 memorandum to the president recommending possible replacements for Connor, John Macy, the administration's chief talent scout, took the occasion to outline his concept of a revitalized Department of Commerce. "The Department," he wrote, "has reached a watershed in its organizational development. It is a department in search of a new role." With the creation of the Department of Transportation in October, Commerce had lost 80 percent of its annual budget, its trust funds, and 15 percent of its personnel. The Office of the Secretary presided over its four remaining components—Science and Technology, Economic Affairs, Domestic and International Business, and Economic Development—"as if it were a benevolent holding company." The department was also largely bereft of "clients." Financial institutions and public utilities had always remained outside its purview.. Industrial giants found it more useful to work with the Justice and Defense departments and the Securities and Exchange Commission. Small business went to SBA, and informed businessmen knew that the commerce secretary had no clout in the formulation of national economic policy. "Thus, the incentive for business leaders to form relationships with the Commerce Department has been shrinking." For a "Commerce Department of the Future," Macy wanted a *"department of economic and commercial services—services* to business, to the consumer, to the country at large." Along with present functions, it would provide

> the commercial services that will become feasible, and in some cases imperative, with the unfolding of new technologies, like: more sophisticated studies of demographic dynamics; training in new management techniques to keep American business modern; consumer services in packaging, credit, and advertising to give freedom of choice to the buyer; weather control and new data on environmental pollution; regional economic development.

> With the diversity of its activities reduced, the Department should also be better equipped to explain the President's objectives and programs to the business community.[6]

President Johnson apparently discussed this memorandum with Macy, in Washington, in a long-distance telephone conversation from the LBJ Ranch on the morning of 29 December 1966.[7] After this conversation, Joseph Califano, budget director Charles Schultze, both at the ranch, and Macy, by telephone, discussed the possibility of merging Commerce and Labor into a department of human and economic development, an expansion of Macy's original idea for an expanded Department of Commerce. In a memorandum to the president that evening, Califano recommended the merger as a move that "makes sense." The idea was "bold" and the Task Force on Reorganization had urged it. Califano had discussed the proposal with his former boss, defense secretary Robert McNamara, who had said it was, as Califano recalled, "clearly correct on the merits." The proposal would "give you another major initiative in Government organization and might help you to maintain the momentum in terms of Government organization." He also noted that there were "serious political problems" with the proposal and requested (and apparently received) permission to discuss the merger with commerce secretary John Connor, labor secretary Willard Wirtz, postmaster general Larry O'Brien, and Ben Heineman, chairman of the president's current Task Force on Government Organization.[8]

With the president indicating initial interest in the merger of Commerce, Labor, and perhaps other bureaucracies, Califano and Schultze set John D. Young, from Schultze's staff, and Fred Bohen, from the Bureau of the Budget (BOB) and liaison with the Heineman task force, to work conducting a "completely confidential" staff review of the proposal. So confidential was the staff work that even Harold Seidman, BOB's top expert on government organization, did not know about the development until he heard it in the State of the Union Message.[9] On 5 January Young and Bohen reported to Califano that there were five major objectives the combination would achieve. First, to create one government agency "to receive, analyze, evaluate, reconcile and report the diverse views, agreements, and recommendations of Labor and Management"; second, to create one department that could "carry out most of the major government provisions and policies for balanced growth of the national economy"; third, to improve the quality of manpower programs; fourth, to implement the statistical services of the government and avoid overlap; and, fifth, to reduce by four the number of agency heads reporting to the president (Commerce-Labor, Small Business Administration, Federal Mediation and Conciliation Service, National Mediation Board). The new department's major functions would be to promote economic growth; to improve labor-management relations, especially through execution of wage-price guideline policies; and to collect, analyze, and disseminate major economic and social data.[10]

Another memorandum to reach Califano's desk at about this time, perhaps also from Young and Bohen, added another interesting rationale for the new department. If its head were able to keep the "special confidence" of the president, "inevitably, he will be a tougher competitor with the Chairman of the CEA [Council of Economic Advisers] on economic matters, especially if he beefs up the analytic staff in the new Department." As was well understood in government at this time, economic policy was largely determined by the "troika" (the budget director, the treasury secretary, and the chairman of CEA) or the "quadriad," if the chairman of the Federal Reserve Board were added to the group. "The new man might well become the spokesman for the private sector, thereby forcing the Council to be the advocate of the needs of the public sector, a role it has, in fact, played during parts of its 20-year existence."[11] The Price task force also believed that the initiatives of the private sector could be stimulated by the department.[12]

With the Commerce-Labor merger idea gaining acceptance in the White House, Califano sent the president another memorandum on the subject in the early afternoon of 5 January as background for a meeting with George

Meany, President of the AFL-CIO. After four days of staff work, he wrote, "our initial recommendation that this makes good sense, is bold, is correct on the merits, and has been recommended by a variety of people including the 1964 Task Force on Reorganization [was confirmed]."[13] Three days later, Califano discussed the proposal with the president, and the day following he sent him another memorandum on the subject. "We still think the best name would be Department of Manpower and Economic Development," Califano wrote to the president in a memorandum. The least desirable name would be the "Department of Commerce and Labor" or the reverse. As he explained:

> The Department will be more than merely a combination of Labor and Commerce. In addition, we would propose picking up a variety of agencies and pieces of agencies, including not only the Economic Development Administration, but the Commissions, such as Appalachia, which the Congress has created as almost independent agencies. Further, one of the main points of the Department is to show your recognition of the relationship of all economic development to the human and manpower problem. Finally, we believe that it is important in terms of history to put your stamp on this Department and to put your stamp on the broad concept of economic development and manpower that you began with the Appalachian Commission and the MDTA training programs.

Califano concluded by asking the president if he approved the name Department of Manpower and Economic Development. Johnson checked the blank space after "Neither approve nor disapprove" and did not fill in the space in "Use Department of ———."[14]

The president's answer came the next day, 10 January when he proposed a "Department of Business and Labor" in his State of the Union Message. The title and the statement of purpose—"a more economical, efficient, and streamlined instrument"—did not convey the expanded objectives the Price task force, Macy, and other advisers had projected for the new department.[15] Johnson had apparently accepted the idea of combination without fully embracing the policy rationales of his advisers.

The proposal made headlines in the morning papers, but it was a "bold" idea that had been quickly staffed and inadequately thought through. Major questions remained concerning the structure of the department, its political support, and the role it would play in economic policy development. Within two weeks the shape of the proposed superbureaucracy would emerge in outline form, but during the same period a group of dissatisfied and sometimes confused politicians and labor leaders would turn back the initiative.

Designing a "New Instrument of Government"

Shortly after the president's message, high-ranking members of the Commerce and Labor departments and BOB formed a task force to determine the purpose, functions, and components of the new department.[16] Unaided by the expert component of BOB on organization, the task force considered the controversial issues. By 28 January, Califano informed the president that there was "little interest in a simple merger of two Departments" and that there was a "general agreement" on the components to be added to a combined commerce and labor department:

Economic analysis and stockpile functions of the
    Office of Emergency Preparedness
Appalachian Regional Commission
Small Business Administration
Bureau of Commercial Fisheries (from Interior)
Federal Mediation and Conciliation Service
National Mediation Board

"Additional candidates" being discussed were:

Equal Employment Opportunities Commission
Export-Import Bank
Export control functions of State, Treasury, Agriculture,
    Atomic Energy Commission and Maritime Administration
Oil Import Administration (Interior)
Oil Import Appeals Board (Interior)
Disaster Relief (Office of Emergency Planning)
Adult vocational and technical education (Health, Education, and
    Welfare–HEW)
Immigration and Naturalization Service (Justice)
A number of minor scientific activities that could be combined with the
    mission of the Environmental Science Services Administration in Com-
    merce.[17]

The "additional candidates" were in some cases hotly contested. In the weeks following the president's speech, there was much discussion in the White House, BOB, and various other parts of the executive branch about what might be included or left out of the new department. Many unresolved questions not alluded to in Califano's 28 January memorandum remained. Some officials in the State Department's high command, for example, preferred to keep the Export-Import Bank outside the new department, but the task force wanted it in. BOB's task force member, assistant director Charles Zwick, developed his own separate views on this and other aspects of the potential reorganization that he communicated directly to Califano. Zwick wanted the bank to remain independent unless the new entity were developed "under the concept of a maxium department." The task force also wanted the Vocational Rehabilitation Administration included, but against the wishes of Health, Education, and Welfare secretary John Gardner. The task force thought that the Equal Employment Opportunities Commission should be included, while its commissioner wanted it to remain out. The BOB staff, which examined the question independent of the task force in tandem with Zwick, felt that the Environmental Science Services Administration (ESSA) (then in Commerce) should be out at least temporarily pending a thorough study.[18] In the White House, staff member William P. Graham disagreed "completely with Fred Bohen's proposed strategy of putting [Consumer Affairs] in HEW and waiting to put in the new Department." He advised Califano that "Consumer Affairs can be made an important part of the strategy for the new department."[19] Califano, however, was unimpressed and did not even mention consumer affairs to the president as an "additional candidate."

Not even the "general agreement" list was exempt from controversy. The head of the Mediation and Conciliation Service was, according to Zwick, strongly opposed to being included, while Zwick, contrary to the task force recommendation, doubted that the Bureau of Commercial Fisheries should be taken from the Department of Interior.[20] Califano did not burden Johnson with these problems; it was his practice to have such debates resolved before they reached the president's desk and to mention only the most significant unresolved issues.

On 6 February Califano reported to the president that major issues about the content of the new department were resolved. The history of this memorandum demonstrates the power Califano wielded within the White House on matters concerning domestic affairs of secondary importance to the president. Sometime in early February, Califano apparently asked Charles Zwick to draft a memorandum to the president for Califano's signature recommending the components of the new department. Zwick sent Califano a draft on 6 February, proposing that Califano inform Johnson that "based on discussion to date, I believe it is important that the new Department *take on the character of a broad new instrument of Government.* This means that its internal organization and name should be designed to overcome the image of a simple merger of the Department of Labor and Commerce. It also argued for bringing additional activities into the Department." Zwick also listed the functions and agencies that "appear to be candidates with significant support for inclusion in the new Department"—thirteen agencies and functions drawn from both the "general agreement" and "additional candidates" list in the Califano memorandum to the president of 28 January.

Following the list of thirteen, Zwick's draft memorandum discussed four controversial candidates for transfer. He noted that, on the one hand, Secretary Wirtz and acting commerce secretary Trowbridge believed that the Export-Import Bank should be included and that under secretary of state Vance had no problem with the transfer. On the other hand, both under secretary of state Nicholas Katzenbach and the chairman and president of the Export-Import Bank were opposed. Zwick proposed that Califano inform

Johnson that "in anticipation of a negative Congressional reaction," he and Charles Schultze recommended that it be left out. Zwick and Schultze proposed, over the objections of under secretary of the treasury Joseph Barr, that the Bureau of Customs be transferred. They recommended that Vocational Rehabilitation programs remain in HEW; John Gardner, secretary of HEW, wanted to keep them in his domain, while the task force recommended inclusion in the new department. Zwick also noted that there was a general agreement that the Oil Import Administration and Appeals Board be included but that it might "open up a major issue on oil imports." The memorandum deleted from Califano's 28 January list all reference to the Bureau of Commercial fisheries or the ESSA, neither of which the Bureau of the Budget wished to see placed immediately in the new department.[21]

Attached to the top of the draft memorandum for the president was a qualifying covering note from Zwick to Califano. "Although the [thirteen] items for inclusion in the draft presidential memorandum are listed as secure positions," he warned, "you should remember that

(1) [Director] Simkin of the Mediation and Conciliation Service is strongly opposed to being included;

(2) [Attorney General] Ramsey Clark has not had a chance as yet to look at the question of the Immigration and Naturalization Service carefully;

(3) I won't have had my talk with [Chairman] O'Neill of the National Mediation Board until tomorrow at 10:30 a.m.

(4) Tony Solomon tells me that Seventh Floor, State, is planning a protest memorandum on the inclusion of Munition Control. We may see that memorandum tomorrow.

(5) [Chairman] Shulman of EEOC still strongly objects, and we haven't gotten hold of Louie Martin, but Bob Weaver has talked to Whitney Young, of the Urban League, who enthusiastically supports the idea.[22]

Califano modified slightly the draft memorandum from Zwick and sent it to the president the same day. He ignored Zwick's qualifications in the cover note. Indeed, Califano went even further in his assurances to Johnson about the agreement within the government over including the agencies and functions in the list of thirteen. Instead of using Zwick's mildly qualifying language noting "significant support for inclusion," Califano assured the president that "*all are agreed* that the following functions and agencies should be included (and will not create many problems) within or without the Government." The portion of the memorandum dealing with the Export-Import Bank, Bureau of Customs, Vocational Rehabilitation, and Oil Import were forwarded largely as Zwick had originally drafted them. Califano followed the substance of the Zwick draft conclusion by requesting authorization to contact "people on the Hill and people in business and labor to get their reactions" and prepare a message and bill to send to Congress during the third or fourth week of February, "depending on how soon we can get a feeling from the labor unions concerning their posture on our proposal for the new Department."

As in many Califano memorandums to Johnson, the words "Approve" and "Disapprove" were typed at the bottom, followed by spaces. The president checked "Approve," meaning only approval for further consideration.[23]

The Department's Organization

With the new department's major components tentatively decided upon, it was still necessary to consider the functions around operating divisions. This job was left to the ad hoc task force. By mid-February, the task force produced an outline that acting commerce secretary Alexander Trowbridge described to a meeting of a Washington Business Council. He mentioned five operating units:

1. *Statistical Services*

2. *International Services* (From Commerce and Labor: Bureau of International Commerce; Office of Foreign Commercial Services; U.S. Travel Service; Bureau of International Labor Affairs. From those two departments as well as other departments and agencies: export control functions of the State Department and Maritime Administration in addition to those in Commerce; Bureau of Customs; Oil Import Administration and Oil Import Appeals Board; possibly immigration functions of the Immigration and Naturalization Service.)

3. *Manpower and Business Development* (Manpower and economic development programs.)

4. *Industry Services* (Business and Defense Services Administration from Commerce; Labor Standards Office from Labor; health and safety functions from the Bureau of Mines; Federal Mediation and Conciliation Service; National Mediation Board; Equal Employment Opportunity Commission.)

5. *Science Services* (Trowbridge included ESSA, which had been omitted from the list Johnson approved on 7 February.) For a sixth service area, Trowbridge mentioned the possible inclusion of the Small Business Administration. SBA, however, was one of the more controversial items proposed in the merger. Senator John Sparkman, chairman of the Senate Banking and Currency Committee and a strong friend of his "clients," had succeeded in blocking introduction of a reorganization plan in 1966 designed to transfer SBA to the Commerce Department.[24]

By the date of Trowbridge's speech, 16 February the entire exercise of organizing the proposed department was becoming increasingly academic.

150

The plan to create it was in grave trouble on Capitol Hill, and the root of its problem lay in the Executive Council of the AFL-CIO.

First Reactions

Within four days after the 10 January message, it was clear that the administration would have a tough fight to win congressional approval for the Labor-Commerce merger. The soundings taken before and immediately after the message had been modestly encouraging. Commerce secretary John Connor and Califano had encouraging contacts with top executives at Campbell Soup, International Business Machines, Pennsylvania Railroad, Kaiser Industries, Columbia Broadcasting System, John Deere, Morgan Guaranty, Pan American, General Motors, Chase Manhattan, Chrysler, and other industries. Not all, however, were pleased. Henry Ford liked it, "but only if a labor man is not named Secretary." Charles Thornton of Litton Industries leaned against it because he feared labor might dominate.[25] Little serious opposition, or support, would emerge from leaders of large industries that had direct contact with the White House and relatively little to do with the weak Commerce Department.

The initial conversations with labor leaders were encouraging but misleading. The first was the 5 January meeting between President Johnson and George Meany. Meany apparently said nothing to Johnson to discourage him from going ahead with the merger. When a presidential aide talked with him after the State of the Union Message, he gave assurances, Califano reported to the president, that he "supports [the proposal] fully" and that he could be counted on to call several other union leaders to gain their support. Lane Kirkland, an influential assistant to Meany, said only that he supported the merger "because George Meany does." Two other union leaders reached immediately after the speech also indicated support. Another, Joe Beirne, an AFL-CIO Council vice-president and head of the Communications Workers Union, was opposed. His "first reaction is one of strong opposition," Califano informed the president. "This may continue but he will reserve judgment until he talks to George Meany. Meany will work on Beirne and bring him around."[26]

Meany's public statements of support were more qualified than were the private assurances he gave the White House. Speaking to a reporter for the *Wall Street Journal,* he said that the proposal was "far-reaching" and deserved "open-minded study." He recalled the days when Labor was a second-class component in a combined department of commerce and labor but was sure "that the President has no intention of returning to that concept." Other union leaders were less restrained in their comments. "It looks like something George Romney would think of," one said. The *Journal* also reported that the president of the United States Chamber of Commerce professed astonishment over the proposal. "Off hand," he said, "the proposal appears to be contrary to the best interests of the country."[27]

Initial reports from Capitol Hill were mixed, but they soon proved to be, on balance, negative. It had been a standard Johnson White House procedure to check with important congressional leaders as well as interested members of the private sector before proposing any reorganization plan. In this case, Congress was taken by surprise. Reporting through a memorandum by Califano aide Larry Levinson, commerce secretary Connor informed the president that Senator Warren Magnuson (D–Wash.), chairman of the Commerce Committee, had a "wait and see" attitude; he was waiting to see the reaction of labor and business leaders in his state.[28] The next day Magnuson expressed public support for the idea if it was "an effort to reduce the size of the Federal Government." Other senators' opinions ranged from cautious acceptance to disapproval. Wayne Morse (D–Ore.), a senior Democrat on the Senate Labor and Public Welfare Committee, told the press that Johnson had not made a case for the merger, though he would be willing to hear more. He agreed to a meeting with labor secretary Wirtz before his committee the following week. John McClellan (D–Ark.), chairman of the Senate Committee on Government Operations, reported Connor, had an "open mind." Senator Abraham Ribicoff (D–Conn.), chairman of the Government Operations Subcommittee on Executive Reorganization, reminded the press that he had offered early support for the establishment of HUD and DOT but viewed the proposed Commerce-Labor merger as only "very interesting" and needing further study.[29]

By 16 January the proposed merger was clearly in trouble. "I am running into indifference and disbelief on the Hill so far as the merger proposal is concerned," Wirtz reported to Johnson. Carl Perkins (D–Ky.) chairman of the House Education and Labor Committee, first told Wirtz that he was flatly opposed but moved to a neutral position when the labor secretary informed him that he, Meany, and the president were for it. "But," continued Wirtz, "Perkins is far from convinced" and was unwilling even to set up an informal session with other committee members. Wirtz reported that other members of the committee friendly to the administration were disposed to "wait a few days" before deciding. They were making it "pretty plain that they have heard nothing from the [House] leadership and nothing from the AFL-CIO, and think I am being a little naive about it."

Wirtz's report from AFL-CIO was inconclusive but not encouraging. "The AFL-CIO people are holding to the George Meany 'take a good look at it' line." He noted that:

*George stopped Joe Beirne from making an announced opposition statement last Friday.

*Joe Curran's statement [in a publicized telegram to Meany opposing the merger]...was made without checking with anybody.
*It is fairly clear that the AFL-CIO staff instructions are to keep the situation neutral for now—although I am always told that "George is all for it."

At the bottom of the Wirtz memorandum, Johnson advised Califano that Wirtz "talk to me and you before going further."[30]

Three days later, on 19 January Wirtz reported more on the merger. He now found that five members of the House Education and Labor Committee were more or less for the merger "unless labor comes out against it," but that it was "pretty clear" that they did not really believe Labor would back the proposal. None of the five members "is presently inclined to take the idea very seriously," he concluded. Wirtz also reported that there was "increasing question about whether George is going to be able to sell this to the [AFL-CIO Executive] Council." Only two members were for it on its merits. Three supported it because the president had prevailed on them in a private meeting and because George Meany was for it. Three were "all out against it." Two others were against it "but would go with the President and George." Wirtz concluded that Meany could control the situation if he wished, but that it might "take a little more arm twisting than he originally expected but not much." He also felt that Lane Kirkland, key aide to Meany, and the AFL-CIO staff were against it but were backing Meany's neutral position.

Wirtz's own assessment was that the "more the proposal is discussed the *righter* it seems .... But it also gets clear than *no one is very anxious to push.*" His judgment was that Johnson could have his department if he were to "put all you have behind it but...*that it is still too early to tell whether it is worth that much* .... [There] is a lot more to be found out before you would make it a *personal issue.*" These conclusions went to the president accompanied by a cover memorandum from Joe Califano noting that Lane Kirkland had called him that night. Kirkland had said that "they were running into 'very serious trouble with the Labor people.'"[31]

Labor Opposes

In spite of the mixed reception for its reorganization proposal, the administration pressed ahead with its advertising, planning, and lobbying. In a 20 January letter to Congress recommending an extension of the Appalachian Program of regional development, the president noted that his proposed department, which would "have the basic responsibility for the Federal government's effort in all of the regional commissions that have been or soon will be established," would take over the program after the department's creation. His 24 January annual Budget Message and his Economic Report, two days later, also peddled the merger as serving to improve government organization. In the latter message Johnson stated that separate Labor and Commerce departments "perpetuate the obsolete notion that there is a fundamental conflict between the interests of business and labor or between the interests of either and that of the Nation." A union of the two would "improve efficiency, reduce costs, simplify the reporting burden on business, provide . . . statistics, and assure that the views . . . of the private sector enter more effectively into decisions on general economic policy."[32]

The president's public statements, however, did not persuade the labor leaders. On 24 January Califano reported that the AFL-CIO Executive Council was still opposed by a margin of fourteen to seven. "Kirkland believes it will be impossible to get the Council to approve the Department. He also believes that Meany should not have to put something this important to a vote where there is any chance he *will be defeated*." Califano detected no room for bargaining and said Kirkland personally did not think the merger was a good idea.[33] After a conversation with Meany and Kirkland the next day, Wirtz reported that Meany was for the idea in principle "but expressed very strong doubts about going ahead with it as a practical matter." Several members of the council were "strongly opposed," nobody else was actually for it, one AFL-CIO official who had been for it had changed his mind, and Walter Reuther was supposed to be for it but did not speak out. "The objections of the Labor people come down to the feeling that they have had their own Department and voice in the Government and that they will lose this." They especially feared loss of all influence under a conservative administration. "There is little discussion of the matter on its merits," he concluded.[34] It is likely that George Meany conveyed the same thoughts directly to the president when he saw him that day.[35]

The significance of Labor's opposition was apparent when the administration examined the political arithmetic on Capitol Hill. In the House, a department bill would go to the Committee on Government Operations. Acting commerce secretary Trowbridge and his legislative assistant, Paul Southwick, called on the committee's chairman and five other "key" Democratic members who happened to be in the chairman's office on 31 January. The committee's Democrats would need to stick together if the bill were to have a chance, since the committee was composed of twenty Democrats and fifteen Republicans. Because all of the Republicans would probably vote against the bill, the defection of three from the friendly side would kill it. When Trowbridge discussed the merits and logic of the proposal, John Moss, a ranking Democrat from California, insisted that the committee's decision would not be based on "logic." Democrat Jack Brooks pointed out that the opposition of one labor union would cause the defection of one or two votes from his side. After the meeting, Trowbridge and Southwick spoke privately with Moss, who said that "as of now, we don't have the votes and . . . all the Republicans would vote against it."[36]

With the fate of the merger proposal apparently resting in the hands of AFL-CIO's Executive Council, Joe Califano decided to make a direct appeal to the labor chiefs when they met at their annual convention in Florida in late February. Califano obtained permission from Johnson to talk to the group in the company of Wirtz and budget director Schultze.[37] Their combined effort proved to be a failure. Wirtz made an appeal for the proposal on 20 February but without success; Meany continued to express doubts about it after the meeting. Wirtz apparently supported the proposal because, among other reasons, it would merge "two special interest" departments into one that was "functional." Meany responded to this by observing that, if labor's "special interest" department had to go, then others, like the Agriculture Department, should be eliminated too. The day after Wirtz's presentation, Califano and Schultze tried their hands at persuasion. To the by now standard list of reasons for support, Califano added a personal plea from the president that the group not take a final position on the merger until he had a chance to talk to them personally. The Executive Council respected Johnson's wish, took no official stand on the proposal, and eventually agreed to meet with Johnson on 9 March.[38]

Two days before the 9 March showdown, Califano and Wirtz maintained some optimism for the proposal's future, whereas the president was inclined to give up. Califano discussed it once more with Kirkland and Andrew Biemiller, the Executive Council's legislative specialist, on 7 March, reviewing the possible components of the new department and stressing that the list was not firm. Kirkland and Biemiller were impressed with its scope but observed that emotion, as distinct from logic, ran deep in the council. The emotion was based on the feeling that they should not dismantle the independent Labor Department that Samuel Gompers had fought so hard to create. They also said that the council was concerned about the loss of a single spokesman and recommended that the new department—were it created—include an under secretary of labor.

After the meeting, Califano discussed the conversation with Wirtz. The labor secretary observed that the best case he could make for the combined department was that its head would have a significant voice in the formulation of economic policy. Wirtz said that he had no influence on economic policy and felt that this was the most compelling reason for people like Meany, with sophistication in the ways of government, to support the merger.[39]

The following afternoon, 8 March Johnson expressed reservations to Califano about discussing the merger with the council the next day (there were several other topics on the agenda as well). This prompted Califano to write the president a memorandum that evening recommending that he

at least mention the new Department at the luncheon tomorrow. I recognize the problem you raised this afternoon, but I believe Meany was able to hold off action by the Council in Florida on the ground that you wanted to talk to them about it first. Some general mention would be helpful, even if you later turn the group over to Secretaries Wirtz and Trowbridge and Charlie Schultze.[40]

The proposal died the following day. Johnson apparently did what Califano asked and no more. He briefly discussed the merger at the end of his visit with the council members, turned the meeting over to his advisers, and left the room. According to a source quoted in the next day's *New York Times*, the union officials "generally left the impression that it would be difficult to work out any modification that would make it acceptable."[41]

A week later, Johnson sent Congress a special message, "The Quality of the American Government," in which he stated that he was asking his Advisory Committee on Labor-Management Policy to consider the proposal. Although the president's press secretary denied that the proposal was dead, most observers viewed this move as a way to quietly bury the merger scheme.[42] Alexander Trowbridge continued to attempt to pump life into the idea for six more weeks, but after his own meeting with industry and labor leaders on 2 May, he advised the president, perhaps unnecessarily, to give up.[43]

Commerce-Labor in Retrospect

The record of events between 27 December 1966, when Macy's letter went to the president, and 10 January 1967, when the president presented the proposal, reveals a feverish pitch in an activist administration's search for new ideas. The haste prevented the advance preparation and staff review that Johnson customarily required. Had labor's rejection not led to a quick death, comparable to the proposal's premature birth, the unresolved issues and the threats to established positions within the executive structure would undoubtedly have been reflected in congressional reaction.

Yet the incompleteness of staff work, both before and after the message, did not deter Califano from pushing the proposal on the president, and Johnson's own schedule must have prevented him from examining the structural issues and considering carefully the soft possibilities for political support. But, aside from the rush, the Commerce-Labor proposal was an anomaly, for it was not directly related to any major policy thrust of the administration. It was more distinctly a structural reform independent of particular presidential policy objectives than any other organizational change proposed by President Johnson. Perhaps this accounts for its untimely appearance and its less than enthusiastic reception.

A DEPARTMENT OF NATURAL RESOURCES

Perhaps no idea for reorganization has received so much attention recurrently as that for the consolidation of the water resources functions of the executive branch. Presidents Harding and Hoover favored transferring the civil functions of the Corps of Engineers to the Department of Interior. President Eisenhower in his final budget message recommended making this transfer and also transferring the river basin planning functions of the Federal Power Commission to Interior. And, similarly, perhaps no idea for comprehensive rearrangement of executive functions has received more attention than the proposal for a unified natural resources department. The Brownlow commission recommended a department of conservation, and a minority of the Hoover commission recommended a department of natural resources. The logic behind the idea for a department with the latter name has been succinctly stated in one of numerous BOB memorandums supporting the idea:

> Three executive departments—Interior, Agriculture, and Defense (Corps of Engineers)—now have independent, overlapping authority with respect to multiple-purpose development and management of water resources. Management of public lands and forests is divided between Interior and Agriculture. Interior has a government-wide responsibility with respect to minerals on all federally-owned lands, thereby dividing surface and subsurface management of the National Forests.[44]

Yet no organizational proposal forces into view a more complete demonstration of the conflicting perspectives on organization and the political limitations on the application of the comprehensive perspective to department structure. It has been said with respect to a single department for planning and action in this area of public policy: "It simply cannot be achieved . . . without a bloody, bone-shattering fight, which would leave the landscape so scarred that the conservation cause would be lost in the critical years immediately ahead."[45] Probably this says too little. There is probably no possibility of marshaling enough political force to achieve the result.

Nevertheless, the idea came off the back burner of the BOB and onto the White House table early in the Johnson presidency, as the legislative program for 1965 was being considered.[46] It was supported at about the same time by a recommendation of the Price task force[47] and was among the items on which Califano sought reports from cabinet and other officials at the end of 1965. The general form of the proposals as stated in the BOB was:

> To create a Department of Natural Resources by transferring to it the natural resources functions of the Department of the Interior, the water resources functions of the Army Corps of Engineers, the Forest Service and the watershed management functions of the Department of Agriculture, and certain water resources functions of the Federal Power Commission not essential to its regulatory functions. The Department of the Interior would be abolished. The Bureau of Indian Affairs and the Office of Territories, now in Interior, would be transferred to the Department of Health, Education and Welfare, a Department better equipped to deal with the urgent human problems found in those areas.

157

The Mississippi River Commission, the California Debris Commission, the Beach Erosion Board, and the Board of Engineers for Rivers and Harbors, which are subsidiary water resources agencies related to the Corps of Engineers, would be abolished and their functions transferred to the Secretary of Natural Resources.[48]

Califano received the responses he could have expected. From Udall, secretary of the interior, "*I strongly favor* the creation of a Department of Natural Resources."[49] From Orville Freeman, secretary of agriculture, disagreement with Califano's suggestions for such a department. The bases: defense of the location of the Forest Service and watershed protection functions in the Department of Agriculture; the anticipated antagonism of Interior, Public Works, and Agriculture committees and the appropriations committees; opposition of interest groups; need for staffing out a detailed study. To this reflection of particularistic perspectives of executive departments, congressional committees, and private interests, Freeman added a more general proposition that deviated from traditional management philosophy: "Competition is a healthy condition provided it is kept within bounds so it *stimulates* improved performance rather than destructive competition." He referred to the present cooperation between secretaries and between services, and he continued his unorthodoxy: "To combine these activities would tend to establish a monolithic government recreation operation which would be monopoly [*sic*] in its nature and would tend towards complacency with a great concentration of power."[50] From Alfred B. Hitt, general counsel, Department of the Army: emphasis on the several aspects of the Corps functions that would need careful attention and a suggestion for study over a three-week period by all affected agencies, with subsequent analysis in BOB and the White House. Hitt, however, made concessions: (1) the case for control over waterways navigation by the Corps was only "that it works," and the question would be a different one if the president were considering a department of transportation; (2) the navigation planning task could be shifted to a department of natural resources. The negative nature of his views was reflected in the comments that "a Department of Natural Resources has an organizational tidiness which is very appealing," but that it "involves an immense upheaval and ought to be articulated in great detail lest it founder on some small but emotionally charged issue."[51]

Udall saw, but perhaps underestimated, the political difficulty of achieving the reorganization he desired. "Hill politics" holds the key, but a "two-bite plan attuned to congressional realities," with the president dividing and conquering his opposition, was suggested. The first bite, for 1966, would be the transfer of water pollution and air pollution to Interior, and a transfer out of it of non-natural-resource functions that logically belonged in other departments. The second bite, for 1967 or 1968, would be the transfer of the

Corps and the change in department name. A postscript suggested for "tactical reasons" leaving out the Forest Service, but said, "At the right time, ripe fruit drops of its own weight."[52]

On yet another aspect of the proposed rationalization of functional allocations—the transfer of the Bureau of Indian Affairs, which handled both resource and educational matters—there was entrenched defense of the status quo. Udall was negative, and adverse reactions were reported from Congress. This more restricted proposal was being separately considered at the same time Califano was exploring opinion on the natural resources department, and Califano reported to the president that he and Lee White recommended that the proposal be deferred a year to give Udall and Gardner time to work out support. But the president responded, "Let's forget it."[53]

In effect, the same verdict was given on the broader proposal. This was revealed in the exploratory hearings held on Senator Moss's bill to create a department of natural resources with functions similiar to those contained in BOB summaries. Freeman opposed the bill, as did representatives of the Army; Wilbur J. Cohen, under secretary of HEW, opposed transfer of air pollution and solid waste disposal functions and thought further consideration should be given to Indian Affairs. Udall's view was also particularistic; he doubted the timeliness of the change in title and questioned whether the benefits from consolidation of water resources and pollution control functions would exceed losses suffered from the changes; he had mixed feelings on the Indian Bureau; and he opposed transfer of the Office of Territories. Senator Ribicoff, appreciative of the secretary's loyalty to the administration's position, remarked to him that, since "you cannot get the approval of the President and the Bureau of the Budget, that you feel you might as well do the best you can with an unhappy situation." The position of the administration was, of course, stated by the representative of BOB: the bill was not favored "at this time."[54] Thus the administration pulled away from "a bloody, bone-shattering fight" in which the odds favored defeat rather than victory.

A Department of Education and Related Matters

While the issue of organization for natural resource functions exhibits—in the Johnson administration and continually—a conflict between rationalization and the politics of particularistic perspectives, the issue of organization for education uncovers, in addition to political factors, a basic conflict in expert opinion on executive structure. Under Johnson, rival suggestions mirrored this conflict, but a more urgent problem with respect to educational administration demanded the immediate attention of the administration.

The conflict of opinion on executive structure, stated simply in managerial terms, was whether the president's span of control ought to be limited by the creation of consolidated departments or superdepartments, within which coordination and direction might be partially achieved without presidential burden, or whether the responsibilities of administration should be divided among a larger number of departments and agencies, with coordination provided by interdepartmental and presidential activity. More broadly, the issue became one between policy and management objectives—whether the policy purpose needs to be emphasized and strengthened by a separate organization with cabinet-level standing, or whether management objectives of coordination and reduced presidential span of control should be dominant. In practical terms the argument was whether departments should represent unified constituency groupings or, as some in BOB believed, multiconstituency interests. These issues were brought to focus on the contest over whether education should have a separate department or be part of a larger assembly of functions.

As in the case of natural resources, the proposal for a department of education surfaced in the White House in 1964 from BOB and task force sources. As early as June 1964, and again the following December, BOB was referring this subject to Moyers for consideration for inclusion in the president's legislative program.[55] Moreover, the President's Task Force on Government Reorganization (the Price task force) recommended creation of a department of education, and the President's Task Force on Education proposed either an independent presidential office, similar to OEO, or a department of education. Both task forces reported in November 1964.

The next month, Congressman John E. Fogarty (D–R.I.), who like Senator Ribicoff had been a strong advocate of a department of education, wrote to the president urging him to adopt this as part of his education program. The president replied that the suggestion was "timely" and would be "carefully considered in the course" of the review of the structure of the executive branch he was conducting.[56] Bills for creation of a department of education were introduced in the Senate and the House in January 1965.[57]

Immediately a more urgent, almost a crisis, situation in educational administration confronted the president. The organizational structure of the Office of Education had been strained by the burdens of recently passed legislation. On 11 April 1965 the president signed the Elementary and Secondary Education Act, which increased the activities of the office enormously and started them in new directions. The president himself became involved in the reorganization of the office that was needed promptly. At a reception for members of Congress on the occasion of signing the act, the president said, "I am asking Secretary [Anthony] Celebrezze and Commissioner [Francis] Keppel to move immediately to prepare the Office of Education for the big job it has to do, just as soon as the funds are appropriated. Upon their recommendation, I am notifying the Secretary that I am going to appoint a task force to carry out his recommendations to assist him in the next 60 days on organization and personnel problems in this area to administer this bill."[58] Moving at once, the president designated for full-time work a task force composed of a representative each from BOB and the Civil Service Commission, with Dwight A. Ink of the Atomic Energy Commission as chairman. With the assistance of BOB and the Civil Service Commission, the cooperation of HEW, and the oversight of Douglass Cater from the White House Office, a new structure for the Office of Education and accompanying personnel requirements were worked out in detail and reported to the president, the cabinet, and the press about mid-July. Although the programs suffered—as is so often the case—from the speed with which organizational arrangements were created, the prompt reorganization of the Office of Education for the administration of the Elementary and Secondary Education Act and other functions was one of the major administrative accomplishments of the Johnson administration.[59]

The proposal for a department was not dead. Fogarty again wrote to the president; and, replying for the president, Cater promised that the question "will be given active review before the next session of Congress."[60] When asked at a news conference on 28 July if the selection of John Gardner as the new secretary of HEW suggested "that there will be less interest now in the creation of a separate department of education," the president replied, "No, not at all."[61] But the question was never put high on the legislative agenda or given the thorough staff study that would have been necessary to shape a proposal. A wide-ranging study on the components of a department of education would have been required. Would, for example, a new department incorporate the National Science Foundation, the educational functions of the National Institutes of Health, and various other educational functions, as proposed in the Price task force report? Would it include, also or alternatively, manpower training and placement functions?[62] The president undoubtedly had an interest in all matters related to his favorite subject—education—but other reorganizations were pending or being urged. BOB understood that the president desired only one proposal for a new department to go before Congress at a time, and legislation to establish HUD had been recommended and was pending. Moreover, a recommendation for a department of transportation had also come to the president's attention.[63]

Nevertheless, there was concern by many over the low status of education in the executive structure, which was believed not to offer attractive positions for educational executives or adequate representation of education before Congress. But the discussion of a form of organization shifted within the administration from a department of education to a superdepartment including education as one of its functions. This was the proposal of Secretary

Gardner in the fall of 1966 and would be' included within the recommendations of the Heineman Task Force on Organization in 1967.[64] While the latter's report had not yet been made, a President's Task Force on Education, reporting 30 June 1967, said it tended "to favor the plan attributed to Secretary Gardner for elevating the status of education by giving it greater rank within the Department of HEW."[65] The proposal, we may note, did not provide for elevation to cabinet status and hence would not have been acceptable to many who desired such a department.

The Task Force on Education of 1967, recognizing the complexity of the problem, proposed "establishment of a high level Task Force or Public Commission to study recommendations concerning the organization of Federal programs in support of education." It should look at such alternatives for elevating status as a separate department, organization within HEW, a coordination agency in the Executive Office—like the Council of Economic Advisers or the Office of Science and Technology (OST) or an advisory group from outside the government for the president and the education agencies.[66] It is not suprising that such uncertainty about executive structure, the issues about what should be collected in a department or subdivision on education, the varied perspectives of interests within and outside government on these matters, and the other pressures on the administration left the president without a position of advocacy, and the issue of organization of educational functions was set aside for future consideration.[67]

ADDITIONAL ADMINISTRATIVE PROPOSALS

Many additional organizational proposals surfaced in the subpresidency but failed either to gain the president's approval (perhaps even his attention) or to obtain the consensus or support necessary for adoption. Yet several received enough attention to merit mention. One that gained presidential approval and got on the track for congressional acceptance was transfer of SBA to the Department of Commerce. The Price task force included the SBA in the components of the Department of Economic Development recommended by it in 1964. BOB included consolidation of SBA and Commerce in lists of reorganizations sent to the White House in 1964 and 1965, and congressional opinions were sounded in early 1966. Though the proposal had other opposition, Senator John Sparkman (D–Ala.) killed it. It was reported to the president that Sparkman wanted him to know that the action would "be harmful to him politically and also unwise administratively."[68] The death of the proposal was signaled in a letter from Sparkman, chairman of the Senate Small Business Committee, reporting a resolution of the committee declaring its opposition.[69]

Another proposal, approved by the president, was for creation of a strong chairman for the ICC, to be designated by the president. He stated in a message to Congress that he would include this in a reorganization plan,[70] but it was never submitted. Tentatively accepted by the president was a proposal, initiated by the Price task force and approved by BOB, for consolidation of bank examination functions. The president also favored a proposal for transfer of telecommunications management from the Office of Emergency Planning to a new executive office.[71]

The Price task force recommended a single administrator instead of the existing commission for Atomic Energy Commission functions, and the approach was favored by BOB and the Office of Science and Technology. The Departments of Commerce and Treasury recommended that civil service positions be substituted for presidential appointees (with Senate confirmation) in the Patent Office and the Bureau of the Mint, and the consequences of such a move were given consideration in the subpresidency. A President's Task Force on Indian Affairs recommended in December 1966, contingent on lack of opposition from Indian leaders, that primary responsibility for Indian Affairs be transferred from Interior to HEW; but, as noted above, the president shelved the idea when opposition developed.

The President's National Commission on Selective Service suggested a radical restructuring of the selective service system, but an interagency task force formed at the direction of the president found the structure of the selective service agency to be satisfactory.[72] The National Labor Relations Board desired a reorganization plan to authorize it to delegate to hearing examiners authority to make determinations on unfair labor practices and to issue orders, subject to discretionary review by the board. BOB proposed abolition of the Bureau of Security and Consular Affairs, with transfer of its functions to the secretary of state, and the transfer of weather modification functions from the National Science Foundation (NSF) to Commerce. OST recommended that a direct channel of presidential authority to NSF be strengthened by vesting power in the director to take final action on individual transactions, subject to policy made by the board. BOB also advocated on various occasions transfer to the secretary of HEW all functions within the department not legally vested in him.

CONCLUSION

The failure of some organizational initiatives under President Johnson was due to conditions in which particularistic points of view were dominant. The proposal for a department of business and labor died because it conflicted with the perspectives of business and labor on the representational purpose to be served. A strong case existed for a structure that would increase the president's ability to mediate disputes between business and labor and that would add a new component to economic advice to the president. Moreover, with the addition of agricultural functions it could become the nucleus of a superdepartment. Yet it was clear that this potential threatened the institutional representation of interests in the government so radically that presidential action could not achieve it. Similarly, a recommendation for a department of natural resources, resurrected by the subpresidency, was defeated because of "proprietary" interests in programs and budgets on the part of affected agencies and congressional committees.

A proposal for a department of education, which received some consideration, was not accepted because of the conflict between those who favored a department with a unified constituency and those who saw education as one of a number of functions in a large and diversified structure. Finally, there were a variety of proposals that received attention in the subpresidency—or were even recommended by the president—that failed because they could not generate widespread interest or support.

SEVEN

PROTECTING THE PRESIDENT'S HIERARCHICAL POSITION

From the comprehensive management perspective, the president is properly endowed with hierarchical controls over the executive structure. Yet the position of the president and the national and public power of his office are threatened by forces that can dilute their influence. Historically, two common methods of weakening the presidency have been to spread national executive power among a number of participants and to create decision-making centers strongly independent of presidential influence.

The president, however, has not been without countervailing resources. The Constitution gives him not only a general caretaker responsibility for the execution of the laws, but also the authority to appoint officers of the United States, with the advice and consent of the Senate, and the power to veto laws encroaching on his authority. The appointment power has been construed to include power to remove at his discretion officers performing executive duties.[1]

On several occasions during the Johnson presidency the president and the subpresidency acted to protect the president as head of the executive branch. The action was against sharing executive authority and influence with Congress, with professional groups, with governors, and with a departmental secretary. The incidents, as well as the policy objectives pursued, illustrate the conflicting forces affecting presidential capability for direction of executive structure.

PROTECTING THE EXECUTIVE FROM CONGRESS

The Price Task Force on Government Reorganization gave attention to types of provisions in law "which either raise constitutional questions or which

165

cumulatively encroach in a serious way . . . on the proper authority of the President."[2] Among these were

> statutory provisions that give particular Congressional committees the opportunity to control executive decisions, either by requiring reports and a waiting period, or by requiring committee approval of specific projects.[3]

Such provisions are distinguishable from the legislative veto by which either house separately or the two concurrently may disapprove executive actions. The constitutionality and the wisdom of the legislative veto have been questioned, and contention over it has been paralleled by the debate over congressional committee authority.

Statutory provisions requiring notice to congressional committees and a waiting period are distinct in legal terms from those requiring committee approval for executive decision. Yet both are often loosely called "committee veto," and the practical effect may be the same. When a committee objects after notice and during a waiting period, an agency is not likely to complete proposed action. Thus, notice or approval provisions create co-administration by executive agencies and congressional committees in place of executive administration.

A study during the Johnson presidency located nineteen statutory provisions that required referral to congressional committees. Of these, twelve were of the notice type; the others required committee approval.[4]

President Johnson strongly defended the executive position against committe approval requirements. In June 1965 he vetoed the Pacific Northwest Disaster Relief Act that contained a committee-approval provision. In justification, he said:

> The Attorney General advises me that this provision is clearly a "coming into agreement" with a Congressional committee requirement. This device requires an executive official to obtain the approval of a committee or other unit of Congress before taking an executive action. It is not only an undesirable and improper encroachment by the Congress and its committees into the area of executive responsibilities—it also leads to inefficient administration. The executive branch is given, by the Constitution, the responsibility to implement all laws—a specific and exclusive responsibility which cannot properly be shared with a committee of Congress.[5]

In signing the Omnibus Rivers and Harbors Act in October of the same year, he stated, "I cannot abide by one provision of the bill which flies in the face of the Constitution." With respect to the provision that required committee approval, he said, "It would dilute and diminish the authority and powers of the President."

The people of this country did not elect me to this office to preside over its erosion. And I intend to turn over this office with all its responsibilities and powers intact to the next man who sits in this chair.[6]

Similarly, Johnson would not accept a notice and waiting provision that seriously interfered with effective administration. In 1965 he vetoed a military authorization bill that provided that no military installation or facility could be abandoned or reduced in mission until 120 days after reports of the proposed action had been made to the committees on armed services of the houses, that provided further that such reports could be submitted only between 1 January and 30 April of each year, and further that in case Congress adjourned sine die within the 120 days the report should be submitted to the next regular session of Congress. The bill in effect would have deprived the president of power to propose for eight months of the year and could have prevented his action for a year or more, and at a minimum for 120 days. The veto message stated: "The times do not permit it. The Constitution prohibits it."[7]

On the other hand, President Johnson acquiesced in notice and waiting provisions that were deemed reasonable in their requirements. He accepted a second version of the military authorization bill that revised the requirement in the vetoed bill to one for thirty days notice and contained a similar provision in another part of the act.[8] Yet the basis for his acceptance was made clear again when he accepted a military construction act that extended the period of notice to thirty days of "continuous session" of the Congress. The president said:

I have serious doubts that the new restriction meets the test of a reasonable waiting period set out in my veto message on the first military construction bill last year. However, ... I am resolving this doubt in favor of approval. Nevertheless, my responsibilities as President and Commander in Chief will require me to seek prompt revision of the restriction if future circumstances prove it to be inimical to the national interest.[9]

PROTECTING THE EXECUTIVE FROM PRIVATE CONTROL

Included in the Price task force's listing of provisions that could encroach on the president's authority were these:

[Provisions that give] representatives of private interests some role (usually in a nominally advisory capacity) in the executive decision-making process.
Statutory provisions that limit the President's authority in appointing or removing officials who will discharge executive functions.[10]

167

There are various kinds of arrangements for private group protection or participation that can affect the potential for presidential influence. The most familiar perhaps is the independence from presidential controls in law and tradition of independent regulatory commissions. It is a form of organization deemed by economic groups to be less threatening to them than one that implies full responsibility to the president. Other protections for group interests are advisory committees, qualifications for agency personnel, or requirements for consent. Sometimes group participation becomes associated with technical expertise and may produce ambiguity on whether the participation is independently professional or associated with economic interest. Whether participation is strictly professional or client-oriented, an issue of presidential responsibility and democratic accountability may arise. The subtleties of the issues in what appear to be narrow choices are exhibited in the history of two laws passed during the Johnson presidency: those creating the national endowments for the arts and the humanities and the Administrative Conference of the United States. Both show group influence, almost determinism, on choice of organizational form, as well as group participation reconciled in law with presidential authority.

The National Endowments for the Arts and the Humanities

Congress in 1965 established the national endowments for the arts and the humanities. The legislation had the endorsement of the president. At a speech at Brown University, whose president had been chairman of the Commission on Humanities that had recommended government support, the president said, "And I look with the greatest of favor upon the proposal by your own able President Keeney's Commission for a National Foundation for the Humanities."[11] Also, the president, who had signed a bill in 1964 for a National Council on the Arts in the Executive Office, said in his State of the Union Message, "I will propose a National Foundation on the Arts."[12] When numerous bills were introduced in the Congress for government support for the humanities and arts through joint or separate foundations, and when joint hearings by Senate and House subcommittees had begun, the president was asked for his recommendations. The administration sent a clean bill to Congress with the president's endorsement on 10 March 1965.[13] It was a very popular proposal in the Congress, but at least one participant believed it would not have been successful without the president's endorsement.[14] The president even intervened personally with the Speaker of the House of Representatives to draw the bill out of a committee tangle and onto the floor of the House.[15]

By the time the president sent his bill to Congress an organizational model had been fixed in the perspectives of clientele or professional groups to be served through the legislation. Their position was that the groups affected should participate in administration so that the norms of the groups would be protected. This position needed to be reconciled with presidential authority.

Similar ideas had set the pattern for the structure of the National Science Foundation. A bill passed by Congress in 1947 to create a National Science Foundation provided for a board with twenty-four members chosen by the president, which was to select an executive committee with nine members, which in turn would designate an executive director. President Truman vetoed this bill, which put two layers between him and the director, because it implied "a distinct lack of faith in the democratic process" and deprived the president of means "for discharging his constitutional responsibilities."[16]

A new bill was accepted by President Truman,[17] though it still contained provisions to ensure independence of the foundation from presidential direction and to guarantee representation of professional groups in government decisions. The foundation's affairs would be conducted by a board of twenty-four members, appointed by the president with advice and consent of the Senate, and a director who would be similarly appointed. The members were to "be eminent in the fields of the basic sciences, medical science, engineering, agriculture, education, or public affairs," "be selected solely on the basis of established records of distinguished service," and "be so selected as to provide representation of the views of scientific leaders in all areas of the Nation"; the president was requested to consider nominations submitted by certain named organizations "or by other scientific or educational organizations." The board would make policies. The director, in accordance with these, would exercise the grant and contract powers of the foundation, but only with approval "in each instance" of the board. Similarly, the director could not be appointed without the board's having opportunity to make recommendations. Thus the act struck a compromise between the constitutional responsibility of the president and clientele administration of a public function.

Although details vary, and advice rather than approval is the usual requirement, the protection of professional and research groups is embodied in other administrative structures, such as the National Institutes of Health (NIH). This pattern also prevailed in the National Council on the Arts established by legislation in 1964—a year before the establishment of the endowments for the arts and the humanities.[18] Located within the Executive Office of the President, the National Council had as members a chairman, the secretary of the Smithsonian Institution, and twenty-four persons from private life appointed by the president—with fixed terms, representing the various arts, and appointed only after nominations from leading professional organizations. The council had only study and recommendation functions, and its chairman, who was appointed with the advice and consent of the

Senate, was to advise the president on federal activities related to the arts. The bills prepared in early 1965 for government grants for support of the arts would include this council. Likewise, the framers of bills for support of the humanities had before them the recommendation of the Keeney commission for a foundation with a board of twenty-four members "to determine and carry out its programs," and a director who would be ex officio a member of the board and appointed after nominations from the board, with both the board and the director to be appointed for fixed terms by the president with the advice and consent of the Senate.[19] The organizational pattern—resembling a form of public/private federalism, or a combination of presidential responsibility and clientele administration—was included in the bills. The form of organization was so widely favored and seemingly so far removed from "big politics" that the president and the subpresidency acquiesced. BOB, reporting to the president on the enrolled bill, said merely that it "questions a number of the amendments affecting administrative arrangements but believes they will not cause serious problems."[20]

The issue before Congress was the authorization of a new program of grants to states, nonprofit organizations and individuals for support of arts and humanities, similar to support for the sciences through the National Science Foundation. Although there was a resolution in opposition by the Republican Policy Committee and though there were procedural snags, the purpose had overwhelming support, and amendments of the administration bill related to details.

The administrative structure adopted was a National Foundation on the Arts and Humanities, including a National Endowment for the Arts and a National Endowment for the Humanities, and a national council and a chairman for each endowment. The Council for the Humanities was to be composed of twenty-six members "to provide a comprehensive representation of the views of scholars and professional practitioners in the humanities and the public throughout the United States." The Council on the Arts would be formed as provided in the act of 1964, except for increase of membership from twenty-four to twenty-six, to include persons "widely recognized for their broad knowledge of or experience in, or for their profound interest in the arts"; "to include practising artists, civic cultural leaders, members of the museum profession, and others who are professionally engaged in the arts"; and "collectively to provide an appropriate distribution of membership among the major art fields." For each council the president would give consideration to persons nominated from time to time by leading national organizations in the fields. The chairman of each council would be appointed for a fixed term by the president with the advice and consent of the Senate and would be responsible for the policies and decisions of the endowment. The council would be appointed by the president for fixed terms and would advise the chairman and make recommendations on all applications for grants.[21]

The act for the National Foundation for the Arts and Humanities modified the pattern of the National Science Foundation Act. The chairman for each endowment, not the council, was responsible for decisions on public expenditures. An amendment by Congressman Ogden Reid, a supporter of the legislation, to require approval of decisions by the councils was defeated.[22] The president was not limited, or burdened, by a requirement of senatorial confirmation of council members, and he was free, despite legal provisions, to choose council members who would provide broad representation for the public.

Thus, the endowments were not independent of the president. As in the committees of NIH, the councils were advisory. It may be assumed also that appointing the chairmen for fixed terms would not legally limit the president's removal power. Yet the advisory function was firmly incorporated in the decision process, and, through council representation, the special clienteles could benefit from the decisions made. In sum, the structure was peculiar. Although the president's prerogatives were maintained, the pattern of organization created a duality in the exercise of power.

There was reference in the hearings to the possibility of placing the foundation under the shelter of the Smithsonian Institution and to the relationship of the new functions to those of the Office of Education. But there was no serious consideration of consolidation with related functions. There was a gesture in the act toward coordination. An interagency committee—the Federal Council on the Arts and Humanities—was created to advise the two chairs and to promote coordination between the endowments and related activities of other agencies.[23]

The Administrative Conference of the United States

An enactment in the Johnson presidency that shows group influence toward choice of organization form that would give the group a continuing influence on public policy, yet that avoided issues of presidential control, was the Administrative Conference Act of 1964. In this act the president's appointive power for administrative functions was combined with an advisory function of a professional group.

The Administrative Conference of the United States was created to study and make recommendations for the improvement of administrative procedure. Such a function could have been located in the Department of Justice or the Bureau of the Budget (BOB). But there were precedents for a different type of organization that would reflect the views of a professional group. The Administrative Conference exemplifies effort to achieve procedural reform through the shared opinion of professional participants, in this case primarily members of the bar. Also, within the bar a distinct perspective had developed

171

on those specialized aspects of government operations defined as "administrative" in the Administrative Procedures Act of 1946, including rule-making and adjudication. From this perspective independence from executive control was viewed as desirable for economic regulatory activities. It is not surprising, therefore, that accord on a professional, semi-independent structure for study of "administrative" procedure should have crystallized before the Johnson presidency.

Twice, temporary administrative conferences had been held—one in the Eisenhower administration and one in the Kennedy administration. The conferences operated with a chairman, a small council, and an assembly of about eighty members. The chairman, assisted by the council, gave leadership to the conference; studies were made by a small staff or through contract with experts; and votes on recommendations for procedural change were taken in the assembly. About two-thirds of the assembly's members were the heads or delegates of administrative agencies; representatives of the public accounted for the remaining seats. The membership—both public and private—was almost exclusively from the legal profession. The recommendations of the conference would go to whoever could carry them into effect—the agencies, the president, the Congress. Agency membership was viewed as crucial to provide knowledge on problems studied and to gain agency support for reforms.

From the American Bar Association and others interested in "efficiency, adequacy, and fairness,"as President Kennedy defined the objectives of procedure,[24] came movement for establishment of a permanent administrative conference, with the structure of previous conferences as a model. BOB supported the legislation and aided in drafting it, even though it has been reported that the president did not regard it as important.[25]

When the Administrative Conference Act of 1964 finally emerged, it provided for a conference composed of a chairman appointed by the president for a five-year term, with the advice and consent of the Senate, a council of ten appointed by the president, with at least one-half from the regulatory commissions or departments, and an assembly of seventy-five to ninety-one members appointed by the chairman with one-third to two-fifths from the public. The anticipation of autonomy for the conference in its advisory function was indicated by the fixed term of office for the chairman and by the provision that "the Assembly shall have ultimate authority over the activities of the Conference."[26]

Comment

The administrative design for the national endowments and the Administrative Conference has the advantage of attracting ability and expertise to government service—especially where actions are particularized, as in awarding grants. There may also be advantages in protecting against political influence. Yet there are important practical considerations that support protection of the president's constitutional position. Even in advisory functions, breadth in representation may safeguard against narrowness in point of view or interests protected; where decisions on public policies and their application are to be made, the representation of the public generally through the position of the president supports confidence in the fairness of government. In creating the endowments, the protection of the president's prerogatives and position were better served than in creating the National Science Foundation: the president's authority was preserved through appointment of a chairman with policy and administrative responsibility. Moreover, the directions in the act with respect to persons to be appointed to the councils were advisory and left him with discretion to select individuals outside professional or clientele groups. The president's authority was similarly protected in the case of the Administrative Conference, even though its functions were advisory only.

PROTECTING THE EXECUTIVE IN A FEDERAL SYSTEM

Federal-state collaboration has become a favored, often necessary, means for achieving, or seeking, public objectives. Nevertheless, when national policies exist, administrative decisions on application of those policies, including those on commitment of national funds, are regularly made by federal officials serving in some hierarchical relation to the president. Thus the article II responsibility of the president is protected.

A challenge to the presidential role in this system was spotted by BOB in the planning for the Appalachian Regional Development Act of 1965. The issues raised then and on consideration of amendments to the act in 1967 were not entirely new but were identical with or extensions of those presented in the developments attending the formation of the Delaware River Basin Commission in 1961. The commission, representing four states and the United States government, was instructed by a compact among the states and the United States to plan and promote coordinated policies for the basin, to construct and operate projects and facilities, and to borrow money for purposes of the project. The compact has been said to have been "an almost unbelievable innovation" in American government in that it created "a government agency which is at once a part of each of the affected states and the United States Government."[27] In doing so, it brought into issue the hegemony of the federal government in federal-state relations. The compact provided that "no project having a substantial effect on the water resources of the basin shall hereafter be undertaken . . . unless it shall have been first . . . approved by the commission."

Objections to this sharing of power were raised within the subpresidency, with the result that the compact as finally approved protected the federal position, and the authority of the president as executive agent of the federal government, through what amounted to a two-stage veto authorization: the federal government would not be bound by any provision of the river basin plan unless the federal member of the commission (appointed by the president) concurred in it; and "whenever the President shall find and determine that the national interest so requires, he may suspend, modify or delete any provision of the comprehensive plan to the extent that it affects the exercise of any powers, rights, functions, or jurisdiction conferred by law on any officer, agency or instrumentality of the United States."[28]

The broadest significance of the "unbelievable innovation" for joint federal-state administration is the potential for expansion of the innovation toward a new system of administration. It would be based on regional commonalities, provide options for decentralization in planning and administration for implementation of broad national purposes, and create new elements of federalism. For any or all of these reasons some planners of administrative structure could see new vision and merit in the attempt. Yet a real decentralization to regional authorities in which governors shared equally with representatives of the president could be expected to meet opposition from those who desired uniform application of national purpose, from agencies desiring to retain planning and administration of separate programs, and from elements of BOB who advised the president on allocation of funds and protected his position as head of the executive branch. The issues inherent in the controversy soon to develop were those of decentralization against the dominance of the federal government and the power of the president as agent of that dominance.

These broad differences in perspective were reflected in specific issues when a program began to be developed by the Kennedy and Johnson administrations for relief of poverty and economic development in the Appalachian region. Poverty and underdevelopment in the area, as well as pleas from several state governors, led President Kennedy to appoint in April 1963 a President's Appalachian Regional Commission, composed of representatives of the Appalachian states and federal agencies, to prepare a plan for economic development of the area. As the commission, chaired by assistant secretary of commerce Franklin Roosevelt, Jr., was reaching conclusions on a large program of public expenditures for national and human resources development, BOB objected on both substantive and organizational grounds.

BOB's objections on substantive issues concerned commitment of national funds and led to conflict in the subpresidency during the first three months of 1964. Parties to the controversy included Roosevelt, John L. Sweeney, executive director of the Appalachian Commission, BOB, and presidential counsel Lee White. Roosevelt and Sweeney were defenders of the plan about to emerge from the commission for greatly augmented and accelerated expenditures for the Appalachian area, with specific obligations for federal funding. BOB objected generally to the inflexibility of the commitments from the federal treasury. Sweeney saw the conflict as whether the commission's report "should conform to existing policy determinations of the Federal executive branch."[29] Lee White became mediator. He reported to Bill Moyers "a hard fought agreement between Frank Roosevelt and Budget with me serving as referee, interlocutor, and King Solomon."[30] Memorandums went to the president from Roosevelt and Sweeney emphasizing the expectations of the governors, with BOB reflecting its view of general government interests and White House personnel mediating the conflict.[31] The president himself made a spectacular trip through Appalachia and sent Congress an enthusiastic acceptance of the goals of the commission. He did not, however, endorse specific budgetary commitments for the future.

BOB also objected to a proposal for a federal-state development corporation with mixed stock ownership. It would be financed largely by federal appropriations and federally guaranteed bonds and would engage in diverse activities, including planning and coordination, promotion of development activities and districts, and use of funds to supplement existing federal programs. A board of directors would be composed of heads of federal agencies designated by the president and governors of states subscribing to the capital stock of the corporation. Within the corporation there would be two votes, one by a federal co-chairman designated by the president, the other by a state co-chairman selected by the governors; a chief executive officer would be selected by the board. Harold Seidman, BOB's director of the Division of Management and Organization, objected in a statement that reflected that agency's position on mixed government corporations:

> The usual justification for a mixed ownership corporation would not apply to the proposed joint Federal-State development corporation. There is no contemplation that the States would be the eventual owners of the Corporation. Indeed, the proposed Corporation would be both in law and in fact a Federal agency created by the Congress for Federal purposes and financed from Federal funds. Mixed ownership is a transparent fiction designed for the sole purpose of permitting State governors to participate in the direction and control of a Federal agency. Thus a limited number of State governors would be accorded authority with respect to Federal programs for which they could not be held responsible or accountable. The designation of governors as corporation directors would appear to conflict directly with Article 2, Section 2 of the Constitution which vests the appointment of Federal officers in the President, the courts of law or the heads of departments.
>
> The proposed arrangements are calculated to impair seriously the executive powers vested in the President and his ability to "take care that the laws be faithfully executed." The Corporation would not be

175

responsive to Presidential direction and control. The President would not have authority directly to appoint or remove any of the Corporation's directors, although he would designate the Federal co-chairman. The Federal directors would serve ex officio and would have to be removed from their other jobs in order to remove them from the Board. State representatives would have 50 percent of the vote and could veto actions desired by the President and agreed to unanimously by the Federal directors. In casting his vote, the Federal co-chairman would be acting "on behalf of the Federal members" not by direction of the President. In creating Government corporations in recent years, Congress has generally provided in specific language that they shall be subject to the direction and supervision by the President. As a mixed ownership Government Corporation, the Corporation would be exempt from annual budget control, although specific requests for appropriations would have to go to the Congress.

The proposed arrangements appear to us to be unworkable and would produce organizational and administrative chaos.[32]

Seidman proposed an alternative: to establish a joint federal-state development planning commission, with a chairman and federal agency representatives selected by the president and a member from each state selected in accordance with state law; to place the new functions, administrative in nature, in the appropriate federal departments or in an Appalachian Development Administration in the Department of Commerce.

This separation of planning from administrative functions was achieved in the act that was passed.[33] The Appalachian Regional Commission created by the act would have responsibility for coordinated planning, for providing a forum for consideration of problems, and for encouraging avenues of development; but it would not have responsibility for execution of federal programs. Although the commission was a joint federal-state organization, the president's position was protected. Decisions were to be made by the affirmative vote of a majority of the states and of the federal co-chairman, thus creating federal veto as well as offering an opportunity for federal leadership. The federal co-chairman was to be compensated at level IV of the federal executive salary classification and appointed by the president with approval of the Senate. The President himself was made responsible for liaison between the federal government and the commission and for a coordinated review within the federal government of plans and recommendations developed by the commission.

Yet the administration of federal programs for Appalachia remained essentially as it had been in the past. The administration bill proposed, instead of a mixed federal-state corporation, the creation of a federal development corporation that could assist in financing projects within the region. The Congress killed this proposal and left the operation of federal programs in the federal line agencies, expending funds from the appropriations in accordance with commission recommendations.

Although no commission recommendations had been rejected by the line agencies—essentially because the federal co-chairman cleared the recommendations with the agencies before giving his approval—the governors were dissatisfied with the arrangements. They desired direct appropriation of federal funds to the commission. They were supported by federal co-chairman Sweeney, who saw disadvantages for Appalachia in uncoordinated budget planning by federal bureaus and departments for expenditures for that area.[34] As the Appalachian Act came up for renewal and revision in 1967, the bill for this purpose introduced by Senator Jennings Randolph contained a provision for direct appropriations to the commission. The commission would make the final determination of amounts and purposes of expenditures, with the agencies remaining as the operating instruments to implement the recommendations.

Again, BOB objected. Although it saw possible constitutional encroachment on the president's appointment power in vesting administrative powers in nonfederal members of the commission,[35] it argued mainly on administrative considerations:

> to appropriate funds and authorities directly to this Commission would set a very dangerous precedent for many other Commissions which are now forming. It would tend to create many independent Commissions with independent Federal representatives directly reporting to the President and outside the supervision and control of any of the President's Cabinet Officers.[36]

In this instance two actors in the subpresidency gave opposing advice. Sweeney urged Califano that the president should be noncommital on the issues raised by the Randolph bill,[37] and he testified in favor of direct appropriations to the commission.[38] But in a letter to the president of the Senate and the Speaker of the House the president asked that the 1965 act be extended in its present form,[39] and he responded favorably to Schultze's suggestion that Califano and Schultze talk to Randolph.[40] He later approved opposition to an amendment with similar content proposed in the House committee.[41]

In the end there was a compromise. The Senate bill, with provisions ultimately to be adopted by Congress, provided for the appropriations for the commission to be made to the president with the understanding that he would pass them on. Moreover, language limiting the president's authority to disapprove commission-approved projects was removed.

Thus the president was protected in two ways. He retained the veto, to be exercised through the federal co-chairman, that had been given to him in 1965. He had, at least technically, a power over appropriations to the commission, and perhaps his position in consideration of budget proposals to Congress for Appalachia was strengthened. Moreover, the line agencies were protected from carrying out any recommendations of the commission in violation of their legal authorizations. Yet BOB was still concerned that the independence of this commission, and perhaps others modeled after it, would leave the president without any instrument, other than the budget examiners in BOB, for direction and oversight and thus would dilute his hierarchical authority over it.

This concern of BOB had been heightened by the creation of other regional commissions. As the Appalachian Commission was being proposed in 1965, members of the Senate from certain other regions were alerted to the possibilities for federal funding for development in their regions. Senatorial logrolling led the administration to submit a bill to allow creation of other regional commissions. BOB's desire that these commissions be integrated into a department prevailed both in the administration's bill and in the action of Congress. Each commission would be similar to the Appalachian Commission in that it would have a federal co-chairman. But the plans of the commissions would go the secretary of commerce, who, after they were submitted to federal agencies for review, would transmit them to the president "for such action as he may deem desirable." The secretary of commerce would coordinate the activities of the federal co-chairmen and serve as liaison between the commissions and the rest of the federal executive establishment.[42]

When the Appalachian extension bill came up for consideration in 1967, the president himself expressed a desire to assign responsibility for federal participation in regional commissions to a department. He said that his proposal for a department of business and labor would

> contain a recommendation that Federal activities relating to regional economic development and depressed areas be coordinated through the new Department. This Department would then have the basic responsibility for the Federal government's efforts in all of the regional commissions that have been or soon will be established, including the Appalachian Regional Commission.[43]

Later, when the proposal for a department of business and labor was dead and the Appalachian renewal bill had passed, Califano sent the president a proposal endorsed by him, Schultze, Alexander Trowbridge, secretary of commerce, and James Gaither, White House aide, for concentrating the directive and supervisory powers of the government over the Appalachian Commission to the secretary of commerce. This would be accomplished by executive order.[44] The president approved, but Califano then advised him that there was opposition in the Senate to such a move. Senators Randolph and John Cooper had expressed strong opposition, other Appalachian senators would probably be opposed, and Senator Edmund Muskie (Maine) thought the timing was poor. The president responded: "Lets [sic] try to sell Randolph & Byrd—Cooper fights us anyway."[45]

A few months later an executive order was issued, tracking closely the proposals that had been transmitted to the president by Califano.[46] The order defined the functions of the secretary of commerce to include coordination and policy guidance to the commissions, including the Appalachian Regional Commission (and the Field committee for Development Planning in Alaska). In carrying out these functions the secretary would

> Review the regional economic development plans and programs submitted to him by the Federal Cochairmen, budgetary recommendations, the standards for development underlying those plans, programs and budgetary recommendations, and legislative recommendations; and advise the Federal Cochairmen of the Federal policy with respect to those matters, and where appropriate, submit recommendations to the Director of the Bureau of the Budget.

The order defined and in some ways strengthened the position of the federal co-chairmen, acting within the context of secretarial guidance and control. It also created, to assist the secretary, a Federal Advisory Council on Regional Economic Development, composed of agency representatives and the federal co-chairmen.

In summarizing the chain of events from 1965 to 1967 with respect to regional commissions, and particularly the Appalachian Commission, it is pertinent to note dual effects. On the one hand, the participation of the states in federal policy and administration is strengthened: in new structures for regional planning, project approval, and project administration; and in the influence of those structures on national administrative decisions and on sympathetic congressmen on favorable committees. On the other hand, the formal machinery for federal hegemony in use of federal funds and for preservation of the hierarchical position of the president is preserved: in the president's power of appointment of federal co-chairmen, the co-chairmen's influence and formal veto, the secretary of commerce's authority for policy direction and coordination, and BOB's examination of expenditure requests. As in the case of the foundations for the arts and humanities, representation of the interests within a pluralistic society gives influence to affected interests in federal administration, but the structure of government preserves formally, and with potential for control, the hierarchical position of the president as the executive agent for the federal government.

PROTECTING THE PRESIDENT FROM EXECUTIVE DEPARTMENTS

Unusual and dramatic, exemplary of the foundations of presidential power and of the will of one president to maintain it, were the events surrounding the issuance and suspension of Secretary Wirtz's order in the waning days of the administration for reorganizing the administration of manpower functions in the Department of Labor. Though not productive of any organizational change, the events yield an intimate view of the Johnson presidency.

The setting was one where the secretary of labor could claim the legal power of reorganization because the powers of the department were vested in him. The situation here differed from those where the powers and functions are legally vested in a bureau within a department or in the president.

Reorganization of manpower functions had been considered below the level of the president in person in 1965, but it was stymied by the opposition of state employment security administrators, several unions, and allied groups in Congress.[47] Reorganization was pressed on the president in 1968, as Wirtz and Stanley Ruttenberg, assistant secretary for manpower and manpower administrator, became committed to a reorganization before the end of their tenure. They gained from the president a directive to reorganize and, at a later date, the support of Califano, who twice recommended to the president that he consummate a reorganization order.

In the view of Wirtz and Ruttenberg, the organization within the Department of Labor for administration of manpower functions prevented unified direction and produced jurisdictional conflicts at headquarters. Conditions were made worse by independent lines of communication and control to separate sets of field officers. There was a Manpower Administration, a Bureau of Apprenticeship and Training (BAT) for on-the-job training programs, a Bureau of Employment Security (BES) that administered the Employment Service and Unemployment Insurance programs, and a Bureau of Work Training Programs (BWTP). BAT, BES, and BWTP all had their own regional directors.[48]

The situation and the reforms being considered were reported to James Gaither in the White House in 1968 in a series of memorandums from within BOB. First, a proposal for additional field offices for the Manpower Administration was evaluated, as well as attempts to locate together the field offices for the different bureaus. BOB officials were in agreement that the lines of communication and control between headquarters and the field offices were "hopelessly tangled." A second memorandum addressed changes being made

180

in the Washington structure but reported problems of diffusion, overlap, and duplication that still remained. BOB recommended taking "final steps to create a unified Manpower Administration" (abolishing BES and BWTP). A few months later, in October, a BOB official reported on Labor's reorganization plan, which proposed consolidating the field offices under a single line of authority from Washington, combining the work training of BWTP and placement functions of the Employment Service (thus splitting the service from the unemployment insurance function of BES), and strengthening the authority of the manpower administrator to produce a more unified operation. The BOB communication—while noting the inadequacy of the department's plan for determining the effect on program execution, raising doubts about monetary savings, and not knowing what personnel changes were contemplated—thought it was, nevertheless, "a move in the right direction." One of BOB's memorandums stated that a unified manpower administration would "require explicit Presidential support" and that political considerations would be inhibiting.[49]

On 11 October 1968, Califano reported the advantages of the reorganization to the president and asked whether he would like to announce it himself or have the secretary of labor do so. The president responded to Califano the same day, "I will have to talk to you about detail—I don't want any quickie."[50] On 14 October Califano wrote again to the president on the advantage of the plan and reported that George Meany, president of the AFL-CIO, Congressman Wilbur Mills (D–Ark.), other key congressmen, and "key state employment service heads" were in agreement, though some "state employment service people will oppose it." To Califano's question whether Wirtz could announce the reorganization the next day, the president replied, "No."[51]

Presidential support, in deference to the firm convictions of a cabinet executive, might have been given in different circumstances. The president had, in fact, in his "Jobs" message to Congress in January, stated that he had "directed the secretary of labor to strengthen and streamline the Manpower Administration";[52] within the Department of Labor the president's support was assumed. But in October, when the Wirtz order was ready to be issued, a combination of special circumstances existed. In 1966 the president, after conferring with state governors, had directed the heads of departments and agencies to provide reasonable opportunity for state and local officials to consult on changes that affected their jurisdictions.[53] To implement this policy, BOB had issued its famous circular no. A-85, giving guidelines on consultation. The president, with his long experience in government, must have been cognizant of the opposition of some state officials to splitting BES and less than assured by Califano's report on the degree of support for the order. Also, election of a new president would occur in a few weeks, and stirring up controversy might have adverse effects on the Democratic candidate's chances. Moreover, under preparation was a statement to departmental executives that the president wanted nothing done at the end of his administration that would complicate the transition to a new administration.

Whatever effect these factors may have had on the president's rejection of reorganization, they supported his position when there was confrontation with Wirtz over the issue. This confrontation was precipitated by Wirtz's issuance on Monday, 21 October of his reorganization order. Strangely, the event did not come to the attention of the White House until late the following day. At 7 P.M. Califano communicated the information by a memorandum that came to the President's attention during his night reading, at about 9:30.[54] Reports of Johnson's reaction, which appear to be authentic, are that he was angry. Unable to reach Wirtz, he talked to James Reynolds, the under secretary of the department, and obtained confirmation that his rejection of the order had been communicated and understood. At seven o'clock the next morning Larry Temple, White House aide, was instructed to arrange a meeting with Wirtz at eleven o'clock and to brief himself on the entire problem by that time.

The White House log shows that the meeting lasted from 1:15 to 2:19 P.M.—a long one in an unusually busy day for the president. Califano was present, and Temple was called in to take notes. Temple later reported on the meeting.[55] The president was deliberate and calm, formal, and came straight to the point. Wirtz also was calm, puffing his pipe. It was a "low voice operation." The formality of the meeting was emphasized by its being held in the cabinet room. The president asked Wirtz to confirm that he had received the information of the president's rejection, and Wirtz did so. The president stated his commitment to confer with governors and his desire that no twelfth-hour changes be made in the government that could be held off until a new president was in office. The president wanted the order rescinded. Wirtz refused. The president declined to discuss the merits of the reorganization, but he was firm that the order was "not going to go in." Temple reports that the president said, "Well, we have to have somebody who makes the decisions in this government, and that's me." With Wirtz refusing and the president insisting that he would find someone to rescind the order, the question of resignation was inevitable. Temple's summary follows:

> The President said, "...if your resignation is here, it's accepted. If it's not, then I will expect to have one from you." Wirtz said, "if you don't have one over here, another one will not be forthcoming. You can fire me if you want to." The President said, "I don't want to fire anybody. That sounds like removing people, like removing demonstrators, and I don't

want to do that. That's not becoming of your office or mine. I will expect a resignation from you." Wirtz again said, "It will not be forthcoming."

At the president's direction Temple located a resignation on file and called Warren Christopher at the Department of Justice for a report on removal of cabinet officials in the past. Temple, remarking on the president's rare gift for instantaneous recall of personal associations and past events, says the president remembered that Christopher, and also Clark Clifford, were friends of the secretary. He called Christopher and asked him to see Wirtz and persuade him to submit a new resignation so that the president would not be in the embarrassing situation of using an undated resignation on file. Christopher's conference with Wirtz that afternoon was successful; Wirtz sent a letter of resignation that night.

But the president wanted something different: the rescission of the order. He asked Clifford to see Wirtz, and knowing of Wirtz's friendship with Humphrey, to bring to his attention the adverse effects the resignation could have on the Humphrey campaign. Ruttenberg reports that Califano, in the meantime, called Reynolds to ask if he would be interested in becoming secretary and rescinding the order, but that Reynolds said he would rescind the order and then resign in protest.[56]

In the meantime, the president was receiving support. Ruttenberg believed the president arranged it by a call to Governor Buford Ellington of Tennessee, but he admitted there was no evidence to support the charge.[57] The president's log did not reveal a call by the president to the governor, or a conversation with the Office of Emergency Planning (OEP), which maintained liaison with the governors, until late in the day. The order, moreover, had been made known by Ruttenberg to field officials and could have been expected to arouse spontaneous protest from some state capitals. In the early afternoon, just before the conference with Wirtz, Califano presented a memorandum to the president telling him that Price Daniel, head of OEP, had reported that some of the governors, naming two, were unhappy over the reorganization.[58] This was followed by a second report by Califano to the president transmitting a summary by Daniel's deputy of past opposition in some state capitals to dismemberment of BES.[59] At roughly the same time (4:55 P.M.) the president and Daniel talked by telephone.[60] A little earlier (3:25 P.M. CST) Governor Buford Ellington, chairman of the National Governor's Conference and former director of OEP, had wired the president protesting failure of consultation, pointing out the past opposition of the Governor's Conference to the proposed reorganization, and asking for rescission of the order. The wire was transmitted from the White House to Wirtz.

The next day—after Wirtz's White House conference and the submission of his resignation—both Clifford and Christopher held long sessions with him. Two things followed: first, Wirtz sent a wire to Governor Ellington, cleared with the White House, stating that the order would be held in abeyance pending conference with governors. Second, the secretary sent word to the president that he would like to withdraw the resignation letter.[61] When a meeting with state officials was held later, there was some uncertainty whether Wirtz said or implied that the order was still under active consideration.[62] In any event, the order was not formally rescinded, but nothing was done to implement it. The secretary's face was saved, the governors had been consulted, and the president's will prevailed. Johnson's claim that only the president could make the decisions for the executive branch was confirmed. Indeed, Johnson's position resembled that of President Jackson, who removed Secretary Duane when he refused to comply with the president's discretionary power.[63] While Johnson did not, as did Jackson, spell out the constitutional basis for his position, the practical foundation in each case was the same: the powers of appointment and removal make the president the head of the executive branch—insofar as the functions are executive in nature and fall within his purview, and to the extent that he is willing to accept the political consequences.

CONCLUSION

The protection of the president's hierarchical position is of major concern to presidents. Power independently located and with a capacity to force presidential attention is a condition that all presidents have resisted. Lyndon Johnson carried on that tradition.

Johnson knew that the expansion of the congressional committee veto would enlarge the particularistic influence of committees and their members on executive decisions, limit the president's power, and delay or prevent effective executive action. He refused to accept requirements for committee approval of executive action, and he accepted only such notice and waiting requirements as would not, in his judgment, prevent effective administration.

In addition to influencing legislation, professional, clientele, or regulated groups may establish a position in the executive decision making structure independent of the presidential guidance system. In legislation sponsored by the Johnson administration for the creation of the national endowments for the arts and the humanities, in which professional or clientele interest would be strong, executive power was vested in an administrator appointed by the president. Unlike the situation with the National Science Foundation, group participation was made advisory only. In the case where advisory functions were given to an Administrative Conference, the president maintained independent control over the executive in the agency.

In establishing the Appalachian Regional Commission the prospect of decisions shared or brokered between the president and the governors was at issue. The states gained influence in the administration of national programs, but the president's authority for oversight of administration of federal law was protected by his power to appoint the federal co-chairmen, the veto power over regional plans possessed by this official, the policy oversight and coordination of the secretary of commerce, and the budgetary controls that could be exercised through BOB.

Department heads, by virtue of their statutory authority and administrative responsibility, have interests that may conflict with presidential policy. On occasion they may resist, or even refuse to follow, presidential instructions when to do so would run counter to strongly held convictions. This was the nature of Wirtz's conflict with President Johnson over reorganizing administration for manpower programs in the Department of Labor. Not only did the president demand Wirtz's resignation, he accepted the intervention of a few state governors to protect his position.

In the dynamics of presidential government, the dominance of the comprehensive management perspective is always at risk. Professional groups, special clienteles, department and agency heads, and executives of other governments have powers and influence that are separate from those of the presidency. The Johnson administration resisted the particularistic efforts of Congress, private groups, federal departments, and regional interests to erode the president's position. Yet, ultimately, its concern went beyond the issue of presidential protection to one of presidential capability. How could a president—removed from the details of administration itself—"take care" through guidance and coordination of the executive branch? That is the subject of the next chapter.

EIGHT

AN EXECUTIVE GUIDANCE AND
COORDINATION SYSTEM

"The White House . . . was talking vaguely about a vast reorganization of the Federal Government," said Richard Harwood in an article in the *Washington Post* on 18 January 1967.[1] This apparent leak of information foreshadowed a new direction in the attention of the subpresidency. It was turning from legislative goals to a central guidance system for the bureaucracy.

The *Post* article stated the problem that had the "White House seemingly on the verge of despair" was the vast and complicated government apparatus through which money must pass to reach constituents from the Great Society programs. Two months earlier the *New York Times* carried an article by James Reston entitled "Washington: Johnson's Administrative Monstrosity."[2] As Johnson began his fourth year, Reston felt:

> one fact is not only clear but undisputed: his administration is poorly organized to administer the domestic programs he has introduced, and the administrative chaos of the state and local governments is even worse. The reasons for this are fairly clear: the Administration has put through more social and economic programs in the last two years than it can absorb.

For the moment Reston placed the blame on Johnson's personal style:

> we have a President who is poorly organized himself, reluctant to delegate power over these homefront activities to the Vice President or anyone else, and suspicious of political institutions of any kind.
>
> He did not work easily with the Democratic caucus when he was in the Senate. He has not made an effective instrument out of the Cabinet or the National Security Council. He all but wrecked the Democratic National

Committee after he got into the White House, and he is still trying to run the Presidency as if it were a Senator's Office on Capitol Hill.

Although Reston had focused on the personal qualities of the president, he had identified an institutional problem of enormous complexity: Could there be an effective central guidance and coordination system for the execution of Great Society programs?

The problem was receiving attention inside the Congress. Senator Abraham Ribicoff (D–Conn.), whose dissatisfaction with the narrow scope of reorganization orders has been noted,[3] from his position as chairman of the Senate Government Operations Committee had hoped for more than a year that the president would place "major emphasis . . . on recommendations for a substantial overhaul of the basic machinery of the executive branch."[4] He looked favorably on the idea of a commission to study the organization and operation of the executive branch. Although a 1965 bill sponsored by thirty-nine senators proposed a commission with representatives from Congress, the executive, and private life appointed by the president, the president of the Senate, and Speaker of the House,[5] Ribicoff was willing to have a presidential commission.[6] Senator Edmund S. Muskie (D–Maine) was concerned over an adequate national structure to coordinate program administration effected through the states and cities. He was holding hearings in November 1966 on his bill to create a national intergovernmental affairs council with responsibility for coordination of activities directly affecting state and local governments, assessing the effectiveness of national domestic policies and programs in the federal system, and eliminating duplication in grant-in-aid programs. The council would be chaired by the president, contain representatives of departments and agencies, and have a secretariat of experts and generalists in program management.[7]

The urgency of attention to the problem of national coordination arose from the discontent of governors and mayors over the problems of administering federal grants-in-aid. In recognition of this discontent the Bureau of the Budget (BOB) organized teams of federal officials, called "flying feds," to visit five states for the purpose of identifying the problems that states and cities were encountering in their relations with the federal government. Shortly thereafter these problems were frankly discussed by Schultze in testimony before the Muskie committee.[8]

Previous Executive Consideration

In the first years of the Johnson presidency, there had been a study and report on the organization of the executive branch. Among the task forces established by Bill Moyers in 1964 was the President's Task Force on

187

Government Reorganization. It was composed of government officials and academicians and was chaired by Don K. Price. Price had served as chairman of a task force for the Hoover commission and had been a member of the President's Committee on Government Organization in the Executive Office during the Eisenhower administration. With five political scientists in its membership, and staffed by BOB, the task force took a comprehensive presidential perspective. Reporting on 6 November 1964, before the numerous legislative enactments that would magnify the problem of coordination and executive direction, the task force began:

> Progress toward the Great Society requires, in addition to substantive social and economic programs, a reorganization of the Executive Branch.[9]

The dual objectives of the presidential management perspective followed immediately:

> to administer policies and programs effectively and economically, and also ... to be responsive to Presidential leadership in developing new policies and programs.[10]

Within the executive branch, "He alone is the General Manager."[11] In the constitutional system, "The President shares with Congress the constitutional responsibility for the general organization of the Executive Branch. But he alone has the perspective to visualize the complex problems of Government organization, and to appreciate how greatly the success of his policies depends on the soundness of the administrative system by which they must be carried out."[12]

The report gave primary attention to departmental restructuring. It recommended five new "major-purpose" executive departments: Transportation, Education, Housing and Community Development, Economic Development, and Natural Resources—with abolition of the Department of Commerce through absorption or transfer of functions, as well as the Department of Interior, possibly the Department of Agriculture, and perhaps later the Department of Labor.

The report recommended other reorganizations: transfers, consolidations, abolitions; full presidential authority over the Executive Office organization; a single transportation regulatory commission; changes in the higher personnel system; presidential "policy guidance, consistent with law," to regulatory commissions; making a permanent grant of authority to the president to propose reorganization plans.

The report was designed for in-house consumption and hence was not distributed publicly. Particular recommendations may have had some influence in moving forward ideas for certain reorganizations—departments of Transportation, Urban Development, Commerce and Labor—and in bringing BOB ideas and studies up to date. But comprehensive reorganization was not part of the Johnson strategy. When the task force met with him after submission of the study, he said nothing about the report and for most of the evening talked about the Vietnam War.[13]

The inattention was to be expected in view of Johnson's involvement in war and Great Society legislation. Concern for reorganization on a broad scale at that time in his administration would have been premature and would have expended political capital on the Hill that was needed for other things. With Roosevelt's experience in mind, presidents are likely to be leery of attempts at comprehensive reorganization; for Johnson at this point it would have made no sense whatever.

After the report of the Price task force in 1964, there was no comprehensive consideration of executive structure until the Heineman task force was created in September 1966. In the interim there was, as previous chapters show, much attention to selective organizational change to apply conventional objectives at the departmental and bureau levels, and to improve program coordination and promote overhead direction in line with departmental or presidential purpose. HUD had been created in 1965, DOT would be signed into law on 16 October 1966, and the president would propose a department of business and labor on 10 January 1967. Also, the subpresidency had brought to the president's attention various proposals for consolidation or transfer of agencies, bureaus, or divisions, or their functions, many of which resulted in structural changes believed to improve opportunities for coordination and central direction. Finally, coordination was being sought by interdepartmental councils, use of lead agencies, convenor orders, and staff assignments for program coordination within departments.

Such particularistic changes—continual in successive presidencies and especially reflecting feverish activism in the Johnson presidency—were significant to the effort to maintain or establish effective program coordination and presidential guidance for the executive branch. There were, additionally, at midstream (1966–67) other moves in action, proposal, or deliberation that were direct efforts to increase responsiveness to centrally coordinated purpose through structural changes in the executive branch. These activities are important in the history of the Johnson presidency because they bring to attention competing and complementary approaches to providing guidance and coordination to an executive establishment so large and complicated that it would appear a "monstrosity" to a competent commentator.

Foreign Affairs

One novel development was a structure for consultation and decision in administration of foreign affairs. A presidential directive on 4 March 1966 created the Senior Interdepartmental Group (SIG) and Interdepartmental

189

Regional Groups (IRGs). The purpose was stated by General Maxwell Taylor, consultant to the president and active in working out the design: "The particular task addressed . . . is the coordination and organization of inter-departmental activities overseas."[14] For such activities a Washington structure for coordination was added to the previously decreed primacy of the ambassador in the field.

General Taylor, in explaining the impact of SIG/IRGs, stressed the obvious fact that coordination was "not inherently or organically a State Department function." By the directive, "The President has taken a portion of his own presidential responsibility and given it to the Secretary of State as his agent."[15]

The president "directed the Secretary of State . . . to assume responsibility to the full extent permitted by law for the overall direction, coordination, and supervision of interdepartmental activities of the United States Government overseas (less exempted military activities)." Implementation of this responsibility was to be achieved by coordination at the subcabinet level.

The president's directive established an interdepartmental committee (SIG), under the under secretary of state as "executive chairman." The other regular members of the group were the deputy secretary of defense, the administrator of the Agency for International Development (AID), the director of the Central Intelligence Agency, the chairman of the joint chiefs of staff, the director of the United States Information Agency (USIA), and the special assistant to the president for national security affairs. The chairman could invite other departmental representatives. In addition, the assistant secretaries of the State Department would serve as chairs of Inter-departmental Regional Groups analogous in membership and responsibilities to SIG. They would work with ambassadors and country teams abroad.[16] Thus, in Taylor's view, the assistant secretaries and the ambassadors were "really wearing a second hat—a Presidential hat."[17]

The unusual feature of this arrangement was that the executive chairman of SIG was given "authority and responsibility to decide all matters coming before his committee, subject to the right of any member to appeal from his decision to higher authority."[18] Executive chairman was the "code name . . . to describe a chairman who not only presides, but also decides."[19]

This was, in sum, coordination by committee consultation, with White House representation, accompanied by grant of decision-making authority to a coordinator acting as presidential agent.

Domestic Field Administration

A great amount of attention was developing in the midperiod to coordination and direction of domestic field operations. One proposal dealt with establishing field offices for BOB.

BOB had maintained field offices in four locations from 1943 to 1953. These had been abolished as part of an economy move in 1953, and their reestablishment had been rejected in 1958.[20] At the request of the director of BOB in 1962, a comprehensive analysis of opinion on the desirability of creating field offices was carried out in BOB. The study was not completed until 30 April 1964. Fifty-six staff members were interviewed or wrote memorandums on the pros and cons of field offices for BOB. About 70 percent of these opposed field offices, with a large proportion feeling that additional staff at headquarters had a higher priority, but with many also doubting the benefits of field offices.[21] Nevertheless—despite these negative views, and after brief discussion with White House staff and further delay— agreement was reached in the top offices of BOB that field offices had merit.[22] Charles Schultze, assistant director, communicated to the White House his approval, after interagency discussions, for regional field representatives within BOB.[23] By this time the idea had support from those concerned with the need for better linkage with states and cities.[24]

Though he supported the concept of regional field representatives, Schultze wished to restrict their function. He rejected "regional representatives of the Executive Office as coordinators, expediters, or trouble-shooters" and pro- jected solution of "serious problems of local and regional coordination" by better definition of agency functions, providing in the case of project-type programs for "overall project management in a single agency," and providing for "specific mechanisms adapted to problems at hand (e.g., Appalachia)." He saw that field offices could provide a two-way flow of information between Washington and field establishments that would supplement the function of Federal Executive Boards, created in and after 1961 in major cities as means of bringing together and promoting cooperation among federal field executives. For this limited function there should be introduced, "initially on a gradual and experimental basis, regional field representatives of" BOB. For even this kind of recommendation, Seidman saw reasons to warn of the danger of undercutting agency representatives.[25]

Schultze's recommendation was followed a year later by a proposal in BOB's budget for 1967 for six two-member field offices. The proposal re- ceived an unsympathetic response in a House Appropriations Subcommittee hearing and was killed at that level.[26]

Growing Concern

At the end of 1966 and the beginning of 1967 there was growing concern about the structure and operation of domestic programs, particularly those reflecting the purposes of the "Great Society." At the first meeting of White House staff to "shake down the State of the Union Message," remarks of this nature were made by top staff persons:

We should primarily stress good administration and avoid speaking of new ideas or new legislative programs.... There is a growing criticism that the President does not know how to administer his programs effectively. There is a great need for consolidation.

He must speak about the work of the next two years which is the "rationalization" of our present programs, and to end the congressional proliferation of agencies and programs.

We must for the present, concentrate on making existing programs work better.

Although Bill Moyers felt that "people now think that the programs are being run more poorly than in fact they are," Califano included "reorganization" among four topics for "next year's program."[27] To prepare for reorganization, Califano sent a memo to departments, agencies, and Executive Office heads asking for suggestions.

These expressions of the opinion that policy advances needed to be followed by improvements in administration were paralleled by several occurrences that produced an agenda for the newly appointed Heineman task force. One was a comprehensive, though succinct, analysis by Schultze, now director of BOB, of problems that confronted the administration in coordinating Great Society programs and of alternative solutions. It was sent to Heineman by Schultze on the very day Ben W. Heineman consented to serve as the task force chairman.[28] The analysis began with an assessment of prospects for Great Society programs: "Their success or failure hinges upon establishing new and effective mechanisms for coordinating planning, evaluation, and execution quite different from any currently available." The *"heart of the problem"* was that, while *"*a successful program in the cities has to be composed of *many* elements," these elements were the responsibility of five agencies in Washington that were coequal, having "no means for central long-range planning and budget allocation" and no way of "putting together and administering a successful 'package'" for *"thousands of day-to-day decisions in thousands of communities throughout the country."* Schultze saw a need for a *"program manager* in each city." Who would be his boss? "Clearly not the President *directly.* Both politically and administratively this would be a nightmare."

In the existing system of federal-state administration, Schultze saw complications in state and local administrative structures but limited his analysis to three alternatives for improving the administrative structure of the national government.

"Alternative One: Establish a 'super-Department' along Defense lines."

The full proposal was, "Merge Labor and Commerce into a Department of Manpower and Economic Development"; reallocate OEO functions to Labor and HEW; "Collect HUD, HEW and the new Department of Manpower and Economic Development under *one* 'super'-Secretary like McNamara"; give each subdepartment a secretary, "like the Army, Navy, Air Force"; and give the supersecretary a staff to plan and evaluate. One advantage of this arrangement would be that the structure "*could be duplicated in each major city and Federal regional office,*" with the city representative being the "*program manager.*" The main disadvantage would be that the superdepartment would be "*extremely* difficult to get by Congress."

"*Alternative Two*: Establish a Council composed of the members of the Departments primarily involved in the Great Society programs—HEW, HUD, Labor, Commerce, OEO." This would be accompanied by an executive secretariat for the council with a representative in each major region and metropolitan area. The weakness of the proposal was said to be the lack of a single decision point, and hence it was proposed that the president would be represented by a special assistant for program management who would be a member of the council. This was seen as "weaker" than the suggestion for a superdepartment and would involve the president in detailed decision. Politically it was more salable than a superdepartment and might serve as "an ideal half-way house on the road to a 'super'-Department."

"*Alternative Three*: Establish in the Executive Office of the President an *Office of Program Management*—probably as part of the Budget Bureau." The office would have a representative "*in each major Federal region and in each major city.*" The alternative of establishment outside BOB was suggested. The major problem with alternative three was that the head of the office, who "must ultimately *coordinate Cabinet members,*" could do this only if he were known as the "President's man" and that this would bring the president into "every sticky situation." Schultze concluded that this solution might work, but that it was less desirable than the other two alternatives. In any case, there would be other problems: realigning the regional structure so it would be consistent among departments and agencies, decentralizing operational decisions and replacing categorical grants with block grants.

To Schultze's comprehensive agenda on Great Society alternatives, others were adding specific suggestions for structural change. One was part of the ferment over organization of OEO activities.[29] Shriver recommended to the president a "Social and Economic Development Council" patterned after the National Security Council (NSC)—a proposal similar to that made by Senator Muskie. The council, which would be most effective if chaired by the president, would be the central focus for the total responsibilities of the Great

Society program. It would have a full-time executive director. Such a structure would absorb the existing central structure for planning and coordinating OEO activities.[30]

Another development that would affect the Heineman task force was the reorganization proposals of Secretary Gardner (HEW). In contrast or supplement to Shriver's conciliar structure within the Executive Office, Gardner advanced a departmental solution for coordination and central direction. At a news conference on 6 November 1966, the president announced:

> At my request, Secretary Gardner has been reviewing ways to streamline the Department to make it more modern and efficient, and economical in its operation.
>
> Dr. Gardner has submitted to me some very far-reaching proposals for major reorganizations of the Health, Education, and Welfare Department. In general, I believe they are worthy of very serious consideration. I have asked Director Schultze of the Budget Bureau and members of my White House staff to join the Secretary in giving these most careful study.[31]

The "far-reaching proposals" were set forth by Secretary Gardner at the same conference:[32]

> I have proposed to the President a major and far-reaching reorganization of the Department of Health, Education and Welfare. Specifically, I have proposed the establishment of three sub-Cabinet departments, each headed by a secretary and each responsible to the Secretary of Health, Education and Welfare: a Department of Health, a Department of Education, and a Department of Individual and Family Services, which would include both social security and welfare, and perhaps other programs.
>
> This will reduce the number of line agencies reporting to the Secretary from eight to three. It will give each of the three primary program fields a stronger national voice and greater prominence, and, at the same time, it will keep the three fields closely related under one management and in a position where they can work very closely.[33]

An event of at least momentary consequence was the president's proposal on 10 January 1967 of a new department of business and labor.[34] Ten days later he recommended including in such a department "basic responsibility for the Federal government's efforts in all of the regional commissions that have been or soon will be established, including the Appalachian Regional Commission."[35]

Finally, in a comprehensive message, "The Quality of American Government," the president, after summarizing the efforts he had made to establish better communication with governors and mayors and the steps being taken for consolidation of grants-in-aid, stated that he had asked the director of BOB "to undertake a comprehensive review of the federal field office structure" and "to recommend a plan for the restructuring of these offices." He added that he hoped "to incorporate the first steps of this plan in my next budget message."[36]

Here, then, were a variety of suggestions for major organizational reform: a domestic council patterned after NSC; a conversion of HEW into a super-department over three departments, similar to the Department of Defense (DOD); a new department to provide coordination of the government's efforts in economic development; a new office for program management in the Executive Office; and restructuring of field operations for programs related to Great Society legislation. The proposals provided a base for a comprehensive evaluation of executive structure.

THE HEINEMAN TASK FORCE ON GOVERNMENT ORGANIZATION

The concern in the Johnson presidency with organization for effective administration was focused by the creation in 1966 of the Heineman task force. Its assessment of the concepts and problems of national executive structure and the possibilities for effective organization for presidential guidance and control merit close attention for several reasons.

First, the task force was an effort of the Johnson subpresidency to develop a plan for rationalizing executive structure for effective administration under presidential control. The task force was composed of persons of wide experience, intelligence, and administrative competence. On this basis alone, its perspectives and proposals should be part of the historical record.

Second, the task force analyzed and recommended solutions for problems of central guidance and coordination at a third stage in the enlargement of national administration. The New Deal had produced the Brownlow study (1937), World War II was followed by a new structure for national security and the report of the first Hoover Commission (1947), and the profusion of Great Society programs now brought the Heineman task force into existence. The Heineman group confronted the problem of management created by centralized domestic policy-making on a scale far beyond that of the New Deal. The moment was ripe and the need was urgent for presidential management to catch up with policy. The routes toward successful presidential management proposed by the task force would be on the nation's long-run agenda.

Third, the task force provided occasion for reexpressing concepts of management in a presidential system. These concepts would not die with the

Johnson administration; some would rise again in the Nixon and Carter administrations. Their scope, precision, and interlinkage—even though removed from the specifics of action—would help define alternatives for successive administrations as each gave attention to presidential responsibility for national policy and executive control.

The formal steps for creation of a Task Force on Government Organization date from 30 September 1966, when Califano recommended to the president establishment of an outside task force on government reorganization "to insure the coordination and effective implementation of federal programs, with particular emphasis on programs designed to meet the problems of the cities."[37] Ten days later Califano reported to the president on a meeting in which Ben W. Heineman had expressed willingness to serve as chairman. The high importance attached to the task force was shown by the selection of Heineman and the other members of the group; by the fact that Secretary McNamara (DOD), Schultze, and Califano met with Heineman to engage his direction of the project; and by Califano's statement to the president that "McNamara, Schultze and I feel that this will be the most productive task force over the next 8 or 12 months."[38]

The president's confidence in Heineman must have been comparable to that of previous presidents when they selected Brownlow and Hoover for reorganization studies. President Johnson earlier had offered him the positions of secretary of commerce and director of BOB and had tried to persuade him to be secretary of HEW. He was at the time of this appointment president of the Chicago and North Western Railway Company. He first had extended contact with the president when he was on a negotiating committee during a threatened railroad strike in 1964. He had helped form a National Independent Committee for Election of Johnson and Humphrey in 1964, had served on a task force on organization of HUD, and had been the president's designee for chairman of the White House Civil Rights Conference in 1966.

The expectations for a meaningful study were further demonstrated in the experience of the members of the task force. The president approved ten of twelve names submitted by Califano and later added McGeorge Bundy, who had served as special assistant to the president for national security affairs under Presidents Kennedy and Johnson, and Nicholas Katzenbach, who had become under secretary of state. The membership included several people in whom the president had a great deal of confidence. The presence and participation of Secretary McNamara was conspicuous despite his heavy responsibilities on Vietnam at the time.

Other members of the task force were Schultze, Kermit Gordon, and William Capron—current or past members of the Executive Office staff; Hale Champion, director of finance, state of California; Richard C. Lee, mayor,

New Haven, Connecticut; Herbert Kaufman, chairman, Political Science Department, Yale University; Bayless Manning, dean, Stanford University Law School; and Harry Ransom, chancellor, University of Texas at Austin. Heineman has reported that "the President couldn't have been more interested." He recalls three meetings of the task force with the president. The president did not give them "a platform," for, in Heineman's view, he regarded the task force as an informed, realistic, and highly confidential group whose ideas he wanted. The president did ask them to take up out of order the question of what should be done about OEO.[39]

The staff director for the task force was Fred Bohen, who was designated from the White House staff. He was assisted by a specially recruited staff of six, to which were added two organization experts from BOB.[40] The task force met seven times for twelve days between 12 November 1966 and 7 May 1967 and sent the president three early reports or letters and four reports that contained its ultimate recommendations.

For its first meeting on 12 November the task force had limited background materials that included the Price task force report and statements on organization problems from the Wood Task Force on Urban Problems, testimony by government officials to the Muskie Subcommittee on Intergovernmental Relations, and submissions related to the Shriver and Gardner proposals for executive reorganization.

Reports on Pending Proposals

The first report of the task force to the president related to OEO and was transmitted by Califano on 15 December 1966 (see pages 101–2). The report found that the existing structure of OEO had "not proved workable"; it recommended transfer at appropriate stages of its operating functions, and preservation of an organization, outside the Executive Office, to run the Community Action Program (CAP), develop new programs, and monitor administration of antipoverty programs. The task force was split on an executive assistant to the president and rejected Shriver's proposal for a domestic NSC.

On 3–4 December the task force focused its deliberations on the Gardner proposal in order to give recommendations to the president concerning an endorsement in the State of the Union Message or as an item in the 1967 legislative program. It had before it replies to Gardner and analyses by BOB, Rufus Miles—long experienced, before 1965, in administration in HEW—and Bohen. After receiving these materials, the task force unanimously recommended to the president on 3 January 1967 that he defer endorsement of any specific proposals for internal reorganization of HEW. It reasoned that additional staff study was needed on the proposal and on alternative ways of achieving the objectives, and that the implications of the proposal for other areas deserved careful analysis. Anticipating its later proposals, it recommended to the president that he declare in the State of the Union Message his intention to press for organizational improvements in and between departments responsible for Great Society programs.[41] The precise recommendation was not followed in either the State of the Union Message or the "Quality of American Government" message that followed in March.[42]

A third report was sent in the form of a letter from the chairman to the president on 31 January 1967 "enthusiastically endorsing" the merger of the departments of Labor and Commerce, recommended three weeks earlier by the president in the State of the Union Message. While most of the arguments were specific to the proposal, there was some language that foretold later task force positions on general organization: "A new Secretary with major, rather than partial government responsibility for the healthy development of the private sector" could resolve problems now going to the president's desk and serve as a more neutral interpreter of diverse needs in the private sector.[43]

The Organization and Management of Great Society Programs

This title of a report of the task force on 15 June 1967 reflected the subject to which the task force had given the major portion of its attention, and which was the compelling reason for its existence. The report agreed that "*organizational criticism is merited.*"[44] It ranged widely, encompassing both Washington and field structure. Professor Wallace Sayre of Columbia University—after reviewing for the task force what presidents beginning with Franklin Roosevelt had done toward leadership, direction, and coordination of the executive branch—had emphasized the larger dimensions of the problem, including field administration:

> The problems before this Task Force apparently include two additional dimensions, for which we have virtually no precedents or experience to guide us.
>
> (1) The regional coordination of the executive agencies in the field. . . . This is a problem exceeding in administrative and political difficulty the task of Presidential leadership over the agencies in Washington.
> (2) When to this problem of federal regional coordination is added the task of direct, authoritative regional relations with state and local governments—particularly governors and mayors—the difficulties are at least doubled for the President.[45]

The task force did not deal with operational relationships in the three-level political system but concentrated on the structural problems within the national government, including field structure. It was aided mainly by a set of staff working papers being developed concurrently with its discussion, dealing with "the President and the Executive Office," "Domestic Departmental Management," HEW, and HUD, and with alternatives in field administration and on various subjects such as BOB's potential functions in program planning.

The report would show rejection of certain approaches to the problem it was considering. The study "The President and the Executive Office" reported on the inadequacy of various forms of interdepartmental structure and of lead agency responsibility. Unmentioned in the report were the interagency structures prominently advanced elsewhere—the domestic National Security Council proposal of OEO director Shriver and the interdepartmental council proposed by Senator Muskie. The report opted for new Executive Office structure and strengthened staff aid within departments, with accompanying strong field representation for both.

The report diagnosed the organizational problems as follows:

(1) The target problems—poverty, discrimination, urban blight, dirty air and water—are not the sole concern of any one Federal department....
(2) ... Federal social programs remain badly coordinated *in Washington and the field*....
(3) ... *administration* of Federal domestic programs *is* centralized excessively in Washington—centralized in autonomous bureaus, and administrations *below the Presidential and departmental level.*

The report saw *"fragmentation in Washington"* that *"in turn, encourages piecemeal effort by State and local government agencies." "The first order of organizational reform in domestic affairs*, therefore, is to forge better interdepartmental and *intergovernmental connections through strong Presidential leadership....* To meet these problems the President needs new staff support."

Two new offices were recommended to provide "institutional staff" support. One was a new, independent Office of Program Coordination in the Executive Office, led by a director and having a field force organized in ten federal regions. The director would, with staff assistance, *"Anticipate, surface, and settle jurisdictional and program arguments between Federal departments"*; *"Monitor the administration of Great Society programs requiring cooperation* between Federal departments"; *"Provide the staff focal point* in the White House ... *for continuing consultation with Governors and Mayors ...";* "Carry *primary* staff responsibility in the Executive Office" for improvements through grant consolidation, and so forth. Particularly emphasized in the report was the *"authority from the President to settle interdepartmental issues"—"a sensitive role, totally dependent on Presidential confidence and support."* It was noted also that the recommendation would "unify current part-time efforts" of BOB, the Office of Emergency Preparedness (OEP), the vice-president and several White House assistants.[46]

The second office would be a new Office of Program Development within BOB "*to provide year-round professional support to the President's personal staff in the vital task of constructing a domestic legislative program.*"

There was some difference of opinion in the task force, not with respect to functions and institutionalization of presidential aid, but on structure. Heineman, McNamara, and Schultze favored location of the Office of Program Coordination as well as the Office of Program Development in a "reorganized and reoriented Budget Bureau." Heineman also favored a director of the Executive Office of the President with responsibility "for the day-to-day operations of the Executive Office, excepting the work of the Special Assistants."

With the same purpose of strengthening presidential "instruments," the report recommended that cabinet secretaries be required to expand staff assistance for "*program planning, review, budget and coordinated field management.*" With respect to field management it was further proposed that cabinet secretaries be directed to unify field operations under departmental regional executives responsible directly to the Office of the secretary, to decentralize to these executives authority for "program operations and specific grant decisions," and that the secretaries of HEW, HUD, Labor, and the director of OEO agree on a plan "to colocate field offices in common regional cities serving common geographical areas." One means of accomplishing this was suggested—with twelve regional offices.

Anticipating the direction of later recommendations, the report stressed the importance of continued efforts to reduce the number of departments "*in the grip of parochial* interests" and resistance of efforts to create new departments dominated "by narrow, specialized interests or professional clienteles (Health or Education)." Finally, it recommended transfer of manpower functions from Labor and OEO to a unified manpower administration in HEW.

In partial summary, it can be seen that the task force envisaged a need for strengthening presidential program development and coordination, to be achieved primarily by expansion of institutionalized staff aid at the presidential level—reducing somewhat the need for personal staff aid, but supported by stronger planning and direction at the departmental level. There was no discussion in the report of whether Great Society programs could be successfully administered without policy change—such as grant consolidation or transfer of some programs to financially aided state governments. Instead, there was an assumption that institutionalized staff aid to the president and departments—aided by field decentralization—could provide coordinated program and policy development.

200

Califano transmitted this report, which he called the "final report," to the president and said, "I urge you to read the report because it is one of the best I have seen." He told the president that the report finds "weaknesses in the way we manage or domestic programs—an 'organization lag' as a result of over 50 major programs launched in 3 years." It "is unusually candid (particularly in its discussion of HEW and HUD) and should be closely held." As for implementation of the report, Califano stated, "The proposals to strengthen the Executive Office of the President are clearly steps in the right direction. Schultze is carrying out his own study of BOB and I will be working closely with him, Heineman and Kermit Gordon to develop a practical and workable plan to modernize BOB, so it can be an instrument of much greater power and use to you." There were "obvious political problems" with many other recommendations in the report, and "Schultze and I will begin staffing them out and come back to you with specific recommendations on a point-to-point basis."[47]

Government Organization for Economic Policy Formulation and Administration

A report to the president with this title was completed 15 September 1967. Three elements in the background explain the concentrations of attention shown in the report. The first was the sequence of events from the report of the Price task force in 1964, which recommended a department of economic affairs whose primary function would be economic development of the private sector, to the recommendation of the president on 10 January 1967 for a department of business and labor.[48] Within this context, consolidation of functions related to development of the private sector and expansion of business services were discussed. A second element was the desire for more effective means of formulating economic policy. Two reports to the task force, one from members of the Council of Economic Advisers (CEA) and the other from an unnamed source, suggested that a strong department of economic affairs could be effective as a fourth member added to the existing triad (the joint advisory mechanism of BOB, CEA, and the Treasury), could expand the data for economic decisions, and could contribute effectively to planning economic policy. A third element was the discussions over previous years of the position of the Federal Reserve Board (FRB) with relation to the president. The task force was authorized by both Califano and the president to include this subject in its considerations and was supplied with the report of the prestigious Commission on Money and Credit and with related arguments by leading authorities.[49]

The task force discussed the Labor-Commerce merger and the organization for economic planning on 21 January and 6 May 1967. Members of CEA joined the meeting. As a result, the staff of the task force prepared a draft report to which was added "as a staff report, whole cloth," with Heineman's approval, a discussion and recommendations on FRB's interagency relationships. At the final meeting of the task force on 26 July seven members who were able to attend discussed the draft report, and a final report was then prepared for task force approval.

The task force report stated that the interagency mechanisms for coordination of administration fiscal policy and consultation with the FRB were "working well." It defined the need for organizational change as follows:

> We continue to feel that *the major organizational problem in the area of economic affairs is the existence of several special-interest executive departments,* each holding a stake in only part of the national economy, and none now capable of serving as a neutral, Presidential instrument of program or policy on broad-gauged economic issues or problems that affect "their" interest or clientele.

It concluded that, "As President Johnson has recognized, *the President and the public interest would be served better by a Department of the Economy,*" especially including activities of the departments of Commerce and Labor.

Specifically, therefore, the task force recommended: "Keep alive" the proposal for merging the departments of Labor and Commerce in a new department of economic affairs; as a "second-best step," provide a new charter to the Department of Commerce, with analytical staff capability to support new responsibilities in long-range economic planning and create "a unified bank of national economic, social, and demographic information to facilitate analysis," and avoid enlarging the triad to include other departments until the creation of a department of economic affairs, at which time it would become a full-fledged member of a new quadriad of economic advisers. To these recommendations were added comments with respect to FRB:

> While we find little to recommend the historic organizational independence of the Federal Reserve Board, effective consultative relationships between key policy-makers in the Kennedy and Johnson Administrations and the Chairman of the FRB have produced a sustained dialogue and more coordinated fiscal and monetary policies in the 1960's than can normally be anticipated from our independent institutions.

The task force concluded, therefore, that, when political considerations permitted, the autonomy of the FRB should be reduced in ways recommended by the Commission on Money and Credit. These included: making the terms of the chairman and vice-chairman of FRB coterminous with that of the president; reducing the size of the board and the length of its members' terms; consolidating policy responsibility for open market operations in FRB by abolishing the Open Market Committee.

A Recommendation for the Future Organization
of the Executive Branch

With the completion of the foregoing reports the task force might have concluded that, with respect to domestic affairs, it had finished its assignment. But in view of broader discussions in meetings of the preceding six months, at its meeting of 9 June it asked the staff to prepare a report containing longer-range organizational recommendations. Such a report, titled "Perspectives for the Future," was prepared, and it was discussed by those who could attend the meeting on 26 July. The members present were able to support one idea in the staff draft: "a small number of line officers to manage the Executive Branch short of the President." A revision on this idea became the six-page report of 15 September 1967, bearing the above title, which was signed by all members of the task force except Katzenbach.

The task force justified this additional report in its beginning sentence: "we remain genuinely concerned about the longer-range administrative viability of the organization of American government, from the Presidency down." What followed was terse, bold, and unequivocal—in concept, assessment of the problem, and remedy. The preceding reports had "been advanced with the goal of increasing the managerial influence of the Chief Executive." The nation expects that the president "will not merely propose but also deliver" the substance of programs. Professor Richard Neustadt was quoted: "His special place in government requires of him, indeed thrusts upon him, a unique responsibility—and opportunity—to oversee and assure execution."

The problem for him was a structural one: "Presidential authority to carry through the measures he proposes is fragmented and circumscribed. The executive branch does not belong exclusively to him: its command and subordination structure is pluralistic in character; its unwieldly size too vast for personal surveillance."

Two basic recommendations were made:

We urge resistance by Presidents to the persistent political pressure to create more executive departments and independent agencies. *Unchecked, these pressures to widen the President's span of control will eliminate the possibility of meaningful direction from, and contact between, the President and the major line officials of his Administration.*

To make the President's administrative job manageable, and to improve the coordination of related Federal programs, *we believe that the future line organization of the executive branch should be shaped over time to provide a small number (4–6) of line deputies (Secretaries) to manage the full range of executive departments and agencies short of the President.*

The task force illustrated the kind of supercabinet it had in mind by listing the following departments: Social Services, Natural Resources and Development, Economic Affairs, Science and Environmental Preservation, Foreign Affairs, and National Security Affairs. It was said, also, that the Justice Department would probably remain. The executive branch, however, should include all activities of the current regulatory commissions that were not quasi-judicial in character.

In justifying these recommendations, the task force stated that it believed they "would enlarge meaningful Presidential authority and influence." It believed that "*organizational reform to steepen and 'presidentialize' the pyramid of top executives who support the President as Chief Executive is indispensable to give the President a fighting chance to perform his management tasks.*" The "Presidential deputies and super-Secretaries, even with legal authority to take action themselves, would inevitably seek policy direction and guidance from the President."

To these recommendations for organization in Washington, the task force added forceful affirmation of its views of field coordination. This would be improved by "*strong regional line executives for each of these super-departmental groups,*" with operating responsibilities paralleling "the full range of functions commanded by the corresponding Presidential deputy in Washington" and reporting directly to him.

In this and preceding reports the task force had attacked the problem of presidential guidance and program coordination with three sets of structural recommendations, which it undoubtedly regarded as complementary. It would expand the institutionalized staff aid in the executive office, it would "presidentialize" the departmental structure by creating supersecretaries with staff help, and it would integrate the field structure with Executive Office and departmental structure. The structural position of the White House staff was not discussed, but it was assumed. The effects of task force proposals on its size were not analyzed. And the arguments that could be advanced against the task force proposals were not mentioned or barely adverted to, the behavioral effects or lack of effects on program actors by such changes were not predicted, and the political difficulties of obtaining approval from those in Congress who would have different perspectives on executive responsibility were left for the president to ponder—if he desired.

Organization for the Management and Coordination of Foreign Affairs

A report with the above title, transmitted to the president on 1 October 1967, was the final report of the Heineman task force. Although he had had an earlier approval from the president to move into the area of foreign affairs, Heineman asked for another by Califano and received a second approval from the president. The high-level support for Heineman's desire to go into this area and the initial views on what might be covered are revealed in Califano's request for approval from the president.

> I think he [Heineman] could do some excellent work for you in this area (as does Nick Katzenbach), particularly with respect to AID and foreign economic activity. He would also give you a good look at the foreign policy formulation process of Government and the relationships between State, Defense and CIA. As you know, McNamara strongly recommends the Task Force go forward in this area.[50]

The introduction of this topic led to Katzenbach's addition to the task force, though he suggested that perhaps Secretary Dean Rusk should be a member instead because McNamara and Bundy were members. As a hesitant member, Katzenbach did not sign the report, but he attended and participated in all the meetings and authorized a statement to the president that he was in general agreement with the recommendations.[51]

The high competence of the task force members on foreign affairs was supplemented by the sophistication of its staff reports. One of these examined the authorities and operations in foreign economic policy. Another dealt with the problems of personnel management. But the papers centered on the "primary" issue—should the secretary of state be the president's agent for coordination of foreign policy? The issue was in essence whether the SIG pattern of using the secretary of state as the president's agent for coordination in overseas administration could be extended to foreign affairs generally. One paper reviewed, first, the expectancy (from the first Congress) that the secretary of state would be fundamentally the agent of the president and occupy a unique position among cabinet officials, and second, the president's legal authority to direct specific government programs in such areas as foreign assistance and government intelligence.[52] Yet other papers reviewed the practical limitations on "primacy" for the secretary in interdepartmental relationships and even the odds against coordination within the Department of State. One paper was very negative on structural reform. A first point was this:

> I think it's high time to give up the fiction that even in principle the Department can and should get exclusive control under the President of foreign policy formulation and management. *It cannot—and it would be wrong if it did*. I think the right strategy for the Department is to focus *less* on its jurisdictional prerogatives, and to try to be *more* energetic and skillful in engaging the right people in the other agencies at the sub-cabinet level in the foreign policy process, thereby imposing foreign policy considerations on the workings of the other departments.[53]

Another point was an argument against formalism—against fixed committees or high expectancy for a single across-the-board committee, such as SIG—and in favor of "overlapping aggregations of *ad hoc* task forces, the informal network of sub-cabinet and cabinet officers," "a system which gives reasonable assurance that right clubs will be formed around right issues at right time with right connections above and below." There was, last, in this forceful paper, an elaboration of the important functions that could be performed by White House staff.

Another paper sought ways to surmount the institutional liabilities against a primary position for the secretary of state. These, it was suggested, could be transcended by (1) creating a four-man team (president, secretary, deputy secretary, under secretary) and delegating many coordination responsibilities to a deputy secretary; (2) strengthening staff capacity in the Office of the Secretary; (3) vigorous exercise of SIG-IRG machinery; (4) expanding State's budgetary role vis-à-vis other foreign affairs agencies. Such steps, another paper stated, would "change the character and reduce the size of the NSC staff" as the complementary functions of NSC and secretarial staff were developed.

This paper supplied the base for the task force's recommendations, which opted for primacy of the secretary of state in interdepartmental foreign policy formulation and administration. The task force saw three "related deficiencies" in organization of the government for the conduct of foreign and national security affairs:

(1) *Neither the White House nor the State Department is equipped to provide continuous, clear-cut policy leadership and guidance to all the various agencies of the government engaged in foreign affairs.*

(2) *No agency in government systematically and regularly* provides the President and other key decision-makers with *comprehensive analysis* of foreign affairs issues . . . .

(3) Outside the annual agency by agency budget review conducted by the Bureau of the Budget, no office or institution reviews the budgets of the foreign and national security affairs agencies from the perspective of the priorities, commitments and requirements of foreign policy.

While reorganization would "not solve all the problems of our foreign affairs," "*we still believe that organizational improvement is a prerequisite for improved U.S. performance in world affairs.*" The primary goals for organizational change were set forth in two paragraphs:

(1) To provide day-to-day leadership in policy and to insure that the diverse programs and activities of the agencies concerned with foreign affairs support established policies, *the President needs a strong chief subordinate*—an individual, not a committee—who can both advise him and act for him across the whole range of his international responsibilities.

(2) In our judgment the Secretary of State should do this job. He should be the President's chief adviser on foreign and national security

affairs, and under the President he should coordinate the programs of all U.S. agencies which support our foreign policies.

To achieve these objectives and enable the secretary of state to discharge these responsibilities, organizational changes would be required at the presidential and the departmental levels. At the "presidential" level, four changes were needed: (1) secretaries of state should be "authorized to free themselves personally, to the maximum extent possible, of social and ceremonial functions and participation in overseas conferences" and be encouraged to reduce their relations with Capitol Hill; (2) the "second-ranking position in the Department of State should be elevated to 'Deputy Secretary'" to provide the secretary with a "true 'alter ego'" and the president with a "top team"; (3) the secretary and his deputy should establish an analytic staff to help them, "somewhat comparable in character and function to the White House NSC staff"; and (4) the Department of State should establish, in consultation with BOB, "programmatic budgetary review" of other agencies whose activities support foreign policy.

For the Department of State, strengthening regional officers, regrouping functional activities under the department's two under secretaries, and broadening the membership and experience of the foreign service were recommended.

The report thus would *"Create a Team at the Top"* with a secretary of state and deputy; supporting staffs to "serve the President and his staff, as well as the Secretary and his Deputy" with the secretary and the deputy in a "direct and personal" and "intimate" relationship with the president. Thus, the specific solution for foreign affairs was different from those proposed for domestic affairs: for the latter, superdepartments with equal status and increased Executive Office staff had been proposed; for the former, leadership of one secretary acting as the agent of the president would be the instrument for the desired guidance and coordination. The objective, nevertheless, was the same: to provide the president with instruments for guidance and coordination of the executive branch.

In transmitting the foreign task force report to the president, Califano wrote, "The group considers this the second most important report they have submitted."[54]

INTERPRETATION OF THE HEINEMAN REPORTS

The ferment over structure of the executive branch midway in the Johnson presidency was program-oriented in its origin. The Great Society programs were recognized to be in trouble, and the interest in organization reflected a desire for their improved administration. These programs were so interspersed through the executive structure for domestic administration that considering how to implement them effectively led inevitably to an appraisal of the total organization for domestic programs. The Heineman task force was led beyond this into the area of administration of economic programs by the current proposal for a merger of the departments of Commerce and Labor, and into the foreign affairs area by the interests of some of its members. Thus the considerations of the task force led beyond immediate program improvement; and despite lack of analysis in such areas as natural resources, public works, and science and technology, the reports presented a comprehensive view of executive structure, placing the task force in a category with the Brownlow committee, the first Hoover commission and the Price task force.

In viewing the executive branch as a whole, it confirmed by restatement the working concepts of executive structure underlying the previous studies. Foremost, fundamental, and pervasive in the reports is the assumption of presidential responsibility. "Guidance," "influence" and "coordination" are the key words rather than "management" (which was the key word in the Brownlow report), perhaps suggesting directional rather than operational influence; but the president's responsibility for leadership and the need for responsiveness of executive units to his direction are, as in previous reports, the unifying concepts. These are the essentials for unity and cohesion, stated as needs in foreign policy, and coordination, deemed important for domestic policy.

The evils to be corrected in departmental and agency structure were "fragmentation" and the influences of special interests—both economic and professional. The objective was to "presidentialize" the department and agency structure—to force an upward look for guidance. Moreover, whereas the Brownlow committee had said the president "needs help," the Heineman task force believed he needed more help, though in this instance the sole emphasis was on institutionalized help.

These concepts were traditional; they reflect the comprehensive view of presidential responsibility, based on interpretation of the grant of executive power and the "take care" clause of the Constitution and the requirements for viability of the political system. Their acceptance in the Johnson subpresidency cannot be surprising, for it clearly viewed the presidency as the center of executive guidance and control.

There was an added concept of decentralization in domestic operations. Although Wallace Sayre had warned the task force that there would be political forces operating toward centralization, it believed that unification in field organization and changes in the relationships between headquarters and field executives could produce decentralization in "program operations and specific grant decisions."

The means proposed to "presidentialize" and achieve guidance, unity, and coordination should be summarized:

1. Noteworthy, first, was the rejection of conciliar approaches. No domestic council, whether on the model of NSC or otherwise, and no other form of interdepartmental collaboration was recommended, even though such proposals were being advanced in the administration and in Congress.

2. Expansion of the Executive Office of the President through two new offices—one for program development within BOB, the other for program coordination through an independent unit—was proposed.

3. The steepening of the domestic department and agency structure by unification in superdepartments with strong line executives adequately supported by staff officers was the option chosen for departmental organization.

4. In foreign affairs, the secretary of state, as the agent of the president, was to have a position of primacy over other departments.

5. Unification of field structures for the departments and agencies engaged most centrally in the implementation of Great Society programs, strengthening of field executives, and the creation of field offices for the Executive Office were recommended.

These were the means for an executive guidance and coordination system for a new phase in government in which multiple new domestic programs had emerged alongside vast foreign policy responsibilities and military involvements throughout the world.

Unfinished Business

The proposals of the Heineman task force (greatly extended institutional staff aid for the president, superdepartmental groupings and increased departmental staff, primacy for the Department of State, unification of field structures) were large in scope but general in analysis. To refine them into specific form for executive or reorganization order and legislation, and to obtain support of government executives, would have required extensive follow-up by other task forces and individuals representative of various in-house constituencies. Approval or acceptance within Congress, and by constituencies external to it and to the executive branch, would have presented obstacles that a president could overcome, even in part, only with great commitment and skill.

The records available to us do not show whether the president was favorably inclined toward the particular proposals or whether he would have thought they were worth the effort that Roosevelt before him and Nixon after him unsuccessfully expended. Yet the last of the reports came to him approximately six months before his announcement that he would not be a candidate for reelection, when he was deeply engrossed in decisions on the Vietnam War and the battle for public support for it. Obviously, the opportunity for President Johnson to turn from large policy issues—his primary concern through his total government experience—to structural

and operational problems in implementation of policy was not present.[55]
Yet there were concurrent or follow-up developments of significance. One
of these related only to the direction and management of a single department,
but is an important part of the legacy of the Johnson presidency. The other
three developments related to issues of government-wide management, such
as were considered by the Heineman task force.

The department was the Post Office. Responding to charges President
Johnson gave to him on his appointment as postmaster general late in 1965,
Lawrence F. O'Brien made a preliminary survey of post office operations and
reported to the president: "I would be derelict if I did not advise you of the
seriousness of this situation which frankly I was not aware of until I arrived
here."[56] O'Brien set up a task force for study of post office problems, which
reported recommendations in March 1967 that included substitution of a
government corporation for the cabinet-level Post Office Department.
O'Brien reported to the president that in his opinion the idea was "right in
logic" and "right politically." He asked for approval to float the idea as a trial
balloon in a public speech. Although Johnson wondered whether this would
endanger a rate bill being considered in Congress, he approved "if OK by
Schultze." Schultze-wrote to the president that he was "enthusiastic" about
the idea of a public corporation, and the speech was given on 3 April.[57]

In the midst of favorable reports received on the suggestion, condemnation
by the House Republican Policy Committee of the quality of postal service,
and a plan of Congressman Morris K. Udall (D–Ariz.) to introduce legislation
for a study commission, O'Brien and Schultze each recommended to the
president the quick appointment by executive order of an executive commission to study the organization of the postal service.[58] The president promptly
approved, and an executive order for creation of "A President's Commission
on Postal Organization" was issued on 8 April 1967.[59] The commission was
composed of highly prestigious private members; it was chaired by Frederick
R. Kappel, former chairman of the board of American Telephone and Tele-
graph Company, and Murray Comarow, staff director of the Federal Power
Commission, served part-time as its executive.

After a year of study the Kappel commission was ready to report severe
condemnation of the current situation and to make numerous recommendations for reform of organization and operations, including the creation
of a postal corporation. The proposal for postal reform was again before the
president and the subpresidency, now composed for consideration of this
proposal primarily of O'Brien, Schultze, Califano, and W. Marvin Watson,
White House aide. Immediately, the subpresidency worked through Comarow to obtain modifications in the draft report to soften denunciation of
Congress and current postal administration for postal difficulties and to
obtain some substantive changes.[60] As the report was being revised and

prepared for release, the subpresidency considered the options for a public position to be taken by the president. Charles J. Zwick, who had become director of BOB, favored support for the corporation as the best route to reform, and the postmaster general thought specific reforms should be supported without clouding the issue by support for a corporation.[61] It was recognized that considerable study needed to be given to the proposals in the report, and hence there was consensus on a suggestion to the president that he praise the commission and call for careful study of its recommendations.[62] This was the course he immediately followed in his statement releasing the report to the public.[63] But in his final State of the Union Message he went further: "I believe we should reorganize our postal system along the lines of the Kappel report."[64] Thus, the initiative of the postmaster general in response to the expression of presidential concern; the deliberations of a subpresidency that included first the postmaster general and the director of BOB, then a task force, and then the postmaster general, BOB, and White House staff; and the interest of the president generated the idea for a corporate structure, led to plans for its structure and operation, and kept the idea alive for adoption in 1970 by Congress and a new administration.[65]

The first of the developments related to governmentwide management was a BOB self-study, stimulated in part by the Heineman task force. The relation between the study and the task force was examined in a memorandum from Bohen to Schultze in December 1966. Bohen expressed awareness of some steps within BOB toward an internal examination of itself and the Executive Office, and he suggested discussion over the choice between an in-house study to be fed into the task force or an inquiry under a prestigious outsider.[66] BOB was skeptical of an external review of its functions and status[67] and opted for an internal study with some outside representation. The study was completed too late to become a part of the deliberations of the task force,[68] and its scope and perspectives were narrower than the recommendations of the task force for two new offices—one for planning within BOB, the other for interagency coordination through an Executive Office structure distinct from BOB. Although much of the BOB study dealt with its internal organization, the research objectives were broader. In program planning: "The development of the President's program is seen as the task of the White House staff, but the Bureau is viewed as having an important supporting role." The support role of the bureau was to "continue to play" traditional roles in legislative clearance, budgeting, and advice on organization and management and to assist in developing economic policy.

Yet negative views toward expansion in some areas were expressed: the Bureau "must perform its current responsibilities in the area of operational coordination more effectively" but avoid "actual . . . involvement in operations"; policy research was discussed briefly and vaguely. The emphasis was on doing present jobs better. To this end a new Office of Executive Management, its status provided by its being headed by an assistant director, could have responsibilities in five areas: government organization, systems design, operational coordination (with a small staff an on an ad hoc basis), financial management and accounting, and special projects (on "Government-Wide Management Problems").

Clearly, BOB's analysis was not coordinated with the task force deliberations. Its restricted view of a management role contrasted with the task force's recommendations for vastly enlarged machinery for policy coordination in the Executive Office and policy planning in BOB itself.

More significant were developments concerning the task force recommendations on field office restructuring. There had been some proposals on field office structure in the Johnson presidency before the report of the task force. Among these was a recommendation by a Task Force on Intergovernmental Cooperation appointed by the director of BOB that a presidential commission be established to recommend common regional boundaries for related programs;[69] and one for greater standardization of regional boundaries from the acting director of OEP—whose numerous contacts with governors undoubtedly pointed up the difficulties states had in dealing with federal field offices.[70] The president in his message to Congress, "The Quality of American Government," after noting that "the cause of intergovernmental cooperation is poorly served . . . when their [field offices] geographic boundaries overlap or are inconsistent," said:

> I have asked the Director of the Bureau of the Budget to undertake a comprehensive review of the federal field office structure and to develop a plan to assure the most effective use and location of these offices.
>
> I have asked him to recommend a plan for the restructuring of these offices, and I hope to incorporate the first steps of this plan in my next budget message.[71]

In response, Schultze recommended establishing common regions for Labor, HEW, HUD, OEO, and SBA. Califano presented these recommendations to the president on 2 December 1967 and recommended approval. The president, however, checked the "disapprove" space and scrawled beneath it, "Hell no! Not this year. L."[72]

A thorough, detailed, and conclusive study called the "Hughes Report" was sent to Califano in May 1968. The plan called for eight regions, with regional offices in Boston, Philadelphia, New York City, Atlanta, Chicago, Austin, Kansas City, and San Francisco. Strong regional office representation would also be provided in seven other cities. Attached were documents that showed the personnel relocations that would result (totaling 3,264), the effect on cities and congressional committees, a suggested press release, and copies of letters that could be used to present the plan to the agencies affected. Obviously this was planning with an objective of prompt action. It was accompanied by a memorandum for the president with respect to the inclusion of Austin as a regional city, believed "to be consistent with your wishes" but possibly productive of "additional controversy." Such locations are normally made in the largest and most accessible cities, and including Austin would require relocating more than a thousand persons in contrast to fewer than three hundred if Dallas or Fort Worth were selected. Califano, quoting from the president's earlier message and noting the effect the action would have in improving administration and strengthening the Great Society programs, recommended approval of the Hughes package as soon as the tax controversy was concluded.[73]

Califano revived the proposal as the end of the Johnson administration was approaching, saying that on 17 May "we decided to postpone a final decision on the plan." He argued it would correct "a patchwork that is incapable of meeting the challenge of the great domestic programs which you have sponsored," and that because of the difficulty in initiating such a program during the first year of a new administration, it was "proper and beneficial for it to be an accomplishment of your Administration." He concluded that "Charles Zwick and I recommend that you approve these plans." Transmitted also was a planned reorganization of the field structure of the Department of Commerce, which its secretary desired, that was consistent with the other plan and could be accomplished without presidential or congressional action. Johnson, not surprisingly, in view of his other actions against late recommendations for reorganization, did not approve the proposals.[74]

A final development occurred in the Congress. Hearings were held in the Senate in 1968 on bills to establish a commission to study the organization and management of the executive branch. S. 47 from Senator James B. Pearson (R–Kans.) and forty-one cosponsors and S. 2832, introduced by Senator George A. Smathers (D–Fla.) and cosponsored by Senator Jacob Javits (R–N.Y.), provided for a commission composed, like the Hoover commission, of persons appointed by the president, the president of the Senate and the Speaker of the House, while S. 2116, introduced by Senator Ribicoff with twenty cosponsors, provided for a presidentially appointed commission.[75] The position of BOB on these bills was negative,[76] as it had been on proposals for a commission in the past. But Seidman, responsible for the application of traditional concepts in BOB organization planning, thought BOB ought to reevaluate its position. His statement of changes that had occurred in government that led him to believe it was time for reevaluation of organization concepts deserves quotation.

Almost seventeen years have elapsed since the report of the first Hoover Commission. We are still preaching the gospel according to Herbert

Hoover and Louis Brownlow, although much of the doctrine is dated and in some respects questionable when applied to current problems of executive branch organization. The use of non-Government entities as managers and operators of Government programs, the size and complexity of Federal grant-in-aid programs and rapidly changing relationships between the Federal Government and elected executives at the State and local level, the geographic and intergovernmental approach to regional development, and technological developments such as ADP have added new dimensions to the problems of executive branch organization and administration which were almost totally unknown at the time of the Hoover and Brownlow studies. I am coming around reluctantly to the view that a comprehensive study of the organization of the executive branch and a reevaluation of our organizational doctrine are needed and could provide the conceptual framework on which to build a consistent approach in developing solutions to current problems. At present we appear to be going off in several different directions at once.[77]

It is not surprising that the frankness of the Heineman task force reports on the conditions prevailing in Great Society program administration should have led to a directive to keep them secret, or that the president should have refused to make them available to President Nixon. Nixon's transition representative had asked Charles S. Murphy, Johnson's transition coordinator, for copies of the reports. Murphy asked Johnson whether he should forward them, saying, "Joe Califano's feeling is that you should not make the report available to the President-elect but should keep it for your own use." Johnson checked "no" on the approval sheet and added, "Hell no. And tell him I'm not going to publish my wife's love letters either."[78]

Later, however, when Nixon appointed the President's Advisory Council on Executive Organization under the chairmanship of Roy L. Ash, Heineman, on its request, made the reports available.[79] The imprint of the Heineman task force reports on the Nixon administration is unmistakable. Nixon's message to Congress after receipt of the Ash council's report condemned "fragmentation" and the difficulty of launching "a coordinated attack on complex problems" and called for decentralization to field structures. The message proposed four new groupings into enlarged departments, three of which seemed to parallel those suggested by the Heineman Report—Human Affairs, Natural Resources, and Economic Affairs. The new departments would be centrally staffed with high-level administrators.[80] Early in the Nixon administration the field organizations of certain domestic departments had already been consolidated with common regional boundaries and headquarters, and these were now to be strengthened to aid in decentralization.

There was also continuity in identification of problems; in concepts of integration, decentralization, and presidential direction; and in belief in

214

larger departments, increased departmental staff, and field office restructuring as means of providing coordination and direction. On the other hand, instead of coordination and program development through institutional (Executive Office) staff—as proposed by the Heineman commission—President Nixon established a Domestic Council embodying the conciliar idea of the Shriver and Muskie proposals.

The Heineman task force had kept alive and preserved for successive administrations a continuing historical tradition of concepts and options for executive coordination and guidance. Yet its work had come too late for the Johnson presidency to act. The political support in Congress that had produced the Great Society legislation had been replaced by anguish over Vietnam and could not have been restored for contests with particularistic interests on executive organization.

NINE

Conclusion

Accomplishment, Process, Legacy

What do the preceding chapters tell us about structural accomplishment of the Johnson presidency, the processes by which changes were effected, and the organizational problems left on the nation's agenda? These are the questions addressed in this final chapter.

Accomplishment

Two new departments were established, a result attained in no other presidency after George Washington until Lyndon Johnson. A new agency (Office of Economic Opportunity—OEO), comparable in scope of purpose to some departments, was created in the Executive Office. Other new agencies with less scope—with mandates to promote the arts and the humanities, to study administrative procedure, to assist in regional development—were initiated. Sixteen reorganization plans were accepted by the Congress. One of these provided a basic reorganization of District of Columbia government. Others consolidated or transferred functions, solved new structural problems (mass transit), modified or abandoned old organization (Customs Bureau, interdepartmental committees, etc.). In addition to these developments in top-level organization, the presidency sometimes intervened in bureau-level changes, proposed or achieved, that could be made by department or bureau heads—as is illustrated by the notable participation of the president in consideration of changes for administration of educational and manpower functions.

The administrative changes under Johnson reflect a decisive presidency in which the White House actively searched for ideas to present to Congress and

216

measured accomplishments numerically—new departments to shape future policy, new agencies to administer new programs, restructuring of established organizations to reflect new purpose or adapt to program changes, new arrangements by which lead agencies (HUD, OEO, Justice, State) could improve interdepartmental coordination. Reorganization plans as well as legislation were used effectively, not usually for the economy and managerial objectives stated in the Reorganization Act of 1949, but for altering organization to conform with policy developments.

As might have been expected, the Johnson presidency included some failures, left some old problems unsolved, and created some new ones. The battle for home rule for the District of Columbia was lost. The president failed to get a department of business and labor, and thus no change was made from the disintegrated structure of the executive branch for economic advice and administration, which serves private interests more than it does the president's. Also, the Johnson administration, like its predecessors, chose not to engage in a "bloody, bone-shattering" and probably futile fight to rationalize the structure for administration of natural resource programs. It chose not to push the consideration of a number of reorganizations—the Small Business Administration, the Bureau of Indian Affairs, designation by the president of the Interstate Commerce Commission chair, a department for education, and others. Meanwhile, it had created an organization for the War on Poverty that had unorthodox features and was attacked from outside and within the executive branch, though the criticism arose more from policy antagonism than from administrative deficiencies.

The Johnson presidency struggled vigorously to preserve the authority of the president and the integrated structure posited for its support in the comprehensive presidential perspective set forth in chapter 1. The president refused to accept new provisions for congressional committee approval of administrative decisions, and he set the standard that requirements for notice to committees, with a waiting period, not unduly impair administrative effectiveness.

The position of the president was formally maintained in his power of appointment of executives with decisional and administrative power for the arts and humanities foundations and administrative functions for the Administrative Conference of the United States. His superior position and that of the federal government were protected in a form of coadministration for the Appalachian region in which governors shared authority over allocation of funds with the president, and thus the states with the federal government. Finally, Johnson established his hierarchical control over a departmental executive who sought to exercise the statutory powers of his office contrary to the wishes of the president.

Of more general significance was recognition midway through the Johnson presidency that the enormous expansion in government programs through Great Society legislation created the need for an examination of executive structure for central guidance and coordination. Although no basic changes for this purpose had been made by the end of the Johnson presidency, the options were clarified for a future administration.

PROCESSES OF DECISION

Organizational changes themselves, within the brief years of a presidency, should be of less concern than how they affect the capacity of the president and the executive branch to attain government purposes. Indeed, consideration and adoption of organizational forms have significant policy implications and encompass origination of ideas, integrated presidential decisions, and dispersed influences on presidential action.

Origins of Change

Issues of government structure got on the agenda of the Johnson presidency as a result of both external and internal pressures. Demographic changes and attendant social problems led to the concept of a department of urban affairs and to movement in that direction before and during the Kennedy administration. The creation of foundations for the arts and the humanities, the Administrative Conference of the United States, and the Appalachian Regional Commission and other economic development agencies resulted from external policy influences, to which Congress and the presidency responded jointly. The continued attention to the structure of the antipoverty program and the attention to the general problem of coordination of Great Society programs were heavily motivated by criticisms from mayors and governors.

Yet much of the agenda was created within the executive branch. The movement for a transportation department arose within the executive branch and had no strong support from outside the government. The idea for a department of business and labor originated with a task force and was developed entirely within the executive branch. All the reorganization plans presented to Congress were executive branch responses to policy and managerial needs as conceived within it. There was some concern within Congress for more or different reorganization plans, but the selection of subjects was recognized as the responsibility of the president.

Task forces were sometimes an important element in the subpresidency for funneling in new ideas, though they did not have influences on government structure, or on the broader subject of government management, comparable to those on policy development. The recommendations of such task forces were part of the background of the proposals for HUD, the Department of Transportation (DOT), a department of business and labor, and a few of the reorganization plans submitted by the president. The Wood task force recommendation for transfer of OEO functions to HUD did not gain acceptance beyond Joseph A. Califano, Jr., staff aide of the president, and the influence of the Price task force report seems to have been small. The Heineman task force had significance in clarifying issues for the future but placed no items on the immediate agenda. An essential role was performed, however, by internal task forces representing affected agencies and by the management aides (BOB, Civil Service Commission) of the president. These developed detailed proposals for the structure of HUD and DOT.

Congress, of course, yielded much of the responsibility for leadership on organization change to the president in the Reorganization Act of 1949 and its renewals. The record of reorganization plans supports the view that adapation of structure to policy and managerial needs is dependent to a large degree on internal forces in the executive branch that force structural issues onto the agenda of government.

Hence the capacity of the presidency for origination, decision, and leadership on executive structure is crucial. It rests on the combined action of the president as a person and the subpresidency.

The Instruments of Policy Integration

The president. Johnson's personal participation comes clearly into view in this study. First, he provided motivation for the subpresidency. This was the activist spirit, continuous from the Kennedy administration, that provided the driving force for new policy initiatives. Although his primary strength was in policy and program, he also had an effect on administration. One reason for this influence was the decision to include proposals for organizational change in the president's annual legislative program.

Second, the president provided a test for choice. "I wouldn't start something I couldn't pass," he told Califano. "Check it out" with those who hold the strategic positions in Congress, and check the votes, were repeated admonitions. Similarly, he expected unity to be developed within the executive branch, and he avoided action where such unity failed to materialize. In this pattern, departments of natural resources or education would not go on the agenda, nor would lesser reorganizations such as administration of Indian affairs. On the other hand, his sense of the dramatic was well known. Califano, realizing this, appealed to it as a basis for supporting transfer of OEO functions to HUD. Yet, success—"coonskins on the wall"—meant for Johnson goals achieved, not policies the president had recommended for consideration.

Third, his participation could be stimulating, decisive, or crucial for the result desired. The demand for a program on transportation, communicated to Califano at the ranch, although it failed to produce a policy agenda, led to

219

the proposal for a department of transportation. On such matters as breaking the irresolution on organization of OEO (by appointing Shriver), killing a manpower reorganization in the Department of Labor, transferring coordinating functions in civil rights enforcement, reorganizing the District of Columbia government, Johnson was determined and manipulative. Particular actions—for example, meetings with committee members, calls to strategically located members of Congress—and his legislative instincts were often critical to the result.

Fourth, Johnson preserved his command position. Although he expected his staff to work out details, even indicating some impatience with certain matters being sent to him, his night reading habits and his intimate knowledge gained through years of experience with government operations and policies enabled him to give attention to significant issues in organization proposals.

Finally, the president's actions—though measured for political effectiveness—did not reflect on overall organizational strategy. In the main, they were piecemeal and reactive. With respect to the two broad studies of government organization and presidential leadership during his administration, he showed little, if any, interest in the first (the Price task force report) and did not follow through on the proposals of the second (the Heineman task force report). Whether under different conditions—no war, a decision to run for reelection—he would have sought implementation of all or part of the Heineman task force report is an intriguing question. Some of the reorganizations were, of course, large and of great significance. They were made within the framework of classic administrative theory as embodied in the comprehensive presidential perspective.

Johnson's reactions to threats to the position of the president were as strong as any since President Jackson's defenses. Yet Johnson had no strategy of organization change, such as Presidents Roosevelt and Truman had after the Brownlow and Hoover reports, or President Nixon after the Ash commission report. He dealt with the structural problems that came to his attention, as result of either his policy initiatives or the choices of the subpresidency.

The subpresidency. The files of the Johnson Library have made it possible to view the elements in and the contributions of the subpresidency, as they relate to organization of the executive branch, more intimately than is ordinarily possible for authors. From these materials it is clear that two components of the subpresidency—one institutional, the other personal—were almost continuously involved in assisting the president on organizational matters. Others were brought in occasionally.

The institutional core, part of what is customarily called the "institutional presidency," was the Bureau of the Budget (BOB), and within it the Division of Management and Organization, headed during most of the Johnson presidency by Charles L. Schultze and Harold Seidman, respectively. Advice to the president on executive structure had been a function of the bureau for almost thirty years when Johnson became president, and it had acquired a reputation for competent and nonpolitical staff work. From administration to administration, it sustained within the presidency the comprehensive presidential perspective, including departmental organization and presidential leadership stressed by the Brownlow committee, delegation of powers to carry out law to departments rather than bureaus by the Hoover commission, and protection of the president from congressional invasion by numerous advocates of a strong president. For protection of the position of the president, Seidman designated two staff members to oversee developments in Congress and the executive branch.[1] In addition to safeguarding the constitutional position of the president and maintaining consistency in concepts of organization, the Bureau was the repository of knowledge on organization history and issues. From its files it could produce on short notice, almost as boiler plate, the history and the pro and cons of an organizational issue. This kind of readiness was valuable to an administration in which organizational consequences needed constant observation as new legislative programs were feverishly conceived.

Usually the Bureau and its division were active through the course of consideration of questions of structure, and normally their perspective governed. The division gleaned from the departments and agencies proposals from which summaries of possible changes could be transmitted to Califano. The Bureau initiated some changes and went along when some of its old ideas—such as a department of transportation—were resuscitated. It transmitted advice to the president as it saw problems arising, for example, within OEO specifically or in administration of Great Society programs generally. The communication flow was from Schultze, Seidman, and others to Califano, and from Schultze and occasionally others to the president directly.

The Bureau was often a link between the White House and task forces. It either created or worked closely with the internal task forces that worked out details of organization for departments or agencies. Also, almost always the administration's position on organization change was presented to committees of Congress by the Bureau.

The Bureau's strategic position on organization changes gave it influence over what went into reorganizations. While concessions to obtain internal support and congressional acceptance were usually necessary, the Bureau's position at the center (with its historical knowledge and clear grasp of agency functions) enabled it to influence from the beginning the content and form of reorganizations.

Despite readiness, oversight, and alertness, the Bureau or its division was occasionally overlooked or the advice of one or the other was not followed.

When assistance to the president was poorly coordinated in the transition following President Kennedy's death, and the Bureau's views on organization for a "War on Poverty" conflicted with others, the president made decisions that were contrary to its recommendations. BOB's suggestions for the internal organization of HUD were rejected when Weaver was appointed secretary. And cooperation of Seidman's division with the Heineman task force was denied and was not sought in preparing the proposal for a department of business and labor. Yet the Bureau had representation in the staff work before the department of business and labor was proposed; it succeeded in persuading the president to keep the HUD legislation free from program proposals; and Schultze gave his views to the Heineman task force. Only occasionally did the Bureau learn late about organizational developments that were occurring.

These, then, were specific contributions of the institutional subpresidency: overseeing developments, maintaining a consistent executive position, protecting the presidency, and supplying information, analysis, and expert guidance. These functions were exercised with concern for the objectives of the president who was in office. The director of the Bureau, appointed by the president, was the agent for reconciliation of persistent institutional and immediate policy objectives. There is no evidence that there was any serious strain between the two functions of representing the president's institutional interests and representing the president personally. The division occasionally met demands for service despite unsympathetic views, for example, preparing justification for a department of business and labor without including arguments it might have regarded as important, or presenting a position of the administration to a congressional committee at variance with its own previous position. Continuously, the division participated in presenting the administration's position to members of Congress. Generally these things were possible because of concordance between the objectives of the institutional and the personal presidency.

The representation of the latter was exercised by a number of staff aides, but increasingly after mid-1965 it was concentrated in Califano, Johnson's special assistant for domestic affairs. This representational role—which encompassed consideration of issues on organization of the executive branch—was served by diverse types of functions that were successfully integrated by Califano. One function was that of change agent. Califano's own drives seemed to conform with those of an activist president. His antennae were out to universities, task forces, and departments and agencies for ideas on organization to go into the president's legislative program. With a general directive from the president to do something about transportation, he proceeded at once to establish a task force to create substance for the president's objective. He pushed for action, even—as in the mass transit negotiations—forcing actors with conflicting positions to continue joint deliberations.

He was also a mediator among the actors. "Can't you reconcile differences before I act," the president wrote to him. In some cases, notably mass transit, the nature of the problems was such that the leadership of a single person deeply absorbed with the actors in the complexities of the problem was required for resolution of specific issues. In other cases, only broad differences in general position required reconciliation. The Johnson message was clear: resolve differences within the executive branch and with the leaders in strategic positions in Congress before sending it to me for approval. Califano had the first part of this assignment and shared the second with others.

Yet he often became an advocate, giving the president alternatives, reporting the positions of others, but also providing his own recommendations. He strongly supported DOT, the proposal for a department of business and labor, reorganization of manpower functions in the Department of Labor, and transferring OEO functions to HUD. Sometimes his views were rejected, sometimes he was asked to check additional items, but usually his advocacy represented the acceptable position within the government and for the president personally.

A necessary function was that of communicator of accurate information and analysis to the president. There were, as would be expected, some slips. The reorganization plan for the Tariff Commission was inaccurately reported as "noncontroverisal," the staff work on the proposed department of business and labor was incomplete, and Califano's reporting in this instance was somewhat inaccurate. Yet his ability for accurate analysis and clear, concise reporting served well the needs of a president who plowed nightly through stacks of memorandums.

The president's dependence on him was great. "Joe. I can't spend my year on these matters," was one of the admonitions to Califano to move ahead himself. Yet in one case, at least, Califano pushed beyond the president's decision ("Joe. I am acting against my judgment" about prospective committee votes) and was warned to clear matters two or three days in advance. The delicate nature of the relationship between a president and a staff coordinator is exhibited in the Johnson-Califano collaboration. The president relied on Califano for initiative, mediation, recommendation, accurate information, and dependable analysis; but the president's knowledge of the government and its programs, including his grasp of details, kept him from passing presidential functions "in commission" to any center or centers of the subpresidency.

Various other units of the subpresidency provided help to the president on organization matters, because this was a duty resulting from their regular functions. The Department of Justice drafted organization plans and other legal documents and gave legal advice. The Civil Service Commission gave advice on classification, needs for additional personnel, or other personnel aspects. Members of the White House staff who had been given responsibilities related to particular policy areas or to designated departments and agencies, and those who had responsibility for congressional liaison, participated as their areas of assignment were affected.

Task forces formed from outside the government and internal task forces became parts of the subpresidency ad hoc. The heads of departments and agencies, and sometimes their subordinates, were likewise drawn into the work of the presidency as their organizations were affected. Their utility to the president as members of the subpresidency was, however, compromised by their loyalties and interests as agency heads or members. They were both within and outside the subpresidency, functioning in a dual capacity as presidential aides and as agency officials. They undoubtedly wanted to be effective and loyal advisers to the president, and they also wanted to protect and promote the effectiveness of their agencies' programs. With these dual motivations, their acceptance of presidential perspectives varied. On occasion they accepted loss of jurisdiction, as the outgoing secretary of the Department of Commerce did when DOT was proposed, or the secretary of the treasury when he accepted transfer of the Coast Guard to DOT. On other occasions, departmental or program protectionism or expansionism was strongly demonstrated. This was patently evident, for example, in the insistence of those representing the Coast Guard that it be preserved intact in the new DOT, in the struggles of departments for jurisdiction over parts of the antipoverty program, and in the hard infighting for jurisdiction over mass transit functions. Rival positions forced representation of the presidency upward to BOB and Califano, whose institutional and personal positions were identified with those of the president.

The Determinants of Decision

We presented in chapter 1 certain perceptions about the relation of history to organization maintenance and change, as well as perspectives that influence the positions of those in authoritative roles. Organization is history that has acquired form and continuity. It congeals the representation of victorious interests and establishes a mechanism for their future dominance. Yet change often challenges history as preserved in present organization. This may lead to political conflicts in which organizational choices will be influenced by the perspectives of those occupying strategic positions.

We set forth four perspectives from which executive organization is viewed. Members of Congress, especially when acting on committees with specialized jurisdictions and supported by interest groups protected in existing administrative structures, tend to look at organization as a means of extending particular policies historically achieved. Such a perspecitve may be reinforced by constituency influences or by desires to protect committee positions. In the bureaucracy, concern over operating programs and the support of their special clienteles limits a comprehensive appreciation of organizational problems. Similarly, the president has his own program and political goals, and he views organization as an instrument for their attainment.

Beyond the three particularistic perspectives, there is a comprehensive perspective that views organization as a rational means for maintaining the constitutional and political position of the president. It considers integrated structure to be the primary objective of executive organization because it creates potential for guidance and coordination by the president and the subpresidency.

The administrative themes, then, that emerge from the Johnson presidency may be stated simply: organizaton is an instrument of new purpose as well as a method of maintaining achieved purpose; it reflects perspectives that motivate actors and institutionalizes them in the decision-making process.

These themes explain the basic issues of controversy in the creation of two new departments. In the case of HUD, the legacy of the Kennedy administration and the persistence of urban problems gave President Johnson an opportunity to elevate the Housing and Home Finance Agency (HHFA) to cabinet status. Yet passage of the enabling legislation was held up until representatives of the private mortgage market were assured that the Federal Housing Administration (FHA) would be preserved. The interests of other federal departments and agencies, paralleled by the interests of the oversight committees of Congress, further limited the scope of HUD to housing and physical assistance programs. These constraints, at times, proved frustrating to the president,whose view of urban policy went beyond specific programs and their host departments. They were also a major setback for those who supported a federal department for the cities—a structure capable of combining both physical development and social services.

As it finally emerged, HUD preserved the particularistic elements of old programs, with their traditional imbalances between central city and suburb and between the private mortgage market and government-owned housing. The new legislation did, however, give full authority to the secretary, who— with the exception of FHA—could readjust administrative structure. At Secretary Weaver's direction, the assistant secretaries were given staff responsibilities, thereby enhancing the secretary's ability to identify overlapping problems and force programs to conform to departmentwide policies.

With the exception of urban renewal assistance and Model Cities, this change may not have produced short-term policy gains, but it at least held some promise for the future.

In the establishment of DOT the president and his aides sought a new focus in transportation policy, one that would give attention to overall national needs and would allocate resources to separate modes of transportation based on an evaluation of those needs. This program objective was a challenge to the independent policies and structures developed for the separate modes of transportation. Hence, two issues were central. First, should there be a transfer of old structures into a department? The Coast Guard was comfortable with its existing dependence; those who had achieved victories for aviation safety and highway construction were concerned that no threat to these objectives be created; those interested in waterways development wanted no new center of influence that would affect government subsidies for this purpose; and maritime labor was unwilling to accept a new organization if its immediate demand for favorable policy was not satisfied. The settlements on this issue turned out to be, except for maritime transport, dependent on a compromise on the second issue: the position of the transferred functions in the new department. In accord with the norms of the comprehensive presidential perspective, the administration wanted powers to be transferred to the secretary of the department with authorization for reallocation, and assistant secretaries to be designated for staff aid to the secretary for planning and resource allocation. Those with particularistic interests wanted the powers to be exercised through existing bureaus or agencies. Essentially, the compromise retained operating responsibilities in the modal structures and created policy development resources in the secretary.

In the antipoverty program there were similar conflicts in a different setting. New objectives were outlined for existing programs, and organizational plans were laid for tactical purposes. Yet the significance of the program to the president's domestic strategy led organization planners to examine its structural role more comprehensively. Since poverty could not be eliminated through an existing categorical program (in any department), the choice was made for an agency directly responsible to the president but with broad coordinating responsibilities. This meant that the struggles between antagonistic bureaucratic interests would continue through the life of the program, with Labor, Agriculture, Interior, and units of HEW contending for jurisdiction in their special areas of activity.

Within the executive branch the strength of particularistic perspectives was clearly illustrated in the brief consideration of a department of natural resources. The departments of Agriculture, Army, and HEW immediately assumed defensive positions. Interior—with the exception of the proposed

226

transfer of the Bureau of Indian Affairs—found it possible to identify generally with the comprehensive presidential objective of BOB and the Price task force. Yet all departmental participants felt that the issue would be determined by interests beyond the executive branch: Secretary Freeman, Department of Agriculture, relied on the opposition that would come from the congressional committees and interest groups, and Secretary Udall, Department of Interior, wrote that "Hill politics" was the key. With congruence in bureaucratic, congressional, and interest group perspectives, the suggestion of a new department died. We saw no evidence to indicate it was seriously considered by the president.

Interest groups can be especially destructive of comprehensive solutions. Their perspectives on organization are almost exclusvely particularistic and gain strength by being shared by Congress and in administrative structures. Organized labor, for example, was able to defeat the proposals for a department of business and labor and for transfer of the Maritime Administration to the Department of Transportation. The particularistic concerns of private groups on natural resource policy stood as a roadblock to the creation of a department of natural resources. Mortgage bankers combined with real estate and business interests to preserve the name and organizational integrity of FHA in the new Department of Housing and Urban Development. Professional groups in the arts and the humanities desired a form of organization that vested grant decision in their representatives. In the case of education, the conflict was between those who supported a particular kind of objective (a department of education) and those who believed that presidential guidance for the executive branch would be promoted by retaining a large department with crosscutting programs (HEW).

On the other hand, reorganization plans, since they have limited objectives and in most cases require low presidential and congressional involvement, are less frequently subject to special group resistance. While there were examples of particularistic representation of constituency interests—conspicuously in pressure for location of the Customs Bureau field offices—and some effort to maintain committee jurisdiction—as in consideration of the District of Columbia reorganization plan—such activities were generally absent.

In all the deliberations on executive structure, the comprehensive presidential perspective was in some way present to influence decision. Economy and managerial efficiency were seldom, if ever, of any significance in the changes of this period. But location of functions in appropriate conjunction with related activities, integrated executive organization, and presidential capability for guidance and coordination were consistent concerns of the subpresidency and the president and provided supporting doctrine that had some conscious appeal outside the presidency.

AGENDA FOR THE FUTURE

President Johnson, like other presidents, inherited an executive structure. It combined unities and disunities that promoted or hampered coordination of its functions, aid to the president in his policy-making role, and guidance by him for its operations. In the years following the Brownlow report, the president had been provided with elements of an institutional staff and White House aides, and after World War II he was given instruments of unification in defense and foreign policy. But the executive structure for policy aid and administration in economic affairs, natural resources, technology, human resources, and other domestic policy areas was diffuse and uncoordinated throughout the executive branch and was poorly designed for presidential control. For discharge of his general caretaker responsibility the president had the potent constitutional power of appointment and removal and the personal influence this created, but he lacked structural support for the functions of executive guidance and control.

The Great Society program, like the New Deal and the international involvements following World War II, put new strains on the executive branch. The rapid development of numerous new programs with their complicated interrelations enormously expanded the administrative problem at two points: the competence of the national government and the state and local governments to handle their new interrelations, and the internal capacity of the national government for administrative coordination and policy direction.

As the structure became more complex, inherited administrative thought was restated, reflecting the comprehensive presidential management perspective. Perhaps in anticipation of the administrative consequences of Great Society legislation, the Price task force was created in 1964, and midway in the Johnson administration concern over the exacerbation of the problems of administrative coordination led to the appointment of the Heineman task force. Both reasserted presidential responsibility for guidance and control.

In both reports, and in the grasping of political leaders for solutions to problems of coordination, the options for strengthening the executive presidency were focused. They included a domestic council, restructuring of departments, superdepartments, expanding the Executive Office, field integration, and primacy of a particular department for a designated policy area. Notably, no one proposed a further expansion of White House staff as the solution to the problems of the executive branch.

While the comprehensive presidential perspective was accepted for the executive branch, there were in the course of the Johnson presidency some suggestions of means of limiting the strains on that branch and concurrently the burdens of executive responsibility. There was vision of increased decentralization of policy choices and administration in the planning for the Community Action agencies, Model Cities, and the Appalachian Regional Commission, and later for bloc grants, grant consolidation, and possible introduction of revenue sharing. There was also implicit in these moves recognition of the integral importance of administrative considerations in policy choices. For various reasons the earlier moves toward decentralization failed to produce any general alternative to national administrative centralization, and accompanying presidential responsibility. By the time the later policy innovations (bloc grants, grant consolidation, revenue sharing) were being adopted or advocated, the sun had begun to set on the Johnson presidency.

The legacy of the Johnson presidency on executive structure included positive attainments: the authority of the president was preserved, the structure of the executive branch was adapted in various ways to particular program objectives, and the capacity of the presidency for leadership in piecemeal organizational change was demonstrated. Nevertheless, policy and administrative coordination, as well as presidential guidance for the executive branch, had been made enormously more difficult, and probably less achievable, with the enactment of Great Society legislation. Solutions for future administrative and guidance problems had not been determined, but options for future consideration had been clarified and in some instances sharply defined.

NOTES

CHAPTER ONE

1. Kendall v. U.S., 12 Pet. 524 (1838).
2. Myers v. U.S., 272 U.S. 52 (1926).
3. For elaboration, see Edward S. Corwin, *The President: Office and Powers, 1787–1957*, 4th ed. (New York: New York University Press, 1957), pp. 242–50.
4. In Re. Neagle, 135 U.S. 1 (1890).
5. *Administrative Management in the Government of the United States* (Washington, D.C.: Superintendent of Documents, 1937). For the background of the study, see Barry Dean Karl, *Executive Reorganization and Reform in the New Deal: The Genesis of Administrative Management, 1900–1939* (Cambridge, Mass.: Harvard University Press, 1963).
6. Quoted in Richard Polenberg, *Reorganizing Roosevelt's Government: The Controversy over Executive Reorganization, 1936–1939* (Cambridge, Mass.: Harvard University Press, 1966), p. 15.
7. *Administrative Management in the Government of the United States*, p. 2.
8. Public Law 162, 7 July 1947, 61 Stat. 246.
9. Frequently, the movement of events in the presidency can be explained more clearly and fully by the activities of the subpresidency than by those of the president personally, because of the extensive documentation in the flow of communications from the subpresidency to the president. This is especially true of structural change, owing to the extensive institutional aid the Bureau of the Budget gives the president on organization and management issues.

CHAPTER TWO

1. U.S. President, "Remarks at the Signing of Bill Establishing a Department of Housing and Urban Development" (9 September 1965), in *Public Papers of the Presidents of the United States: Lyndon B. Johnson, 1965* (Washington, D.C.: Government Printing Office, 1966), p. 985, hereafter cited as *Public Papers*.

231

2. Reorganization Plan no. 3, 1947.

3. *Administrative History of the Department of Housing and Urban Development,* 1:1–6, LBJ Library; Judith Heimlich Parris, "Congress Rejects the President's Urban Department, 1961–62," in *Congress and Urban Problems,* ed. Frederic N. Cleaveland (Washington, D.C.: Brookings Institution, 1969), pp. 174–76; John B. Willman, *The Department of Housing and Urban Development* (New York: Praeger, 1967), pp. 5–14; U.S. Congress, Senate, Committee on Government Operations, *Establish a Department of Housing and Urban Development: Hearings before the Subcommittee on Executive Reorganization,* 89th Cong., 1st sess., 1965, pp. 16–20; Mark I. Gelfand, *A Nation of Cities: The Federal Government and Urban America 1933–1965* (London: Oxford University Press, 1975), pp. 105–56.

4. U.S. Congress, Senate, Committee on Government Operations, *Establish a Department of Housing and Urban Development,* p. 16.

5. See U.S. Congress, Senate, Committee on Banking and Currency, *Federal Housing Programs,* Committee Print, 81st Cong., 2d sess., 24 February 1950.

6. Ibid.

7. Reorganization Plan no. 3, 1947.

8. *Housing Act of 1949, Statutes at Large* 63, chap. 338, part 1 (P.L. 81-171).

9. *Administrative History of HUD,* 1:7.

10. U.S. Congress, House, Committee on Government Operations, *Creation of a Department of Urbiculture, Hearings before a Subcommittee on Government Operations,* 84th Cong., 1st sess., 1955.

11. U.S. Congress, Senate, Committee on Government Operations, *Create a Commission on Metropolitan Problems: Hearings before the Subcommittee on Reorganization and International Organizations,* 86th Cong., 1st sess., 1959.

12. Interview with Harold Seidman, Austin, Texas, 14 June 1979.

13. Draft memo for the president, prepared by PACGO, 2 July 1957, "PACGO Records" folder, box 13, LBJ Library; see also, Mark Gelfand, *A Nation of Cities,* p. 261.

14. W. K. Brussat, Memo to Mr. Peterson, "Meeting on Metropolitan Problems with Messrs. Deming, Gulick and Norton in New York," 22 September 1960, 9-23-60, BOB R4-27.

15. "Statement by Nixon on Housing Program," *New York Times,* 29 September 1960.

16. Ibid.

17. Robert Wood, "The Case for a Department of Urban Affairs" (speech delivered at the annual meeting of the American Political Science Association, September 1960), BOB R4-27.

18. R.E.N. [Richard E. Neustadt], memo to Theodore C. Sorensen and Myer Feldman, "Department of Urban Affairs," 25 January 1961, BOB R4-2/65.1.

19. Parris, "Congress Rejects the President's Urban Department, 1961–62," p. 183.

20. Ibid.

21. Staff memo, "Analysis of Programs Which Might Be Transferred to A New Department of Housing and Urban Development," 3 January 1961, BOB R4-20, vol. 1.

22. Parris, "Congress Rejects the President's Urban Department, 1961–62," p. 186.

23. Ibid.

24. Memo for the president from Harold Seidman, 23 January 1961, BOB R4-2/

65.1; See also Parris, "Congress Rejects the President's Urban Department, 1961–62," p. 186.

25. Reorganization Plan no. 1, 1962.

26. Transcript, Robert C. Weaver Oral History Interview, 19 November 1968, tape 1, p. 23, LBJ Library.

27. Other members of the task force included Jerome P. Cavanaugh, mayor, city of Detroit; Nathan Glazer, University of California at Berkeley; Norman Kennedy, University of California at Berkeley; Saul B. Klaman, National Association of Mutual Savings Banks; Ralph E. McGill, *Atlanta Constitution*; Karl Menniger, Menniger Foundation; Martin Mayerson, University of California at Berkeley, Raymond Vernon, Harvard University; Catherine Bauer Wurster, University of California at Berkeley; and Paul Ylvisaker, Ford Foundation.

28. Report of the President's Task Force on Metropolitan and Urban Problems, transmitted to the president on 30 November 1964, p. 32, Task Force Collection, LBJ Library.

29. Ibid., p. vi.

30. Ibid., p. 32.

31. Ibid.

32. Ibid., p. 35.

33. Report of the President's Task Force on Government Organization, transmitted to the president on 6 November 1964, pp. 2–3, Task Force Collection, LBJ Library.

34. Ibid., pp. 3–4.

35. Hugh Sidney, "The White House Staff vs. the Cabinet," interview with Bill Moyers, *Washington Monthly*, February 1969, p. 80.

36. Robert C. Weaver Oral History, p. 32.

37. Memo, Robert C. Weaver to Bill Moyers, 3 December 1964, "Legislative Proposals, 1965" folder, book 4, box 100, Files of Bill Moyers, LBJ Library.

38. Ibid.

39. See "Legislative Proposals, 1965," books 3, 4, 5, boxes 99–100, LBJ Library.

40. Ibid.

41. William K. Brussat, memo to Harold Seidman, "Agency Comments on HUD," 17 February 1965, BOB R4-27/65.1.

42. Ibid.

43. Ibid.

44. "Annual Message to the Congress on the State of the Union" (4 January 1965), *Public Papers, 1965*, book 1, p. 93.

45. "Annual Budget Message to the Congress, Fiscal Year 1966" (25 January 1965), *Public Papers, 1965*.

46. "Annual Message to the Congress on the State of the Union," p. 9.

47. Memo, Harold Seidman to Phillip S. Hughes, "Draft (2-1-65) Housing Message," 5 February 1965, BOB R4-27/65.1.

48. Ibid.

49. "Special Message to Congress on the Nation's Cities" (2 March 1965), *Public Papers, 1965*, 1:231.

50. Ibid., pp. 233–34.

51. U.S. Congress, Senate, Committee on Government Operations, *Establish a Department of Housing and Urban Development: Hearings before the Subcommittee on Executive Reorganization,* 89th Cong., 1st sess., 1965, p. 75.

52. Ibid., p. 112.

53. Ibid., pp. 109–10.
54. Ibid., p. 242.
55. 2 May 1965, "Reports on Legislation" folder, Lawrence O'Brien's Office Files, LBJ Library.
56. Ibid.
57. U.S. Congress Senate, Committee on Government Operations, *Establish a Department of Housing and Urban Development: Hearings . . . Executive Reorganization,* p. 205.
58. Ibid.
59. Ibid., p. 206.
60. Ibid., pp. 199, 157.
61. Memo, William K. Brussat to Mr. Schnoor, "S. 1599 as Passed in the Senate," June 1965, BOB R4-27/65.1.
62. 17 August 1965, "Reports on Legislation" folder, Lawrence O'Brien's office files, LBJ Library.
63. Memo, Phillip S. Hughes to Lawrence O'Brien, 17 August 1965, "S. 1599 as passed by the Senate" folder, LBJ Library.
64. Ibid.
65. Memo, Mike Manatos to Lawrence O'Brien, 19 August 1965, "Manatos: Leg. 1965; Mr. O'Brien-Sept. (Desautels)" folder, box 3, files of Mike Manatos, LBJ Library.
66. Department of Housing and Urban Development Act, P.L. 89-174.
67. U.S. Congress, Senate, Committee on Government Operations, *Establish a Department of Housing and Urban Development, Hearings . . . Executive Reorganization,* p. 121.
68. Interview with Harold Seidman, Austin, Texas, 14 May 1979.
69. "Special Message to Congress on the Nation's Cities" (2 March 1965), *Public Papers, 1965,* 1:236.
70. Robert C. Weaver Oral History, p. 33.
71. Ibid., p. 41.
72. Dwight A. Ink, "The Department of Housing and Urban Development—Building a New Federal Department," *Law and Contemporary Problems* 32, no. 3 (Summer 1967): 377.
73. *Administrative History of HUD,* p. 25.
74. Ibid.
75. Ibid., p. 26.
76. Robert C. Weaver Oral History, p. 42.
77. Ink, "Department of Housing and Urban Development—Building a New Federal Department," p. 379.
78. Robert C. Weaver Oral History, p. 42.
79. Correspondence from Dwight A. Ink, 29 November 1979, pp. 1–2.
80. *Administrative History of HUD,* p. 13.
81. Ibid., pp. 13–14.
82. Ibid., p. 13.
83. Robert C. Weaver Oral History, p. 3.
84. Correspondence from Dwight A. Ink, 29 November 1979, p.1.
85. For an authoritative account of the relations between the regional offices of AEC and headquarters, see Harold Orlans, *Contracting for Atoms* (Washington, D.C.: Brookings Institution, 1967), pp. 119–23.

86. Ink, "Department of Housing and Urban Development—Building a New Federal Department," p. 379.

87. Ibid.

88. Transcript, Robert C. Wood Oral History Interview, 19 October 1969, pp. 19–20, LBJ Library.

89. Ibid., pp. 19–21.

90. Ibid., pp. 19–20.

91. Ibid., p. 19.

92. The President's Task Force on Urban Problems, "Proposed Plan of Organization for the Department of Housing and Urban Development," *Report of the Task Force Subcommittee*, 14 December 1965, p. 1, Task Force Collection, LBJ Library.

93. Ibid.

94. Also recommended was the transfer of the Veterans Administration Mortgage Guaranty and Direct Loans program to HUD, and the transfer of HHFA's college housing program to HEW.

95. President's Task Force on Urban Problems, "Proposed Plan for HUD," p. 4.

96. Ibid., pp. 2–9.

97. Harold Seidman, *Politics, Position and Power* (London: Oxford University Press, 1970), p. 78.

98. Memo, Harold Seidman to Charles Schultze, "Organization of Department of Housing and Urban Development," 18 February 1966, BOB R4-27/66.

99. Ibid.

100. Ibid.

101. *Administrative History of HUD*, pp. 18–19.

102. Ibid., p. 19.

103. Interview with Harold Seidman, Austin, Texas, 14 May 1979.

104. Robert C. Weaver Oral History, p. 35.

105. Ibid., p. 34.

106. Ibid.

107. Executive Order no. 11297, 11 August 1966.

108. On 30 September 1966, Executive Order no. 11307 gave the secretary of agriculture "convener" authority for rural programs.

109. The President's Task Force on Urban Problems, transmitted to the president on 21 December 1965, 5, Task Force Collection, LBJ Library.

110. Bernard J. Frieden and Marshall Kaplan, *The Politics of Neglect: Urban Aid from Model Cities to Revenue Sharing* (Cambridge, Mass.: MIT Press, 1975), p. 76.

111. James L. Sundquist with the collaboration of David W. Davis, *Making Federalism Work* (Washington, D.C.: Brookings Institution, 1969), pp. 86–87.

112. Ibid.

113. Frieden and Kaplan, *Politics of Neglect*, p. 72.

114. Ibid., p. 80.

115. Ibid., pp. 80–81.

116. Ibid.

117. Correspondence from Dwight A. Ink, 29 November 1979, pp. 2–4.

118. Frieden and Kaplan, *Politics of Neglect*, p. 150.

119. Correspondence from Dwight A. Ink, 29 November 1979, p. 4.

120. Ibid., p. 2.

121. Frieden and Kaplan, *Politics of Neglect*, p. 156.

122. Ibid., p. 157.

123. Secretary's Order no. 22 (Revision no. 1), 5 February 1968, Department of HUD, roll 62, LBJ Library.
124. Frieden and Kaplan, *Politics of Neglect*, pp. 104–5.
125. Ibid., p. 81.
126. Robert C. Weaver Oral History, pp. 7–8.

CHAPTER THREE

1. For a detailed review of proposals for a department of transportation, see Grant Miller Davis, *The Department of Transportation* (Lexington, Mass.: D. C. Heath, 1970), chap. 2.
2. Commission on Organization of the Executive Branch of the Government, Report no. 10, Department of Commerce, H. Doc. 100, 1949. The Task Force Study on Transportation was filed with this report.
3. Interview, one of the authors with Alan Dean, BOB staff member in 1957, 9 July 1979.
4. See the account in Emmette S. Redford, *Congress Passes the Federal Aviation Act of 1958* (University: University of Alabama Press, 1961), pp. 4–15.
5. "Annual Budget Message to the Congress, Fiscal Year 1962," *Public Papers of the Presidents, Dwight D. Eisenhower, 1960–61*, p. 414.
6. Transmitted to the president on 16 November 1964 by George W. Hilton. Copies available in the LBJ Library.
7. *Report of the President's Task Force on Government Reorganization*, transmitted to the president on 6 November 1964. Copies in the LBJ Library.
8. Neither the president nor White House aides discussed the contents of the report with Price. Interview with Don K. Price, October 1977.
9. The words were quoted from Emmette S. Redford, *The President and the Regulatory Commissions* (prepared for the President's Committee on Government Organization, 1960; located in Bureau of the Budget files).
10. Hilton report, note 6.
11. The "subsystem" concept, though implied earlier in studies by Pendleton Herring and others, was developed in J. Lieper Freeman, *The Political Process: Executive-Bureau Committee Relations* (Garden City, N.Y.: Doubleday, 1955). It had been called "whirlpools or centers of activity" by Ernest S. Griffith, *The Impasse of Democracy* (New York: Harrison-Helton Books, 1939), p. 182, and "subgovernments" by Douglass Cater, *Power in Washington* (New York: Random House, 1964). For an analysis of subsystem influences, see Emmette S. Redford, *Democracy in the Administrative State* (New York: Oxford University Press, 1969), chap. 4.
12. Redford, *Congress Passes the Federal Aviation Act.*
13. Robert T. Norman et al., "The Promotion of Civil Aviation," 28 February 1964, Federal Aviation Administration records, as cited in Gary Lee Rosenthal, "The Politics of Reorganization: Creating a Department of Transportation" (honors thesis, Harvard University, 1971), pp. 5–7. Rosenthal's useful study was based on extensive interviews and Washington, D.C., documentary sources but was complete before records were available in the LBJ Library.
14. Memo, Dean to Halaby, "Items for Discussion with Don K. Price," 15 September 1964, Federal Aviation Administration records, cited in Rosenthal, "Politics of Reorganization," p. 27.
15. Letter, N. E. Halaby to the president, 30 June 1965, in *Administrative History of the Department of Transportation*, appendix to part I, LBJ Library. Though the

originals of the documents cited in this study are in a variety of files, many of the memoranda and letters can be found assembled in three boxes labeled Legislative Background, Transportation Department, boxes 1, 2, and 3, LBJ Library.

16. Letter, John T. Connor to the president, 15 August 1965, Ex TN, WHCF, LBJ Library.

17. Memo, Charles L. Schultze to Joseph A. Califano, 20 August 1965, Ex FG 175, WHCF, LBJ Library.

18. Joseph A. Califano, Jr., *A Presidential Nation* (New York: W. W. Norton, 1975), p. 47.

19. As recorded by one who attended the meeting with the president. Memo, Arthur Okun to Gardner Ackley, 11 September 1965, "Foundation for Action—1965, Task Force," Legislative Background, Transportation Department, Box 1, LBJ Library.

20. The meeting, after postponements, came to include Connor, Boyd, Secretary Weaver of HUD, and top officials from the Treasury Department, CEA, BOB, the Office of Science and Technology, two members of Boyd's staff, and several White House staff members.

21. Memo, Joseph A. Califano to Alan S. Boyd, 12 August 1965, in *Administrative History of the Department of Transportation*, appendix, part 1, LBJ Library.

22. Memo, Joseph A. Califano to Alan S. Boyd, in *Administrative History of the Department of Transportation*, appendix, part 1, LBJ Library.

23. "Annual Message to the Congress on the State of the Union," 8 January 1964, in *Public Papers of the Presidents, Lyndon B. Johnson, 1963–1964* (Washington, D.C.: U.S. Government Printing Office, 1965), pp. 112–18.

24. See, for details, transcripts of Alan S. Boyd, Oral History Interview, 20 November 1968, pp. 1–3, LBJ Library.

25. Memo, Alan S. Boyd to members of Transportation Task Force, 7 September 1965, Ex FG 600/T, WHCF, LBJ Library.

26. Ibid.

27. Alan S. Boyd to Joseph A. Califano, 2 September 1965, transmitting nine papers and summarizing some of the contents. "Foundation for Action—1965, Task Force," Legislative Background, Transportation Department, box 1, LBJ Library.

28. Transcript, Alan S. Boyd Oral History Interview, p. 27, LBJ Library.

29. See on Boyd's views, ibid., pp. 13 ff.

30. See memos: William M. Capron on "Meeting of the Transportation Task Force," Friday, 10 September 1965; Arthur Okun to Gardner Ackley, "Transportation Program: High Road or Low Road," 11 September 1965; Capron to the director of BOB, "Transportation Chaos," 13 September 1965—all in Legislative Background, Transportation Department, box 1, LBJ Library.

31. Memo, Califano to president, 22 September 1965, Ex LE, WHCF, LBJ Library.

32. Memo, Califano to president, 12 October 1965, filed with Califano memo to Jack Valenti, 14 October 1965, C.F. LE, WHCF, LBJ Library.

33. Memo, Alan S. Boyd to Joseph A. Califano, 22 November 1965, Ex FG 999-15, WHCF, LBJ Library. Also in Legislative Background, box 1, LBJ Library.

34. Memo, Phillip S. Hughes to Califano, 24 November 1965, Legislative Background, Transportation Department, box 1, LBJ Library.

35. Memo, Charles L. Schultze to Lee C. White, 9 November 1965, Ex FG 175, WHCF, LBJ Library.

36. Reports of these conversations are in memos in "Decision on Transportation,"

Legislative Background, Transportation Department, box 1, LBJ Library.

37. Memo, Califano to president, 13 December 1965, Ex FG 999-15, WHCF, LBJ Library.

38. Memos: Lee C. White to president, 10 January 1965, for Magnuson, Ex LE/TN, WHCF, LBJ Library; for Staggers, Ex FG 999-15, WHCF, LBJ Library.

39. Memo, Connor to Califano, 22 December 1965, C.F. FG 175, WHCF, LBJ Library.

40. Memo, Califano to White, 20 December 1965, Ex FG 999-15, WHCF, LBJ Library.

41. Memo, Califano and White to president, 28 January 1966, Ex FG 175, WHCF, LBJ Library.

42. Memo, Califano to president, 24 January 1966, transmitting Nicholas Johnson's statement. Ex FG 999-15, WHCF, LBJ Library.

43. Memo, Califano and White to president, 1 February 1966, "Decision on Transportation," Legislative Background, Transportation Department, box 1, LBJ Library. The president's approval is marked on the memo.

44. Califano and White to president, 28 January 1966, Ex FG 75, WHCF LBJ Library.

45. Memo, Califano and White to president, 1 February 1966, op. cit.

46. For fuller analysis of the distinction, see Robert Salisbury and John Heinz, "A Theory of Policy Analysis and Some Preliminary Applications," in Policy Analysis in Political Science, ed. Ira Sharkansky (Chicago: Markham Publishing, 1970), pp. 39–60.

47. Interview, one of the authors with Alan Dean, 5 July 1979.

48. Memo, Califano and White to president, 28 January 1966, Ex FG 175, WHCF, LBJ Library.

49. Memo, Fowler to Schultze, printed in Administrative History of the Department of Transportation, U.S. Coast Guard, vol. 4, part 1.

50. For discussion on these points, see memo, Califano and White to the president, 28 January 1966, Ex FG 175, WHCF, LBJ Library.

51. Memos summarized in Administrative History of the Department of Transportation, U.S.Coast Guard, vol. 4, part I, chap. 1, pp. 3–5.

52. Memo, William F. McKee to Schultze, 4 February 1966, Legislative Background, Transportation Department, box 1, LBJ Library.

53. Administrative History of the Department of Transportation, vol. 1, part 1, chap. 1, pp. 28 ff., LBJ Library. The quotation is from the subcommittee proposals.

54. Ibid., vol. 1, part 1, chap. 1.

55. For a summary of the events surrounding the adoption of 1964 criteria see memo, Byron Nupp (Office of the Secretary, U.S. Department of Commerce) to Cecil Mackey, 28 March 1966. In "Legislative Struggle—Vol. I," Legislative Background, Transportation Department, box 2, LBJ Library.

56. See memo, Califano to the president, 10 June 1966 Ex FG 999-15, WHCF, LBJ Library.

57. Memo, White to president, 10 January 1966, Ex FG 175, WHCF, LBJ Library.

58. Letter transmitted by Califano to the president, 22 January 1966, C.F. FG 175, WHCF, LBJ Library.

59. Memo, 1 March 1966, Ex SP 2-3/19/66/TN, WHCF, LBJ Library.

60. Memo, Mike Manatos to Califano, 19 February 1966, in "The Message—Vol. II," Legislative Background, Transportation Department, box 2, LBJ Library.

61. Memo, Paul Southwick to Henry Wilson, 11 February 1966, "The

Message—Vol. II," Legislative Background, Transportation Department, box 2, LBJ Library.

62. Memo, Zwick to Califano, 24 December 1965, *Administrative History of the Department of Transportation,* vol. I, part 1, chap. 1, appendix, LBJ Library. His italics.

63. "Special Message to Congress on Transportation," 2 March 1966, *Public Papers of the Presidents, Lyndon B. Johnson, 1966,* (Washington, D.C.: U.S. Government Printing Office, 1967), pp. 250–63.

64. *Hearings before the Committee on Government Operations,* U.S. Senate, 89th Cong., 2d sess., on S. 3010, part 1, p. 74. Also, see p. 88.

65. Ibid., p. 10.

66. Joseph W. Sullivan, "Bill to Set up Transportation Department Is Likely to Be Watered down by Congress," *Wall Street Journal,* 17 May 1966.

67. *Hearings* on S. 3010, p. 62.

68. Ibid., pp. 58–78.

69. Ibid., pp. 252–53, quotation at p. 253.

70. Ibid., pp. 325–26.

71. Ibid., pp. 293–301.

72. Ibid., p. 132.

73. Ibid., for example, pp. 310–18.

74. Ibid., for example, pp. 310–18.

75. 13 May 1966, Ex FG 170-6, WHCF, LBJ Library.

76. Memo, Califano to president, 30 August 1966, Ex FG 175, WHCF, LBJ Library.

77. Public Law 89-670, 80 Stat. 931, 15 October 1966.

78. See, for example, testimony of Frederick B. Lee, National Pilots Association, 3 May 1966, and Senator Monroney, 4 May 1966. *Hearings* on S. 3010, pp. 287–392 and 293–330, respectively.

79. Memo, Boyd to Connor, 6 June 1966, Ex FG 175, WHCF, LBJ Library.

80. *Hearings* on S. 3010, part 1, p. 65.

81. Ibid., part 2, p. 327.

82. Memo, Schultze to Califano, 13 May 1966, Ex FG 170-6, WHCF, LBJ Library.

83. He considered (*Congressional Record,* 112:24397) that his testimony in hearings had been in favor of a department of transportation; but, as shown herein, the administration forces were uncertain about his support. He is reported to have said that he "was informed by the White House that the FAA could expect cuts of twenty-five per cent in its budget requests if it remained independent . . . basically there was little I could do. I was between a rock and a hard place." Interview with Monroney by Rosenthal, "Politics of Reorganization," p. 139.

84. *Congressional Record,* 112:24398.

85. Conference Report to accompany H.R. 14963, 89th Cong., 2d sess., Report no. 2235, 12 October 1966.

86. *Hearings before a Subcommittee of the Committee on Government Operations,* House of Representatives, 89th Cong., 2d sess., 6 April 1966, part 1, p. 76.

87. Ibid., part 1, pp. 323–29 (BOB response); part 1, pp. 101–27 (statement of William F. Cassidy, chief of engineers, Corps of Engineers, 7 April 1966); *Hearings* on S. 3010, part 1, pp. 109–17 (statement of Maj. Gen. R. G. MacDonnell, acting chief of engineers, 29 March 1966).

88. *Hearings* on S. 3010, 4 May 1966, part 1, pp. 298–99.

89. Memo, Boyd to Connor, 11 April 1966, sent the same day by Connor to

Schultze, filed with Califano letter to Rear Adm. John Harllee, 12 May 1966, Ex FG 175, WHCF, LBJ Library.

90. Memo, Schultze to Califano, 13 May 1966, Ex FG 170-6, WHCF, LBJ Library.

91. Memo, Califano and Barefoot Sanders to president, 13 June 1966, Ex FG 175, WHCF, LBJ Library.

92. Memo, Califano for the record, recording his and Manatos's conversation with McClellan, 21 June 1966, Ex FG 175, WHCF, LBJ Library.

93. Memo, Sanders to Califano, 17 June 1966, Ex FG 175, WHCF, LBJ Library.

94. Memo, Zwick to Califano, reporting meeting held by him and Boyd with Holifield, 1 June 1966, "Legislative Struggle—Vol. I," Legislative Background, Transportation Department, box 2, LBJ Library.

95. Committee on Government Operations report to accompany H.R. 15963, Report no. 1701, House of Representatives, 89th Cong., 2d sess., 15 June 1966.

96. *Congressional Record*, 30 August 1966, 112:21235.

97. Committee on Government Operations report on S. 3010, Report no. 1659, Senate, 89th Cong., 2d sess., 27 September 1966.

98. Conference Report to accompany H.R. 15963, 12 October 1966. Report no. 2236, House of Representatives, 89th Cong., 2nd sess.

99. *Congressional Record*, 30 August 1966, 112:21247–48.

100. Memo, Connor to Califano, 29 July 1966, Ex FG 175, WHCF, LBJ Library.

101. Califano to Speaker of House, 23 August 1966, Ex FG 175, WHCF, LBJ Library.

102. Memo, Califano to president, 31 August 1966, stating that Larry Levinson had prepared the chronology, had read it to Larry O'Brien, "who agrees with it as do I." Ex FG 155-11, WHCF, LBJ Library.

103. Memo, Secretary Wirtz to president, 25 August 1966, Ex FG 155-11, WHCF, LBJ Library.

104. *Baltimore Sun*, 19 August 1966, p. C9.

105. *Congressional Record*, 30 August 1966, 112:21248–49.

106. Memo, Connor to Califano, 29 July 1966, Ex FG 175, WHCF, LBJ Library.

107. *Congressional Record*, 30 August 1966, 112:21262.

108. Ibid., 112:21263.

109. Memo, Henry H. Wilson to president, 1 October 1966, Ex FG 999-15, WHCF, LBJ Library.

110. Memo, Califano to president, 30 August, 1966, Ex FG 175, WHCF, LBJ Library.

111. Wilson to President, 1 October 1966, Ex FG 999-15, WHCF, LBJ Library.

112. See House Report no. 1701, pp. 9–10, and Senate Report no. 1659, pp. 14–15.

113. "Remarks of the President upon signing a bill creating a Department of Transportation," 15 October 1966, press release from Office of the White House Press Secretary, in "Passage and Signature," Legislative Background, Transportation Department, box 3, LBJ Library.

114. Califano, *Presidential Nation*, p. 51.

Chapter Four

1. Of the extensive literature dealing with the origins and operations of OEO, the following works are especially useful: John Bibby and Roger Davidson, *On Capitol*

Hill: *Studies in the Legislative Process* (New York: Holt, Rinehart and Winston, 1967), especially pp. 225–51, "The Executive as Legislator: The Economic Opportunity Act of 1964"; Richard Blumenthal, "The Bureaucracy: Anti-poverty and the Community Action Program," in *American Political Institutions and Public Policy: Five Contemporary Studies*, ed. Allan P. Sindler (Boston: Little, Brown, 1969), pp. 129–79; Robinson O. Everett, ed., *Anti-poverty Programs* (Dobbs Ferry, N.Y.: Oceana Publications, 1966), especially "Coordination of the War on Poverty," by Michael S. March, pp. 114–41; John C. Donovan, *Politics of Poverty*, 2d ed. (New York: Bobbs-Merrill, 1967); Joseph A. Kershaw, *Government against Poverty* (Washington, D.C.: Brookings Institution, 1970); Louise Lander, ed., *War on Poverty* (New York: Facts and File, 1967); Robert A. Levine, *The Poor Ye Need Not Have with You* (Cambridge: M.I.T. Press, 1970); Sar A. Levitan, *The Great Society's Poor Law* (Baltimore: Johns Hopkins University Press, 1969); Peter Marris and Martin Rein, *Dilemmas of Social Reform* (New York: Atherton Press, 1967); Dorothy Buckton James, ed., *Analyzing Poverty Policy* (Lexington, Mass.: D. C. Heath, 1975), especially chap. 6, "Administrative Politics and the War on Poverty," by James E. Anderson; Daniel P. Moynihan, *Maximum Feasible Misunderstanding* (New York: Free Press, 1969); Robert D. Plotnick and Felicity Skidmore, *Progress against Poverty* (New York: Academic Press, 1975); James L. Sundquist, ed., *On Fighting Poverty: Perspectives from Experience* (New York: Basic Books, 1969); James L. Sundquist, *Politics and Policy: The Eisenhower, Kennedy, and Johnson Years* (Washington, D.C.: Brookings Institution, 1968), especially pp. 111–54, "For the Poor, Opportunity"; U.S. Advisory Commission on Intergovernmental Relations, *Intergovernmental Relations in the Poverty Program* (Washington, D.C.: Advisory Commission on Intergovernmental Relations, 1966); Christopher Weeks, *Job Corps: Dollars and Dropouts* (Boston: Little, Brown, 1967).

2. Walter W. Heller, "American Poverty: Its Causes and Cures," address delivered at the Seventh Annual Public Affairs Forum, Indiana State College, Indiana, Pa., 25 March 1965, as quoted by James L. Sundquist, *Politics and Policy*, p. 137.

3. Notable were Michael Harrington, *The Other America* (New York: Macmillan, 1962); John Kenneth Galbraith, *The Affluent Society* (Boston: Houghton Mifflin, 1958); Leon H. Keyserling, *Poverty and Deprivation in the United States* (Washington, D.C.: Conference on Industrial Progress, 1962). A summary of the strands of thought and experience that formed the background for the War on Poverty is in Sundquist, *Politics and Policy*, pp. 111–54.

4. Heller, "American Poverty," as quoted in Sundquist, *On Fighting Poverty*, p. 7.

5. Arthur M. Schlesinger, Jr., *A Thousand Days* (Boston: Houghton Mifflin, 1965), p. 1009.

6. Memo, Heller to the secretaries of Agriculture, Commerce, Labor, HEW, the director of the Bureau of the Budget, the administrator of the Housing and Home Finance Agency. "CEA Background Papers on Poverty-B" folder, Legislative Background, Economic Opportunity Act of 1964, War on Poverty, box 1, LBJ Library.

7. "CEA Background Papers on Poverty-B," Their italics.

8. Typed addition to the Cannon-Hughes memo, "CEA Background Papers on Poverty-B."

9. W. B. Cannon, Draft for Insertion in CEA memo to Sorensen, "Bureau of the Budget Background Papers on Poverty-C," in Legislative Background, Economic Opportunity Act of 1964, War on Poverty, box 1, LBJ Library.

10. See memos, Heller to Sorensen, 20 December 1963, and Schultze to Sorensen, 23 December 1963, "CEA Background Papers on Poverty-B."

11. Lyndon Baines Johnson, *The Vantage Point–Perspectives of the Presidency 1963—1969* (New York: Popular Library, 1971), pp. 73–74.

12. U.S. President, *Public Papers of the Presidents of the United States: Lyndon B. Johnson, 1963–64* (Washington, D.C.: Government Printing Office, 1965), 1:114, hereafter cited as *Public Papers*.

13. *Public Papers, 1963–64*, 1:184.

14. See Cannon draft of 17 December 1963, cited in note 9 above.

15. Memo, Gordon and Heller, for cabinet secretaries and the administrator of the Housing and Home Finance Agency, "BOB Background Papers on Poverty-C."

16. But Secretary Celebrezze has said that he did not want it. Transcript, Oral History Interview, 26 January 1971, p. 12, LBJ Library.

17. Memo, Cohen to Kermit Gordon and Walter Heller, 10 January 1964, "Bureau of the Budget Background Papers on Poverty-C."

18. Memo, Harold Seidman to Schultze, 8 January 1964, "Bureau of the Budget Background Papers on Poverty-C."

19. Memo, Seidman to Gordon, 27 January 1964, summarizing Wirtz's proposals and giving his views. "Bureau of the Budget Background Papers on Poverty-C."

20. Memo, Seidman to Schultze, 31 January 1964, "BOB Background Papers on Poverty-C."

21. Transcript, James L. Sundquist Oral History Interview, 7 April 1969, p. 23, LBJ Library.

22. For Shriver's description of his conversations with the president before the appointment, see transcript of interview of Richard Schott and William Stotesbury with Sargent Shriver, 27 April 1977, pp. 8–15, LBJ Library.

23. For the president's actions and statements, see *Public Papers, 1963–64*, pp. 255, 272, 366–67, 379.

24. See "Possible Changes in Poverty Bill Draft," 26 February 1964, "Bureau of the Budget Background Papers on Poverty-C," p. 7.

25. For a partial list of those who participated or were consulted, see Shriver's testimony on "Economic Opportunity Act of 1964" at *Hearings before the Subcommittee on the War on Poverty Program of the Committee on Education and Labor*, House of Representatives, 88th Cong., 2d sess., part 1, pp. 23–25. For more detailed discussions of the work of the Shriver task force, see Bibby and Davidson, *On Capitol Hill*, pp. 230–38; Blumenthal, "Antipoverty and the Community Action Program," in *American Political Institutions*, ed. Sindler, pp. 129–79; Donovan, "The Executive Writes a Bill," in *Politics of Poverty*, pp. 27–38; Levine, *The Poor Ye Need Not Have with You*, pp. 47–52; Levitan, *Poor Law*, pp. 29–37; Moynihan, *Maximum Feasible Misunderstanding*, pp. 82–89; Adam Yarmolinsky, "The Beginnings of OEO," in *On Fighting Poverty*, ed. Sundquist, pp. 34–51; Sundquist, *Politics and Policy*, pp. 142–45.

26. U.S. Statutes at Large, 78 (1964): 508–34.

27. Interview with Shriver, pp. 16, 18–19, 22.

28. *Public Papers, 1963–64*, 1:379.

29. 29 FR 14764.

30. 37 FR 4589; amended with respect to the Special Impact program to provide delegations to the secretaries of Labor, Commerce, and Agriculture, 27 June 1968. 32 FR 9850. See, for details, Transcript, Stanley H. Ruttenberg Oral History Interview, 25 February 1969, pp. 1–13, LBJ Library.

31. 32 FR 9592.

32. Report to the Congress by the Comptroller General, *Review of Economic*

Opportunity Programs, 91st Cong., 1st sess., 1969, p. 26. Printed for the Senate Committee on Labor and Public Welfare and the House Committee on Education and Labor.

33. 78 Stat. 516.

34. Task force report on *Intergovernmental Program Coordination,* with covering letter to Charles L. Schultze, 22 December 1965.

35. James L. Sundquist, with the collaboration of David W. Davis, *Making Federalism Work: A Study of Program Coordination at the Community Level* (Washington, D.C.: Brookings Institution, 1969), pp. 19–20.

36. Ibid., p. 23.

37. Letter, Orville Freeman to Frank Bane, 21 October 1965, filed with letter from Freeman to Califano, same date, Ex WE 9, WHCF, LBJ Library.

38. Comptroller General, *Review of Economic Opportunity Programs,* pp. 22, 26.

39. See a memo from Theodore M. Berry to Shriver, 14 April 1967 on the effect of OEO on the Employment Service, and the accompanying USES Program Letter, Ex LA 2, WHCF, LBJ Library; and note the following statement from a Department of Labor executive: "the existence of the pressure from OEO helped us at the top bring pressure upon the old established organizations within the Department of Labor like the Employment Service to really do the job and do the job better." Oral History of Stanley H. Ruttenberg, 25 February 1969, p. 11, LBJ Library.

40. "Special Message to the Congress Proposing a Nationwide War on the Sources of Poverty," 16 March 1964. *Public Papers, 1963–64,* 1:378.

41. 78 Stat. 516, Sec. 202(a) (1964).

42. Sundquist, *Making Federalism Work,* p. 32.

43. Ibid., p. 40.

44. 81 Stat. 697 (1967).

45. "Annual Budget Message to the Congress, Fiscal Year 1968," 24 January 1967, *Public Papers, 1967,* 1:52.

46. For comments on the relations of the two structures, see Sundquist, *Making Federalism Work,* pp. 128–29.

47. "Transition of Administration," November 1968 (revised 10 December 1968), Office of Economic Opportunity, book I, CF 1660 (box 11), Files of Charles Murphy, LBJ Library.

48. Memo, vice-president for the president, 2 December 1965, filed with Valenti memo to the president, 7 December 1965, Ex WE 9, WHCF, LBJ Library.

49. Senate Report 563, 90th Cong., 1st sess. (1967).

50. Transcript, C. Robert Perrin Oral History Interview, 7 March 1969, pp. 3–5, LBJ Library.

51. 81 Stat. 718, 23 December 1967.

52. "Transition of Administration" gives a list of the committees.

53. See pp. 212–13.

54. "Transition of Administration."

55. Interview with Bernard Boutin by John Schultze, LBJ School of Public Affairs, Austin, Texas, 17 March 1977, p. 18.

56. Bertrand Harding, the new deputy director, had a long career in management in the federal government, including service in the Veterans Administration, the Atomic Energy Commission, and the Internal Revenue Service, where he ultimately became deputy commissioner.

57. Public Law 89-253, sec. 16, amending sec. 209(c).

58. Sec. 210(a) and (d), Public Law 90-222, 81 Stat. 691-2 (1967).

59. Memo, Hazel Guffey to Mr. Seidman, 7 January 1965, BOB Files on OEO E 1-12/1.

60. Memo, Shriver to Califano, 24 January 1965, "Reorganization Proposals-5" folder, box 95, files of Joseph Califano, LBJ Library.

61. Memo, Douglass Cater to Lawrence O'Brien, 1 February 1965, Ex WE 9-1, WHCF, LBJ Library.

62. Memo, Hazel Guffey to Mr. Seidman, 17 March 1965, BOB files 8 7-1, BOB; John W. Macy to Charles L. Schultze, 17 August 1965, BOB file, BOB.

63. See the summary in John C. Donovan, *The Politics of Poverty*, 2d ed. (Indianapolis and New York: Bobbs-Merrill, 1973), pp. 54–57.

64. See *Special Report: The Office of Economic Opportunity and Local Community Action Agencies*, U.S. Conference of Mayors, attached to memo from the vice-president to the president, 2 December 1965, filed with Valenti memo to the president, 7 December 1965, Ex WE 9, WHCF, LBJ Library.

65. Memo for the president, 15 June 1965, Ex WE, WHCF, LBJ Library.

66. Memo for the president, 2 August 1965, Ex ST/MC, WHCF, LBJ Library.

67. See letter from Orville L. Freeman to the vice-president, 4 October 1965, attached to a memo from Harry C. McPherson, Jr., to Califano, 12 October 1965, FG CF 11-15, WHCF, LBJ Library.

68. Memo, W. Willard Wirtz for Califano, 3 January 1966, Ex WE 9, WHCF, LBJ Library.

69. Memo, Schultze for the president, 18 September 1965. Ex WE 9, WHCF, LBJ Library.

70. The story is told fully in a memo, Schultze for the president, 6 November 1965, Ex WE 9, WHCF, LBJ Library, and a wire to the president at the ranch from Shriver on the same date.

71. Ex FG 170, WHCF, LBJ Library.

72. See memo for the president from Harry C. McPherson, Jr., who worked with the task force, 9 December 1965. Ex FG 170, WHCF, LBJ Library.

73. McPherson to the president, 23 December 1965, confidential file for the Department of Housing and Urban Development, Ex FG 170, WHCF, LBJ Library.

74. Letter, Young to Robert C. Wood, chairman of the task force, 24 December 1965, filed with a memo from Harry C. McPherson, Jr., to Califano, 27 December 1965, Ex FG 170, WHCF, LBJ Library.

75. For the draft orders see memo, Robert A. Schlei to Califano, 20 December 1965, Ex WE 9, WHCF, LBJ Library. The orders had been transmitted 18 December.

76. Memo, Califano for the president, 18 December 1965, Ex WE 9, WHCF, LBJ Library.

77. McPherson to the president, 23 December 1965, confidential file for the Department of Housing and Urban Development, Ex FG 170, WHCF, LBJ Library.

78. The recommendation of the Task Force on Urban Problems leaked out. In addition to the usual outside membership and White House/BOB representation, it worked with the cooperation of officials from HHFA and Senator Ribicoff and a member of his staff. A special report to the *New York Times* stated that it was understood the president desired to keep the dispersed OEO program under his control and that he believed the main political problems were over. Special Report, John D. Pomfret, 7 January 1966, p. 11.

79. See, on the events and Shriver's reactions, *1966 Congressional Quarterly Almanac*, 89th Cong., 2d sess., vol. 22 (Washington, D.C.: Congressional Quarterly, 1967), pp. 250 ff.

80. There was some flak at this time over whether the criticism of OEO's administration conveyed to Shriver, more severe than that in the report, originated with Mayor Lee, and both Heineman and Shriver asked for conferences with the president. Lee remained on the task force.

81. See Report, "Presidential Involvement," "Economic Opportunity Act Amendment of 1967" folder 1739, box 34, files of Joseph Califano, p. 1, LBJ Library.

82. "Annual Message to Congress on the State of the Union," *Public Papers,* 1967, 1:2–3 ("I recommend that we intensify our effort"); "Annual Budget Message to the Congress, Fiscal Year 1968," 1:54 (recommending increase of obligational authority for OEO of $448 million over 1967 level); "Special Message to the Congress: America's Unfinished Business, Urban and Rural Poverty," 14 March 1967, 1:333 (supporting the various OEO programs).

83. Report, "Presidential Involvement," p. 4.

84. Ibid.

85. Califano to the president, 15 February 1967, Ex FG 1–2, WHCF, LBJ Library.

86. For comments, see transcript of interview of Richard Schott with Bertrand Harding, 2 March 1977, p. 32, filed in LBJ Library. "The classic example was Head Start—and, certainly, if anything by that time had been developed, showed potential, it would have been Head Start—so it was a natural thing to take and put over into HEW. Sarge very frankly said, 'Christ, we can't give that up. That's the one way we justify our budget.'"

87. Memo, assistant attorney general to Larry Temple, 1 April 1968, Ex FG 11-15, WHCF, LBJ Library.

88. Memos, Jim Gaither to Joe Califano, 21 March 1968 and 19 April 1968, accompanying in library files a memo from Califano to the president, 19 April 1968, Ex FG 11-15, WHCF, LBJ Library.

89. Memo, Cohen to the president, 9 March 1968, Ex FG 165, WHCF, LBJ Library.

90. 82 Stat. 1097–98, sec. 308 and 309.

91. Memo, Califano to the president, with notation by the president, 20 December 1968, Ex WE 9, WHCF, LBJ Library.

92. Memos, Califano to the president, with the president's notations, 31 December 1968 and 6 January 1969, Ex WE 9, WHCF, LBJ Library.

93. "Annual Budget Message to the Congress, Fiscal Year, 1970," 15 January 1969, *Public Papers, 1968–69,* book 2, p. 1301.

94. Ibid., p. 1300.

95. "Annual Message to the Congress on the State of the Union," *Public Papers, 1968–69,* book 2, p. 1266.

CHAPTER FIVE

1. See a report, O'Brien to Jenkins, 8 January 1964, "Reorganization Act" folder, box 16, files of Mike Manatos, LBJ Library.

2. U.S. Congress, House, *Hearings before a Subcommittee of the Committee on Government Operations on Further Amending the Reorganization Act of 1949*

(H.R. 4623), 89th Cong., 1st sess., 1965, and *Hearings before a Subcommittee on Executive Reorganization of the Committee on Government Operations* (S. 1134 and S. 1135), 89th Cong., 1st sess., 1965.

3. Harvey C. Mansfield, Sr., "Federal Executive Reorganization: Thirty Years of Experience," *Public Administration Review* 29:336.

4. The president is allowed since 1977 to send forward amendments within a specific period. "Reorganization Act of 1977," 91 Stat. 29.

5. Now to the Governmental Affairs Committee in the Senate, 91 Stat. 29 (1977).

6. 2 July 1964, 78 Stat. 240. The provisions in the text are those in effect during the Johnson presidency.

7. Above, p. 6.

8. Useful in the preparation of this account of the Customs Bureau was "Section C" of *Reorganization by Presidential Plan: Three Case Studies* (Washington, D.C.: National Academy of Public Administration, April 1971).

9. U.S. President, "Message to the Congress Transmitting Reorganization Plan I of 1967" (25 March 1965), *Public Papers of the Presidents of the United States: Lyndon B. Johnson, 1965* (Washington, D.C.: Government Printing Office, 1967), pp. 313–15, hereafter cited as *Public Papers*.

10. Memo, G. d'Andelot Belin to secretary, 18 December 1964, OMO Reorganization Plan 1 of 1965, Bureau of the Budget Records, Record Group 51, Washington National Records Center, Suitland, Maryland (hereafter cited as BOB Records, WNRC).

11. Memo, Dillon to Kermit Gordon, 11 January 1965, OMO Reorganization Plan 1 of 1965, BOB Records, WNRC.

12. Route slip, W. D. Carey to Howard Schnoor, 13 January 1965, OMO Reorganization Plan 1 of 1965, BOB Records, WNRC.

13. Memo, Stover to James A. Reed, assistant secretary, Treasury Department, 18 January 1965, OMO Reorganization Plan 1 of 1965, BOB Records, WNRC.

14. Memo, J. P. Hendrick to file, 19 February 1965, OMO Reorganization Plan 1 of 1965, BOB Records, WNRC.

15. See letters, Seidman to director, 26 February and 26 March 1965, OMO Reorganization Plan 1 of 1965, BOB Records, WNRC.

16. Memo, Dillon to Kermit Gordon, 11 January 1965, OMO Reorganization Plan 1 of 1965, BOB Records, WNRC.

17. Memos of 19 and 24 February, 1965, OMO Reorganization Plan 1 of 1965, BOB Records, WNRC.

18. The legislative history is contained in *Reorganization Plan No. 1 of 1965 (Bureau of Customs)*, hearings before subcommittees of the committees on government operations, House of Representatives, 12, 13, and 28 April 1965, and U.S. Senate, 12 and 14 May 1965. The interchange between Senator Pell and Secretary Fowler is in Senate hearings, p. 38. The quotation from Senator Holland is in *New York Times*, 25 May 1965, p. 17.

19. *New York Times*, 9 May 1965, p. 88.

20. Ibid., 22 May 1965, p. 62.

21. For a summary of the complicated considerations at that time, see a memo, Harold Seidman to director, 13 April 1962, R5-21/65-66-67, BOB Records, WNRC. Interestingly, Seidman comments on political factors that suggest that embarrassment for the president would be avoided if the legislative rather than the reorganization route were taken, the president not being as fully involved in the former alternative.

22. Contained in various listings from BOB of proposals for consideration of reorganization, as shown in files R5-21/65-66-67, BOB Records, WNRC.

23. See a memo attached to memo from Hazel Guffey to Seidman, 4 May 1965, OMB Proposed Reorganization Program, BOB Records, WNRC.

24. Draft memo, Douglass Cater to president, 25 January 1966, Ex SP 2-3/ 1966/HE, WHCF, LBJ Library.

25. "Special Message to the Congress on Domestic Health and Education" (1 March 1966), *Public Papers, 1966*, p. 239.

26. U.S. Congress, House, *Hearings before a Subcommittee of the Committee on Government Operations on Reorganization Plan No. 3 of 1966*, 89th Cong., 2d sess., 1966, pp. 26–30.

27. Ibid., p. 13.

28. Secretary of HEW to Califano, 22 April 1966, "Reorganization Proposals—1" folder, box 99 files of Joseph Califano, LBJ Library.

29. The cast of characters is reviewed in a memo, Califano to president, 20 April 1966, "Reorganization Proposals—1" folder, box 99, files of Joseph Califano, LBJ Library.

30. "Message from the President of the United States, Transmitting Reorganization Plan No. 1 of 1968—Creating a New Bureau of Narcotics and Dangerous Drugs" (7 February 1968), *Public Papers, 1968*, p. 197.

31. U.S. Congress, House, *Hearings before a Subcommittee of the Committee on Government Operations on Reorganization Plan 1 of 1968*, 90th Cong., 2d sess., p. 40.

32. "Several weeks ago, Bill Pfleger told me that there was some agreement that the Bureau of Narcotics (Treasury) and the Bureau of Drug Abuse Control (FDA/ HEW) would be transferred to Justice. Apparently, the agencies involved had discussed the matter with Mr. Califano. I have had no further word on the matter." Memo, Schnoor to Hughes, 10 January 1968, F2 90/67.1, BOB Records, WNRC.

33. Califano's statements on these matters are in a memo, Califano to president, 29 January 1968, Ex FG 135-13, WHCF, LBJ Library. The memorandum from Fowler to the president was attached.

34. See House, *Hearings ... Reorganization Plan No. 1 of 1968*, pp. 27, 59, and U.S. Congress, House, *Congressional Record*, 90th Cong., 2d sess., 1968, 114:8601–29.

35. A good analysis of the history of water pollution legislation is in a staff memorandum printed in U.S. Congress, Senate, *Hearings before the Subcommittee on Executive Reorganization of the Committee on Government Operations on Reorganization Plan No. 2 of 1966*, 89th Cong., 2d sess., 1966, pp. 12–16.

36. Memo, Irving J. Lewis to Staats, 17 December 1965, and draft by C. L. Berg, "Organization for Control of Water Pollution," P2-20, BOB Records, WNRC.

37. Memo, Schultze to president, 11 January 1966, Ex FG 165 6-3, WHCF, LBJ Library.

38. Memo, Gardner to Califano, 27 December 1965, Ex FG 165 6-3, WHCF, LBJ Library.

39. Letter, Muskie to Udall, 7 February 1966, Ex FG 165 6-3, WHCF, LBJ Library.

40. Memo, Califano to president, 14 January 1966, Ex FG 165 6-3, WHCF, LBJ Library.

41. Memo, White to president, 12 January 1966, Ex FG 165 6-3, WHCF, LBJ Library.

42. Memo, White to president, 25 January 1966, Ex FG 165 6-3, WHCF, LBJ Library.

43. Memo, Califano to president, 10 February 1966, Ex FG 165 6-3, WHCF, LBJ Library.

44. Memo, Califano to president, 18 February 1966, Ex FG 165 6-3, WHCF, LBJ Library.

45. Memo, Califano to president, 26 February 1966, Ex FG 165 6-3, WHCF, LBJ Library.

46. "Special Message to the Congress Transmitting Reorganization Plan No. 2 of 1966: Water Pollution Control" (28 February 1966), *Public Paper, 1966*, p. 230.

47. For a discussion of the antecedents, see "Water Quality and the Interior Department," in *Reorganization by Presidential Plan*, prepared for the National Academy of Public Administration (Washington, D.C., 1971).

48. U.S. Congress, House, *Hearings before a Subcommittee of the Committee on Government Operations, on Reorganization Plan No. 2 of 1966*, 89th Cong., 2d sess., 1966, and Senate, *Hearings . . . Reorganization Plan No. 2 of 1966*.

49. For illustration of the president's interest in correcting river pollution, see memorandum from Hornig for the record, 11 August 1965, which states that the president had directed him and Udall to develop an overall pollution control plan.

50. Letter, president to vice-president-elect, 2 December 1964, Ex HU 2, WHCF, LBJ Library.

51. Memo, Katzenbach to vice-president-elect, 23 November 1964, Ex HU 2, WHCF, LBJ Library.

52. Letter, president to vice-president, 6 February 1965, *Public Papers, 1965*, pp. 152–53. The executive order was no. 11197, 30 F.R. 1721 (1965 supplement).

53. Memo, Lee C. White to president, 20 September 1965, transmitted to the president with a covering memo by Marvin Watson, 20 September 1965, Ex FG 731, WHCF, LBJ Library.

54. For a summary on this, see Christopher Pyle and Richard Morgan, "Johnson's Civil Rights Shake-up," *New Leader*, 11 October 1965, pp. 3–6.

55. For the first suggestion, see memo, vice-president to president, 21 June 1965, "Executive Order Ending President's Committee on Equal Employment Opportunity" folder, box 4, files of Lee C. White, LBJ Library; for the second, see memo, Seidman to director, 20 May 1965, F1-1, BOB Records, WNRC.

56. Memo, White to president, 20 September 1965, Ex FG 731, WHCF, LBJ Library.

57. U.S. President, "Equal Employment Opportunity," E.O. 11246 (24 September 1965), and "Providing for the Coordination by the Attorney General of Enforcement of Title VI of the Civil Rights Act of 1964," E.O. 11247 (24 September 1965); *Weekly Compilation of Presidential Documents* 1 (27 September 1965): 305–10.

58. See memo, White to president, 20 September 1965, Ex FG 731, WHCF, LBJ Library.

59. See section 1002 of P.L. 88-352 (2 July 1964), Civil Rights Act of 1964, 88 Stat. 241.

60. News Conference Transcript no. 119A, 24 September 1965, Ex HU-2, WHCF, LBJ Library.

61. Status Memorandum, 11 October 1965, R2-10/66, BOB Records, WNRC.

62. U.S. Congress, Senate, *Hearings before the Subcommittee on Executive Reorganization of the Committee on Government Operations on Reorganization Plan No. 1 of 1966*, 89th Cong., 2d sess., 1966, pp. 75–76.

63. *New York Times*, 24 March 1966.

64. For an account of the transfer, based largely on interviews, see Allan Wolk, *The Presidency and Black Civil Rights: Eisenhower to Nixon* (Cranbury, N.J. Fairleigh Dickinson University Press, 1971), chap. 5.

65. U.S. Congress, House, *Hearings before a Subcommittee of the Committee on Government Operations on Reorganization Plan No. 1 of 1966*, pp. 43, 51.

66. Memo, Henry Wilson to president, 23 March 1966, Ex FG 135-12, WHCF, LBJ Library.

67. Memo, Katzenbach to president, 18 April 1966, Ex FG 155-18, WHCF, LBJ Library.

68. See U.S. Congress, *Congressional Record*, 89th Cong. 2d sess., 112:8516, 7843.

69. Transcript, Robert C. Weaver, Oral History Interview, 19 November 1968, p. 17, LBJ Library.

70. Memo, Boyd to Califano, 4 January 1966, "Reorganization Proposals—4" folder, box 99, files of Joe Califano, LBJ Library.

71. Transcript, Robert C. Wood Oral History Interview, 19 November 1968, p. 30, LBJ Library.

72. "Special Message on Transportation" (2 March 1966), *Public Papers, 1966*, p. 255.

73. "Act to Establish a Department of Transportation," 80 Stat. 931.

74. Memo, Califano to Weaver and Boyd, 28 August 1967. "Transportation 1968" folder, box 53, files of James Gaither, LBJ Library.

75. Memo, Schnoor to director, 6 November 1967, T9-2 (vol. 1), BOB Records, WNRC.

76. Memo, Califano to president, 1 December 1967, Ex TN-2, WHCF, LBJ Library.

77. For references to documents on the matters discussed in the text, see *Administrative History of the Department of Transportation*, vol. 1, part 3, LBJ Library, and file T9-2 (vol. 1), BOB Records, WNRC.

78. See memo of meeting between the two secretaries and their under secretaries on 25 January 1968 in *Administrative History of the Department of Transportation*, vol. 1, part 3, LBJ Library.

79. See letter, Dwight A. Ink, assistant secretary of administration, HUD, to Phillip S. Hughes, deputy director, BOB, 14 February 1968, and attached draft reorganization plan, T9-2 (vol. 1), BOB Records, WNRC.

80. U.S. Congress, House, *Hearings before a Subcommittee of the Committee on Government Operations on Reorganization Plan No. 2 of 1968*, 90 Cong., 2d sess., 1968.

81. Ibid., pp. 28–29.

82. Letter, Patman et al. to president, 23 January 1968, T9-2 (vol. 1), BOB Records, WNRC.

83. U.S. Congress, House, *Hearings before a Subcommittee of the Committee on Government Operations on Reorganization Plan No. 3 of 1967*, 90th Cong., 1st sess., 1967, p. 217.

84. 66 Stat. 824 (1952).

85. Data in the files of Charles Horsky, President Johnson's aide for district affairs, show that in 1966 no city of more than 500,000 population had retained the commission system, and that only three between 250,000 and 500,000 and twelve between 100,000 and 250,000 were governed under that system.

86. "Televised Statement by the President concerning the Signing of the D.C. Home Rule Petition by a Majority of House Members" (3 September 1965), *Public Papers, 1965*, p. 967.

87. See *Congressional Record* 112:25879, and 26676.

88. Memo, Horsky to Nicholas G. Maklary, 12 December 1966, box 1107, files of Charles Horsky, WHCF, LBJ Library.

89. For example, a telegram from the president of the Washington Home Rule Committee, accompanied by a list of sixty-eight supporting organizations.

90. See memo, Seidman to Staats, 15 June 1964, box 1124, files of Charles Horsky, WHCF, LBJ Library.

91. As summarized in a memo, Horsky to John Macy, 5 April 1966, E 5-20 (66-67), vol. 1, BOB Records, WNRC.

92. Memo, Califano to president (transmitting Horsky's proposal), 16 November 1966, Ex FG 216, WHCF, LBJ Library.

93. "Special Message to the Congress: The Nation's Capital" (27 February 1967), *Public Papers, 1967*, pp. 226 ff.

94. Memo, Horsky to Califano, 7 February 1967, Ex FG 211/A, WHCF, LBJ Library.

95. Telegram, O'Brien to president, 4 March 1967, Ex FG 216, WHCF, LBJ Library.

96. Memo, president to Califano, 4 March 1967, Ex FG 216, WHCF, LBJ Library.

97. U.S. Congress, House, *Hearings before a Subcommittee of the Committee on Government Operations on Reorganization Plan No. 3 of 1967*, 90th Cong., 1st sess., 1967, p. 33.

98. See the long report on the progress of the plan sent by Califano to president, 16 May 1967, Ex FG 216, WHCF, LBJ Library. The meeting was held by O'Brien, Stephen J. Pollak, and Henry Wilson of the White House staff with eight members of the House District Committee on 2 May 1967. Memo, O'Brien to president, 2 May 1967, Ex FG 216, WHCF, LBJ Library.

99. "Special Message to the Congress Transmitting Reorganization Plan No. 3 of 1967: Government of the District of Columbia" (1 June 1967), *Public Papers, 1967*, pp. 858 ff.

100. See attachment to memo, Califano to president, 23 June 1967, Ex FG 216, WHCF, LBJ Library.

101. Some of the relevant documents are: *Administrative History of the Department of Commerce*, vol. 2, part 4; memo, Lawrence and Berg to director, 21 August 1964, P 1-20/64, BOB Records, WNRC; letter, Hodges to Gordon, 12 January 1965, P 1-20/64, BOB Records, WNRC; letter, Connor to Gordon, 7 March 1965, OMO Reorganization Plan 2 of 1965, BOB Records, WNRC; memo, Moyers to president, 12 May 1965, "Environmental Science Services Administration" folder, box 6, files of Bill Moyers, LBJ Library; and U.S. Congress, House, *Hearings before a Subcommittee of the Committee on Government Operations on Reorganization Plan No. 2 of 1965*, 89th Cong., 1st sess., 1965.

102. See the "Special Message to the Congress Transmitting Reorganization Plan 2 of 1967 (United States Tariff Commission)" (9 March 1967), *Public Papers, 1967*, p. 294; memo, Califano to president, 7 March 1967, Ex FG 297, WHCF, LBJ Library.

103. Memo, Schultze to president, 3 March 1967, "Reorganization Pro-

posals—2" folder, box 99, files of Joseph Califano, LBJ Library.

104. Memo, Schultze to Califano, 20 February 1967, Ex FG, WHCF, LBJ Library.

105. Memo, Califano to president, 7 March 1967, Ex FG 297, WHCF, LBJ Library.

106. Memo, Valenti to president, 5 April 1966, Ex FG 165-4-1, WHCF, LBJ Library.

107. Memo, Hughes to president, 9 May 1967, Ex FG 297, WHCF, LBJ Library.

108. Above, p. 6.

109. See chapter 4.

Chapter Six

1. U.S. President, "State of the Union Message" (10 January 1967), *Public Papers of the Presidents of the United States: Lyndon B. Johnson*, 1967 (Washington, D.C.: Government Printing Office, 1968), p. 4; hereafter cited as *Public Papers*.

2. "Remarks at a reception honoring Secretary Trowbridge," *Public Papers, 1968–69*, p. 401.

3. For a thorough analysis of the history of the evolution of the two departments, see an unsigned, undated study entitled "Historical Perspective on the Creation of the Department of Commerce and Labor (1903) and the Department of Labor (1913)," in "Proposed Department of Business and Labor: Backup Material" folder, box 16 (1595), files of Fred Bohen, LBJ Library.

4. 1964 Outside Task Force on Government Reorganization, pp. 7–9, "1964 Task Force on Government Reorganization" folder, box 151, files of James Gaither, LBJ Library. For information on the creation and scope of the recommendations of the Price task force, see pp. 187–88.

5. *Administrative History of the Department of Commerce*, vol. 1, part 5, p. 607, LBJ Library.

6. Memo, John Macy to president, 27 December 1966, "Califano: Labor-Commerce (2)" folder, box 15 (1419), files of Joseph Califano, LBJ Library.

7. Telephone call noted in the president's daily diary, 29 December 1966, LBJ Library.

8. Memo, Califano to president, 29 December 1966, "Califano: Commerce-Labor (1)" folder, box 15 (1419), files of Joseph Califano, LBJ Library.

9. Interview, one of the authors with Harold Seidman, 12 May 1979.

10. Undated report "A Department of Manpower and Economic Development," filed with undated memo, Califano to the president, "Califano: Labor-Commerce (2)" folder, box 15 (1419), files of Joseph Califano, LBJ Library. The Heineman task force enthusiastically endorsed the merger through a letter from its chairman to the president on 31 January 1967, stating the purposes from a draft prepared for it by Bohen.

11. Memo, "A Department of Manpower and Economic Development," in "Califano: Commerce-Labor (2)" folder, box 15 (1419), files of Joseph Califano, LBJ Library.

12. 1964 Outside Task Force on Government Reorganization, p. 12, "1964 Task Force on Government Reorganization" folder, box 168, files of James Gaither, LBJ Library.

13. Memo, Califano to president, 5 January 1967, Ex LA, WHCF, LBJ Library.

14. Memo, Califano to president, 9 January 1967, "Califano: Commerce-Labor

(1)" folder, box 15 (1419), files of Joseph Califano, LBJ Library.

15. Annual Message to the Congress on the State of the Union, *Public Papers, 1967,* 1:4.

16. *Administrative History of the Department of Commerce,* vol. 1, part 5, p. 7, LBJ Library.

17. Memo, Califano to president, 28 January 1967, "Califano: Commerce-labor (1)" folder, box 15 (1419), files of Joseph Califano, LBJ Library.

18. Memo, Zwick to Califano and Schultze, 2 February 1967, TI-60/67, vol. 2, Bureau of the Budget Records, Washington National Records Center, Suitland, Maryland (hereafter cited as BOB Records, WNRC).

19. Memo, Graham to Califano, 27 January 1967, "Califano: Commerce-Labor (1)" folder, box 15 (1419), files of Joseph Califano, LBJ Library. John Macy had also suggested consumer affairs as an area of interest for his revitalized Commerce Department in his 27 December 1966 memo to the president.

20. Memo, Zwick to Califano and Schultze, 3 February 1967, TI-60/67, vol. 2, BOB Records, WNRC.

21. Draft memo for the president, 6 February 1967, TI-60/67, Vol. 2, BOB Records, WNRC.

22. Memo, from Zwick, 6 February 1967, TI-60/67, vol. 2, BOB Records, WNRC.

23. Memo, Califano to president, 6 February 1967, "Califano: Commerce-Labor (1)" folder, box 15 (1419), files of Joseph Califano, LBJ Library. Emphasis added.

24. Below, p. 162.

25. Memo, Califano to president, 1 January 1967, and memo, Califano and Levinson to president, 11 January 1967, Ex FG 999-22, WHCF, LBJ Library.

26. Memo, Califano to president, 5 January 1967, Ex LA, WHCF, LBJ Library; memo, Califano and Levinson to president, 11 January 1967, Ex FG 999-22, WHCF, LBJ Library.

27. *Wall Street Journal,* 12 January 1967, quoted in *Administrative History of the Department of Commerce,* vol. 1, part 5, pp. 2–3.

28. Memo, Levinson to president, 12 January 1967, Ex FG 999-22, WHCF, LBJ Library.

29. Memo, Wirtz to president, 16 January 1967, "Califano: Commerce-Labor (1)" folder, box 15 (1419), files of Joseph Califano, LBJ Library.

30. Memo, Wirtz to president, 16 January 1967, "Califano: Commerce-Labor (1)" folder, box 15 (1419), files of Joseph Califano, LBJ Library.

31. Confidential memo, Wirtz to president, 19 January 1967, filed with memo, Califano to president, 19 January 1967, "Califano: Commerce-Labor (1)" folder, box 15 (1419), files of Joseph Califano, LBJ Library.

32. "Letter to the president of the Senate and the Speaker of the House recommending extension of the Appalachian Program" (20 January 1967); "Annual Budget Message to the Congress—Fiscal Year 1968" (24 January 1967); and "Economic Report of the President" (26 January 1967), *Public Papers, 1967,* pp. 31, 57, 86.

33. Memo, Califano to president, 24 January 1967, "Califano: Commerce-Labor (1)" folder, box 15 (1419), files of Joseph Califano, LBJ Library.

34. Memo, Wirtz to president, 24 January 1967, Ex FG 999-22, WHCF, LBJ Library.

35. Meeting recorded in president's daily diary, 5 January 1967, LBJ Library.

36. Memo for the record by Paul Southwick, 31 January 1967, filed with memo from Trowbridge to Califano, 1 February 1967, "Califano: Commerce-Labor (1)" folder, box 15 (1419), files of Joseph Califano, LBJ Library.

37. Memo, Califano to president, 6 February 1967, "Califano: Commerce-Labor (1)" folder, box 15 (1419), files of Joseph Califano, LBJ Library.

38. *New York Times*, 21 February 1967, p. 29; ibid., 22 February 1967, p. 15. The meeting was initially set for 8 March. See memo, Califano to president, 24 Februry 1967, "Califano: Commerce-Labor (2)" folder, box 15 (1419), files of Joseph Califano, LBJ Library.

39. Memo, Califano to president, 7 March 1967, Ex MA 2/M*, WHCF, LBJ Library.

40. Memo, Califano to president, 8 March 1967, Ex MC, WHCF, LBJ Library.

41. *New York Times*, 10 March 1967, p. 22.

42. "Special Message to the Congress: The Quality of American Government" (7 March 1967), *Public Papers, 1967*, pp. 358–68; *New York Times*, 17 March 1967, p. 16; *Administrative History of the Department of Labor*, 1:21–22, LBJ Library.

43. Transcript, Alexander Trowbridge Oral History Interview, pp. 5–6, 10–14, LBJ Library.

44. Attachment to memo from Gordon D. Osborn and H. Schnoor to the director, BOB, 6 October 1968, F2-4, BOB Records, WNRC.

45. Frank Smith, *The Politics of Conservation*, quoted by Senator Ribicoff in *Redesignate the Department of Interior as the Department of Natural Resources*, Hearings before the Subcommittee on Executive Reorganization of the Committee on Government Operations, U.S. Senate, 90th Cong., 1st sess., on S. 866, 17, 19, and 20 October 1967, p. 22.

46. Memo, BOB to the president, 1964 December, "Legislative Program 1965, Book 3, Task Force Briefs, No. 1" folder, box 99, files of Bill Moyers, LBJ Library.

47. *Report of the President's Task Force on Government Organization,*1964, LBJ Library.

48. Attachment to memo, Hazel Guffey to Harold Seidman, 4 May 1965, OMO Proposed Reorganization Program, BOB Records, WNRC.

49. Memo, Stewart L. Udall to Joe Califano, 27 December 1965, "Reorganization Proposals—4" folder, box 99, files of Joseph Califano, LBJ Library. His italics.

50. Memo, Freeman to Califano, 27 January 1966, "Reorganization Proposals—4" folder, box 99, files of Joseph Califano, LBJ Library.

51. Memo, Hitt to Califano, 29 December 1965, "Reorganization Proposals—4" folder, box 99, files of Joseph Califano, LBJ Library.

52. Memo, Udall for Califano, 27 December 1965.

53. Memo, Califano for the president, 10 February 1966.

54. *Redesignate the Department of Interior as the Department of Natural Resources*, Hearings before the Subcommittee on Executive Reorganization of the Committee on Government Operations, U.S. Senate, 90th Cong., 1st sess., on S. 866, 17, 19, and 20 October 1967.

55. BOB documents on "Task Force on the 1965 Legislative Program" (17 June 1964) and "Legislative Program, 1965, book 3, Task Force Briefs, #1" (December 1964) folders, box 94 (1395) and 99, files of Bill Moyers, LBJ Library.

56. Letter, Fogarty to the president, 31 December 1964, Ex FG 999, WHCF, LBJ Library, and letter, the president to Fogarty, 5 January 1965, Ex FG 999, WHCF, LBJ Library.

57. S. 200 by Ribicoff, H. R. 1000 and 2088 by Fogarty and Congressman Herman Toll (D–Pa.) respectively. And see statement of Senator Ribicoff, 6 January 1965, *Congressional Record—Senate*, vol. 3, part 1, pp. 222–26.

58. See memo, Douglass Cater to Secretary Anthony Celebrezze, 15 April 1965, Ex FG 165-4, WHCF, LBJ Library.

59. On this reorganization, see Stephen K. Bailey and Edith K. Mosher, *The Office of Education Administers a Law* (Syracuse: Syracuse University Press, 1968).

60. Letters, Fogarty to the president, 15 July 1965, and Cater to Fogarty, 27 July 1965, Ex FG 999, WHCF, LBJ Library.

61. President's news conference, 28 July 1965, *Public Papers*, 2:803.

62. For elaboration of a suggestion for a cabinet-level department of education and employment, see Rufus E. Miles, Jr., "The Case for a Federal Department of Education," *Public Administration Review*, 27 (March 1967): 1–9.

63. Fogarty's letter to the president was dated fifteen days after Halaby's letter to him recommending a department of transportation, above p. 50.

64. See the discussion of the Heineman task force, p. 202. Gardner's proposal was announced by the president, and Seidman recalls that Gardner told him his purpose had not been to provoke an announcement but to suggest to the president a viable alternative to a department of education. Interview, one of the authors with Seidman, 12 May 1979.

65. *Report of the Task Force on Education*, p. 129.

66. Ibid., p. 130.

67. With the strong support of President James Carter, those favoring the creation of a department succeeded in obtaining legislation for it in 1979.

68. Memo, Douglass Cater to the president, 19 February 1966, Ex FG 283, WHCF, LBJ Library.

69. Letter, Sparkman to president, 8 March 1966, "Reorganization Proposals—2" folder, box 99, files of Joseph Califano, LBJ Library.

70. *Public Papers, 1966*, 1:98.

71. Memo, Moyers to Kermit Gordon, 31 March 1965, "Reorganization and Economy" folder, box 3 (1340), files of Bill Moyers, LBJ Library.

72. "Special Message to the Congress on Selective Service" (6 March 1967), *Public Papers, 1967*, 1:285–86; *Report of the Task Force on the Structure of the Selective Service System*, 16 October 1967, LBJ Library.

CHAPTER SEVEN

1. Myers v. U.S., 272 U.S. 52 (1926).

2. Report of the President's Task Force on Government Reorganization, 1964, p. 19, LBJ Library.

3. Ibid., p. 20.

4. Norman Jerome Small, *The Committee Veto: Its Current Use and Appraisals of Its Validity* (Washington, D.C.: Congressional Research Service, Library of Congress, 1967), pp. 6–7. There is extensive literature in law journals on notice and approval provisions and the issues they raise.

5. U.S. Congress, Senate, *Congressional Record*, 89th Cong., 1st sess., 3:12669–70.

6. U.S. President, "Omnibus Rivers and Harbors Bill" (26 October 1965), *Weekly Compilation of Presidential Documents*, 1 (1 November 1965): 432–33.

7. U.S. President, "Veto of the Military Authorization Bill" (21 August 1965),

Public Papers of the Presidents: Lyndon B. Johnson, 1965, 2:907–9; hereafter cited as *Public Papers*.

8. 90 Stat. 793, sec. 611 (a), pp. 818–19, and sec. 501, 811. The recommendations of Harry McPherson, the president's general counsel, on veto or signature of the bill are printed in McPherson, *A Political Education* (Boston and Toronto: Little, Brown, 1972), pp. 276–78.

9. Signing the Military Construction Authorization Act of 1967, in *Weekly Compilation of Presidential Documents*, 2:1278–79.

10. Report of the President's Task Force on Government Reorganization, 1964, pp. 19–20, LBJ Library.

11. 28 September 1964. *Public Papers, 1963–64*, 2:1141.

12. 4 January 1965. *Public Papers, 1965*, 1:8.

13. *Administrative History of the National Endowment for the Arts*, vol. 1, LBJ Library.

14. Transcript, Barnaby Keeney Oral History Interview, 14 April 1969, pp. 17–18, LBJ Library.

15. *Administrative History*, 1:20.

16. 6 August 1947. *Public Papers, 1947*, pp. 368–69.

17. National Science Foundation Act of 1950, 64 Stat. 149, 10 May 1950.

18. National Arts and Cultural Development Act of 1964, 78 Stat. 905, 3 September 1964.

19. "National Arts and Humanities Foundations," Joint Hearings before the Special Subcommittee on Arts and Humanities of the Committee on Public Welfare, U.S. Senate, and the Special Subcommittee on Labor of the Committee on Education and Labor, House of Representatives, 89th Cong., 1st sess., part 1, pp. 205, 207.

20. Memo, Phillip S. Hughes to president, 24 September 1965, "Enrolled Legislation File," P.L. 89-209, S. 1483 folder, LBJ Library.

21. National Foundation on the Arts and Humanities Act of 1965, 79 Stat. 845, 29 September 1965.

22. *Congressional Quarterly Almanac*, 89th Cong., 1st sess., 1965 (Washington, D.C.: Congressional Quarterly, 1966), 21:627.

23. The act of 1964 creating the National Council on the Arts illustrated two additional questions of executive organization. The first is whether the president benefits from the representation of interests in the Executive Office. Full functional representation of interests in a diverse and pluralistic nation would be impossible. Moreover, moves in that direction could burden the president and change the character of his office by blurring the distinction between advocacy and expertise. The second question is whether Congress ought to prescribe the organization of the Executive Office. For cabinet departments, Congress has at times shown a willingness to allow secretaries to change structure within their departments. At other times it views prescription of intradepartmental organization as necessary for achieving its policy objectives. Congress also does this on occasions for the Executive Office, which raises the question whether the nation would be better served by allowing successive presidencies full flexibility in organizing the Executive Office.

24. Executive Order 10934, 13 April 1961.

25. Statement of a top White House official, Interview, 14 December 1976.

26. Administrative Conference Act, 78 Stat. 615, 30 August 1964. In numerous instances where nonpublic organizations are created to provide effective administration for public policy, issues of public control arise. An example in the Johnson presidency was the creation of the Public Broadcasting Corporation. The act declares

it is not "an agency or establishment of the United States Government," but public funds could flow to it and it was to be an instrument for public purpose. A national commission recommended that the corporation be governed by a board of directors with twelve members, six appointed by the president with Senate concurrence, the other six by the presidential appointees, all serving for staggered terms—to preserve independence from political influence. The administration recommended presidential appointment with Senate confirmation of fifteen members, and Congress accepted the recommendation, with inclusion of provisions for staggered terms and bipartisan membership. The corporation would report annually to the president, for transmission to Congress, and the comptroller general would participate in audits if federal funds were used. The study commission in this instance exhibited interesting features: it was part of the subpresidency for consideration of one matter, and it was a private commission, but its chairman was selected in the White House and a list of members was drawn up there, with the president advising his staff that he doubted he should be involved. See particularly P.L. 90-129, 81 Stat. 365; memos, Douglass Cater, Jr., to the president, 24 June 1965, "Original Idea: Appointment of Carnegie Commission," Legislative Background, Public Broadcasting Corporation, LBJ Library, and 1 October 1965, ibid.; and the report and recommendations of the Carnegie Commission on Educational Television, *Public Television: A Program for Action* (New York: Harper and Row, 1967).

27. Frederick L. Zimmermann and Mitchell Wendell, "New Horizons on the Delaware," *State Government* 36 (summer 1963): 157, 163, quoted in Martha Derthick, *Between State and Nation: Regional Organizations of the United States* (Washington, D.C.: Brookings Institution, 1974), pp. 52, 47.

28. See, for summary of these events, Derthick, *Between State and Nation*, chap. 3.

29. Memo, John L. Sweeney to the president, 27 January 1964, Ex BE 5-5/CO1 (Appalachia), WHCF, LBJ Library.

30. Memo, Lee C. White to Bill Moyers, 7 February 1964, Ex BE 5-5/CO1 (Appalachia), WHCF, LBJ Library.

31. See particularly memos, Franklin D. Roosevelt, Jr., to the president, 5 February and 13 March 1964, John L. Sweeney to the president, 27 January 1964, Kermit Gordon for the president, 28 January 1964, Lee C. White for the president, 3 February 1964, Ex BE 5-5/CO1 (Appalachia), WHCF, LBJ Library.

32. Memo, Seidman to director, 12 November 1963 attached to memo, Seidman to White, 5 December 1963, Ex BE 5-5/CO1 (Appalachia), WHCF, LBJ Library.

33. Appalachian Regional Development Act of 1965, 79 Stat. 5.

34. *Hearings before a Special Subcommittee on Economic Development of the Committee on Public Works*, United States Senate, 90th Cong., 1st sess. on S. 602, pp. 90–94.

35. Memo, Charles L. Schultze to the president, 26 January 1967, Ex LE/BE 5-5, WHCF, LBJ Library.

36. Memo, Charles L. Schultze to the president, 17 January 1967, Ex LE/BE 5-5/001, WHCF, LBJ Library.

37. Memo, John L. Sweeney to Joseph A. Califano, Jr., 12 January 1967, Ex LE/BE 5-5, WHCF, LBJ Library. Transmitted by Califano to the president, 17 January 1967, same citation.

38. *Hearings before a Special Subcommittee on Economic Development*, pp. 91–94.

39. *Public Papers, 1967*, 1:31.

40. Memo, Charles L. Schultze to the president, 26 January 1967. Ex LE/BE5-5, WHCF, LBJ Library.
41. Memo, Joe Califano for the president, 10 July 1967, Ex LE/BE 5-5/CO1, WHCF, LBJ Library.
42. For Public Works and Economic Development Act of 1965, see 79 Stat. 552; and for information on the history of its passage, see Derthick, *Between State and Nation*, chap. 5.
43. Letter to the president of the Senate and the Speaker of the House, 20 January, *Public Papers, 1965*, 1:31.
44. Memo, Joe Califano for the president, 5 October 1967, EX LE/BE 5-5/CO1, WHCF, LBJ Library.
45. Joe Califano for the president, 30 October 1967, Ex LE/BE 5-5/CO1-WHCF, LBJ Library.
46. Executive Order 11386, 28 December 1967, Code of Federal Regulations, Title 3, 1966–70 Compilation, p. 697.
47. See transcript, Stanley Ruttenberg Oral History Interview, 29 February 1969, p. 27, LBJ Library; and Harold Seidman, *Politics, Position, and Power: The Dynamics of Federal Organization* (New York: Oxford University Press, 1970), pp. 150–51.
48. Ruttenberg Oral History, p. 28.
49. Memo, Mueller to Gaither, 28 June 1968; memo, Mueller to Gaither, 23 July 1968; memo, Carey to Gaither, no date; "Labor Department Reorganization and Manpower Administration" folder, box 19, files of James Gaither, LBJ Library.
50. Memo, Califano to president, 11 October 1968, "Department of Labor—Reorganization Plan" folder, box 1852, files of Larry Temple, LBJ Library.
51. Memo, Califano to president, 14 October 1968, "Department of Labor—Reorganization Plan" folder, box 1852, files of Larry Temple, LBJ Library.
52. U.S. President, "To Earn a Living: The Rights of Every American," Special Message to Congress (23 January 1968), *Public Papers, 1968*, p. 51.
53. "Memorandum on the Need for 'Creative Federalism' through Cooperation of State and Local Officials," *Public Papers, 1966*, pp. 1366–67.
54. Memo, Califano to president, 22 October 1968, "Department of Labor—Reorganization Plan" folder, box 1852, files of Larry Temple, LBJ Library.
55. For a full report of the actions and words of the President, see transcript, Larry Temple Oral History Interview, 12 June 1970, pp. 26–31, LBJ Library. See also, for supplement, transcript, Clark Clifford Oral History Interview, 16 June 1970, LBJ Library, and Ruttenberg Oral History.
56. Ruttenberg Oral History, pp. 37–38. Ruttenberg recalls that he was in Reynolds's office at the time.
57. Ibid., pp. 39–40.
58. Memo, Califano to president, 23 October 1968, "Department of Labor—Reorganization Plan" folder, box 1852, files of Larry Temple, LBJ Library.
59. Memo, Califano for the President, Ex FG 160, WHCF, LBJ Library.
60. President's daily diary, 23 October 1968, LBJ Library.
61. For a report on Christopher's conference with Wirtz and the follow-up actions, see memo, Temple to president, 24 October 1968, "Department of Labor—Reorganization Plan" folder, box 1852, files of Larry Temple, LBJ Library. For a report on Clifford's conference with Wirtz, see Clifford Oral History, pp. 2–8.
62. See memo, Daniel to Temple, 12 November 1968, "Department of Labor—Reorganization Plan" folder, box 1852, files of Larry Temple, LBJ Library.

63. For a summary of the events in the Jackson administration, and the accompanying legal issues, see Edward S. Corwin, *The President: Office and Powers, 1787–1957*, 4th rev. ed. (New York: New York University Press, 1957), chap. 3.

Chapter Eight

1. *Washington Post*, 18 January 1967.
2. *New York Times*, 23 November 1966.
3. See p. 140.
4. See his statement in the Senate, *Congressional Record*, vol. 3, 27503, 20 October 1965.
5. S. 2411 by James B. Pearson and others.
6. See the reference to later bills at our p. 213.
7. S. 3509, 89th Cong., 2d sess., 1966. See Muskie's explanation in "Creative Federalism," *Hearings before the Subcommittee on Intergovernmental Relations, Senate Committee on Government Operations*, 89th Cong., 2d sess., 16 November 1966, part 1, p. 5.
8. "Creative Federalism," *Hearings before the Subcommittee on Intergovernmental Relations, Senate Committee on Government Operations*, 89th Cong., 2d sess., 1966, part 1, p. 388.
9. *Report of the President's Task Force on Government Organization*, p. 4.
10. Ibid.
11. Ibid., p. 7.
12. Ibid., p. 26.
13. Personal letter from Don Price to one of the authors. Harold Seidman, BOB liaison with the task force, does not even recall such a meeting. Interview with authors, Seidman, 12 May 1979.
14. *The Secretary of State and the Problems of Coordination: New Duties and Procedures of March 4, 1966*, Committee Print, Committee on Government Operations, U.S. Senate, 89th Cong., 2d sess., p. 7.
15. Ibid.
16. Ibid., pp. 1–2, quotation from White House Announcement, *Weekly Compilation of Presidential Documents*, 7 March 1966, vol. 2, no. 9.
17. Ibid., p. 21.
18. Ibid., White House Announcement, p. 1.
19. Ibid., Taylor, p. 7.
20. Memo, Ziehl to Maurice H. Stans, 27 January 1958, B2-7, series 65.6, BOB Records, RG51, NA.
21. *Desirability of Field Offices for the Bureau of the Budget*, 30 April 1964, transmitted on that date with a summary by Harold Seidman to the director. F2-40, series 65.5, BOB Records, RG51, NA.
22. See memo, William Carey to Elmer Staats, 11 August 1965, B2-7, series 65.6, BOB Records, RG51, NA.
23. Memo, Schultze to Redman, the White House, 19 January 1965, F2-40, series 65.5, BOB Records, RG51, NA.
24. For example, see memo, Schultze for the president, 28 January 1965, reporting on the recommendations of the Task Force on Intergovernmental Cooperation; and, for later support, memo, Franklin B. Dryden, acting director, Office of Emergency Planning, to Joseph A. Califano, Jr., 21 January 1966, folders 4 and 5

respectively, box 99 (1843), files of Joseph A. Califano, Jr., LBJ Library.

25. Memo, Seidman to Schultze, 13 January 1965, F2-40, series 65.5, BOB Records, RG51, NA.

26. U.S. Congress, House, *Treasury, Post Office and Executive Office Appropriation Bill, 1967,* H.R. 1412, 89th Cong., 2d sess., 1967, p. 15.

27. Report on the meeting was made in a memo, Redman to Moyers, 2 December 1966, Ex SP 2-4/67, WHCF, LBJ Library.

28. Letter, Schultze to Heineman, with an attachment entitled "The Organization and Administration of the Great Society Programs," 10 October 1966, box 43 (1749), files of Joseph A. Califano, Jr., LBJ Library. Italics in quotations in text as in Schultze's copy.

29. See chapter 4, pp. 99–104.

30. Memo, Shriver for the president, "Subject: Suggestions concerning OEO," 13 December 1966, attached to memo, Califano for the president, 15 December 1966, box 43 (1749), files of Joseph A. Califano, Jr., LBJ Library.

31. *Public Papers of the Presidents of the United States: Lyndon B. Johnson, 1966,* 2:1335, hereafter cited as *Public Papers.*

32. The motivation, according to Seidman, was a desire to ward off a department of education. Interview, one of the authors with Seidman, 12 May 1979.

33. *Public Papers, 1966,* p. 1337.

34. See chapter 6, pp. 142 ff.

35. Letter to the President of the Senate and the Speaker of the House Recommending Extension of the Appalachian Program, 20 January 1967, *Public Papers, 1967,* 2:31.

36. *Public Papers, 1967,* 17 March, 1:367.

37. Califano for the president, Ex FG 749, WHCF, LBJ Library.

38. Ibid.

39. Interview, Joe B. Frantz with Ben W. Heineman, 16 April 1970, LBJ Library Oral History Collection, pp. 24–26, 28.

40. The participation of Harold Seidman, director of BOB's Division of Management and Organization was rejected by the task force, and he in turn vetoed participation by a top member of his staff. Interview, authors with Seidman, 12 May 1979.

41. Memo to Califano transmitting the report with a letter to the president, 3 January 1967, box 43 (1749), files of Joseph A. Califano, Jr., LBJ Library.

42. *Public Papers, 1967,*1:2, 367.

43. Letter, Heineman to president, 3 January 1967, "Final Task Force Report to President on Labor-Commerce Merger" folder, box 1093, files of Fred Bohen, LBJ Library.

44. Throughout this discussion, the italics follow the emphasis in the reports. The reports of the task force are in the LBJ Library.

45. "Some Notes on Presidential Leadership of Executive Agencies," written summary of remarks to the task force on 26 February 1967, box 1094, files of Fred Bohen, LBJ Library.

46. A paper prepared for the task force by Rufus E. Miles, Jr., dated 7 April 1967, had developed similar proposals: an office of special studies to coordinate information for the president and top assistants to aid him "operational coordination." Copy supplied to the authors by Miles.

47. Memo, Califano for the president, 11 July 1967, Ex FG 749, WHCF, LBJ Library.

48. See chapter 6.

49. *The Report of the Commission on Money and Credit* (Englewood Cliffs, N.J.: Prentice-Hall, 1961).

50. Memo, Heineman to the president, 3 February 1967, box 43 (1749), Files of Joseph A. Califano, LBJ Library.

51. The Foreign Affairs Task Force was somewhat smaller than the one for domestic affairs, including only Katzenbach, McNamara, Bundy, Gordon, Schultze, Capron, and Manning, all of whom except Katzenbach signed the report. See letter from Frederick M. Bohen to Califano, 9 March 1967, box 43 (1749), files of Joseph Califano, LBJ Library.

52. For the staff papers on conduct of foreign affairs referred to here, see files of James Gaither on "Presidential Task Force on Government Organization," box 251, LBJ Library.

53. Francis M. Bator, "Draft Notes on Presentation to President's Task Force on Government Organization" folder, 15 April 1967, box 251, files of James Gaither, LBJ Library.

54. Memo, Califano for the president, 14 October 1967, Ex FG 749, WHCF, LBJ Library.

55. Heineman has said that he was informed the president included the report(s) in his night reading on at least two occasions and sent for it on other occasions, "and I am sure that if he had remained in office he would have tried very hard to do something about this," putting "his own experience and knowledge into it." Interview, Frantz with Heineman, pp. 26, 25.

56. Memo, Lawerence F. O'Brien for the president, 9 December 1965, Ex FG 140-PO, WHCF, LBJ Library.

57. Memos, O'Brien to the president, 22 March 1967 and Schultze for the president, 25 March 1967, Ex FG 787, WHCF, LBJ Library.

58. Memo, Schultze for the president, 5 April 1967, Ex FG 787, WHCF, LBJ Library.

59. Executive Order 11341. *Code of Federal Regulations*, 1966–70, 3:632.

60. See memos, O'Brien to Califano, 20 April 1968, and Fred Bohen to Califano, 22 April 1968, "President's Commission on Postal Organization: Report 2 of 2" folder, box 29, files of John E. Robson/Stanford G. Ross, LBJ Library.

61. Memo, Zwick for the president, 16 November 1968, "Postal Reorganization" folder, box 44, files of Joseph A. Califano, LBJ Library.

62. Memo, Califano for the president, "President's Commission on Postal Organization: Report 1 of 2" folder, box 29, files of John E. Robson/Stanford G. Ross, LBJ Library.

63. "Statement by the President on the Report of the President's Commission on Postal Organization," 16 July 1968, *Public Papers, 1968–69,* 2:814–15.

64. 14 January 1969, *Public Papers, 1968–69,* 2:1266.

65. "Postal Reorganization Act," 84 Stat. 719.

66. Memo, Frederick M. Bohen to Charles L. Schultze, 28 December 1966, "Task Force on Government Organization," BOB Records, WNRC.

67. See, for summary of past proposals and conflicts, Larry Berman, "The Office of Management and Budget That Almost Wasn't," *Political Science Quarterly* 92 (summer 1977): 282–303.

68. *The Work of the Steering Group on Evaluation of the Bureau of the Budget: A Staff Summary,* July 1967, BOB files.

69. See memo, director of BOB for the president, 28 December 1965, folder 4, box 99 (1842), files of Joseph A. Califano, Jr., LBJ Library.

70. Memo, Franklin B. Dryden to Califano, 21 January 1966, in response to Califano's request of 15 January for recommendations on reorganization, folder 5, box 99 (1843), files of Joseph A. Califano, Jr., LBJ Library.

71. 17 March, *Public Papers*, 1967,1:367.

72. Memo, Califano to president, 2 December 1967, "Quality of Government Study, Field Office Structure" folder, box 205, files of James Gaither, LBJ Library.

73. Memo, Califano to the president, 17 May 1968, attaching the Hughes Report, "Government Organization (General)" folder, box 8, files of James Gaither, LBJ Library.

74. Memo, Califano for the president, 3 December 1968, ibid.

75. "Establish a Commission on the Organization and Management of the Executive Branch," *Hearings before the Subcommittee on Executive Reorganization of the Committee on Government Operations*, 90th Cong., 2d sess., 22, 23, 24, 31 January; 1 February; 4 April; 15 May 1968.

76 Ibid., pp. 547–48. Testimony of Phillip S. Hughes, deputy director, BOB.

77. Memo, Harold Seidman to the Records, 5 April 1967, F2-9, series 61.1, BOB Records, WNRC. Seidman's own views of the limited utility of traditional concepts in the setting of American politics were given later in Harold Seidman, *Politics, Position, and Power: The Dynamics of Federal Organization* (New York, London, and Toronto: Oxford University Press, 1970).

78. Memo, Charles S. Murphy to the president, 22 November 1968, Ex FG 11-18, WHCF, LBJ Library.

79. Interview, Frantz with Heineman, p. 26.

80. *Papers Relating to the President's Departmental Reorganization Program: A Reference Compilation* (Washington, D.C.: Government Printing Office, 1971).

CHAPTER NINE

1. Interview, one of authors with Seidman, 12 May 1979.

GLOSSARY OF ACRONYMS

AEC	Atomic Energy Commission
AID	Agency for International Development
BAT	Bureau of Apprenticeship and Training
BES	Bureau of Employment Security
BOB	Bureau of the Budget
BWTP	Bureau of Work Training Programs
CAA	Community Action Agency
CAB	Civil Aeronautics Board
CAP	Community Action Program
CDA	Community Demonstration Agency
CEA	Council of Economic Advisers
CFA	Community Facilities Administration
CIA	Central Intelligence Agency
CRS	Community Relations Service
CSC	Civil Service Commission
DOD	Department of Defense
DOT	Department of Transportation
EEOC	Equal Employment Opportunities Commission
ESSA	Environmental Science Services Administration
FAA	Federal Aviation Authority
FBI	Federal Bureau of Investigation
FHA	Federal Housing Administration
FNMA	Federal National Mortgage Association
FRB	Federal Reserve Board
HEW	Department of Health, Education, and Welfare
HHFA	Housing and Home Finance Agency
HUD	Department of Housing and Urban Development

ICC   Interstate Commerce Commission
IRGs   Interdepartmental Regional Groups
NHA   National Housing Agency
NIH   National Institutes of Health
NSC   National Security Council
NSF   National Science Foundation
OEO   Office of Economic Opportunity
OEP   Office of Emergency Planning
OST   Office of Science and Technology
PACGO President's Advisory Committee on Government Organization
PHA   Public Housing Administration
PHS   Public Health Service
SBA   Small Business Administration
SIG   Senior Interdepartmental Group
URA   Urban Renewal Administration
USES   United States Employment Service
USHA   United States Housing Authority
USIA   United States Information Agency
VISTA   Volunteers in Service to America

INDEX

techniques of, 92, 105
through community planning, 93
with state and local governments,
96–97
creation of, 84
discontent with, 98–99
funds for, 87–88, 102
governor's veto in, 96–97
operating functions of, 85, 87, 101,
105
programs of, 85, 87
reorganization of, 160
structural revision of, 99
Office of Emergency Planning, 90, 98,
183
Office of Executive Management, recommended, 212
Office of Management and Budget
(OMB), 2
Office of Program Coordination, recommended, 199
Office of Program Development, recommended, 200
Office of Science and Technology (OST),
136, 152, 163
Office of Transportation Policy Development, 59
Office of Urban Program Coordination,
30
Okun, Arthur, 54
Omnibus Rivers and Harbors Act,
Johnson statement on, 166
Organization
alternative of decentralization,
228–29
alternatives for, 195
bureaucratic perspective on, 9, 64
change in, 218–19
classic theory on, 228
competition in organization defended,
158
comprehensive presidential management perspective on, 4, 9, 165,
185, 188, 208, 227
congressional perspectives on, 7,
64–65, 141
continuity in problems of, 196
departmental interests in, 185
diagnosis of problems of, 199
for foreign affairs, 189–90, 204–7

fragmentation of, 48
Heineman task force concepts of, 208
history and, 1–2, 225
increased concern with, 228
miscellaneous proposals on, 162–63
new dimensions of problem of, 198
options for strengthening president's
position in, 228
particularistic perspectives on,
158–59, 225–27
perspectives on in creation of DOT,
226
perspectives on in creation of HUD,
225
power to create, 2–4
stages in the national problem of, 195
tactical presidential perspective on, 7,
141

Pacific Northwest Disaster Relief Act,
166
Panama Canal Company, 49
Pastore, Senator John, 112
Patent Office, 163
Patman, Congressman Wright, 129
Peace Corps, 88, 98, 101
Pearson, Senator James B., 213
Pell, Senator Claiborne, 112
Perkins, Congressman Carl D., 104, 152
Perrin, Robert, 95
Perspectives on organization. See Organization
Policies, structural and allocative distinguished, 58, 75
Pollak, Stephen J., 133–34
Postal Organization, President's Commission on, 210
Post Office, organization reform of,
210–11
President
and instruments of unification of
foreign policy, 228
authority of, 184–85
constitutional position of, 1–3
expanded staff support for, 228
importance of appointment and removal authority of, 3, 184, 228
lack of structural support for, 228
position of, 175–76
power and position of, 2–3, 5, 7, 9